CW00347173

PATRICK ANTHONY'S
INTERNATIONAL MENU
DICTIONARY

PATRICK ANTHONY'S INTERNATIONAL MENU DICTIONARY

Lennard Publishing 1988

Lennard Publishing
a division of Lennard Books Ltd

Lennard House
92 Hastings Street
Luton, Beds LU1 5BH

British Library Cataloguing in Publication Data

Anthony, Patrick
   Patrick Anthony's International menu
   dictionary
   1. Food – encyclopaedias
   I. Title
   641.3′003′21

   ISBN 1-8529-1055-0

First published 1988
© Patrick Anthony 1988

Phototypeset in Plantin by Goodfellow & Egan Ltd,
Cambridge

Cover design by Pocknell and Co.

Printed in Yugoslavia

CONTENTS

CONTENTS

INTRODUCTION

Twenty-eight years ago, there seemingly being no chance at all of fulfilling my heartfelt ambition to become an actor, I followed the example of a boyhood friend and embarked on a career in 'High Class' catering. Little did I realise then that kind fate was preparing me for my present role in life, because eventually I did enter the theatre and subsequently television broadcasting where, in addition to the usual tasks of announcing, newsreading, interviewing and presenting, for the past ten years, following the simple demonstration of an Irish Coffee, I have been privileged to 'Educate, Inform and Entertain' indigestible amounts on the subject of food, for ITV's East of England News Magazine programme 'About Anglia', and nationally since 1985 with TV AM. The loyal interest and response of collectively many millions of viewers and thousands of correspondents has apparently caused mine to be the longest-running programme item of its kind in television history, and therefore it is with gratitude to those faithful millions that this book is dedicated. Hopefully the information, advice, comment and history contained here will be a useful source of fact, interest and occasional amusement. The world is a marvellous place and I believe the more we learn about its natural bounty the better we can all enjoy and appreciate it.

HOW TO USE THIS BOOK

Foreign menus present terrible problems. Long streams of uncomprehensible words can be completely baffling. This book unravels menu mysteries in several ways.

The At A Glance Translator (page 3) gives you in alphabetical order *individual* words, with an indication of their nationality, that you will find on the menu, so that you can understand the basics, ingredients' of the menu. For example, Potage means soup in French; Ryz means rice in Polish; Farci is stuffed in French; Frito is Spanish for fried.

The Menu Dictionary (page 23) explains in detail the character and ingredients of particular dishes, together with information on their preparation. Dhansak, for example, is a widely served Indian dish, and you will find that it is a meat or chicken dish, with lentils, potato, spinach and aubergine, that has an unusual spicy sour flavour. Churros, a Spanish favourite, are fried batter loops, which are most commonly chopped into cups of hot chocolate at breakfast.

The Key Translator (page 150) gives a checklist of commonly found ingredients in French, Spanish, German and Italian. If you either love, or loathe fennel, for example, you can look out for Fenouil, in France; Trout lovers will find their favourite as Trucha in Spain.

AT A GLANCE TRANSLATOR

À la Grècque	(Fr)	Greek style – marinaded in oil
A la plancha	(Sp)	Grilled
À la vapeur	(Fr)	Steamed
Aal	(Du)	Eel
Aardappel	(Du)	Potato
Abacate	(Br/P)	Avocado
Abobora	(Br/P)	Pumpkin
Abu-abu	(Indo)	Tuna
Acarajé	(Lat/Am)	Black-eyed pea fritters
Acciughe	(It)	Anchovies
Aceite de oliva	(Sp)	Olive oil
Aceitunas	(Mex)	Olives
Aceto	(It)	Vinegar
Aderezar de	(Sp)	Garnish with
Aeble	(Da)	Apple
Aeg	(Da)	Egg
Aeggekage	(Da)	Omelette
Aglio	(It)	Garlic
Agneau	(Fr)	Lamb
Agnello	(It)	Lamb
Agua	(Sp)	Water
Aguacate	(Lat/Am)	Avocado
Aigre-doux	(Fr)	Sweet and sour
Ail	(Fr)	Garlic
Ajiaco	(Lat/Am)	Chicken stew
Ajo	(Sp)	Garlic
Al	(Da)	Eel
Al forno	(It)	Baked
Al horno	(Sp)	Baked
Albondigas	(Mex)	Meat balls
Alebele	(Ind)	Pancake filled with spiced coconut mixture
Alho	(Por)	Garlic
Alla griglia	(It)	Grilled
Almejas	(Sp)	Clams
Almendra	(Mex)	Almonds
Aloo ki tikiya	(Ind)	Potato patties
Alote	(Lat/Am)	Corn
Alu	(Ind)	Potato
Ameijoas	(Por)	Clams
Ameixas	(Br/P)	Prunes
Anatra	(It)	Duck
Ancho	(Lat/Am)	Mild dried pepper
Anchois	(Fr)	Anchovy
Anchova	(Por)	Anchovy
Anginares	(Gr)	Artichokes
Anho	(Por)	Lamb
Anigola	(US)	Rocket, a pungent salad herb
Antipasti	(It)	Hors d'œuvres
Apelsin	(Rus)	Orange
Apfelsine	(Aus)	Orange
Arakas	(Gr)	Peas
Arenque	(Por)	Herring
Arepa	(Lat/Am)	Venezuelan tortilla
Arni	(Gr)	Lamb
Arrosto	(It)	Roast
Arrosto di agnello	(It)	Roast lamb
Arrosto di castrato	(It)	Roast mutton

Arrosto di ferri	(It)	Grilled meat
Arroz	(Sp)	Rice
Asado a la parrilla	(Sp)	Grill
Asparges	(Da)	Asparagus
Asperge	(Du)	Asparagus
Assaisonné	(Fr)	Seasoned
Astakos	(Gr)	Lobster
Atum	(Por)	Tuna
Au four	(Fr)	Baked
Au gratin	(Fr)	With cheese
Au gratin gratinée	(Fr)	With cheese
Auff	(Is)	Chicken
Au poivre	(Fr)	Peppered
A vapore	(It)	Steamed
Avec	(Fr)	With
Aves	(Sp)	Poultry
Avgo	(Gr)	Egg
Ayam	(Indo)	Chicken
Ayran	(Is)	Yoghurt drink
Azeitonas	(Por)	Olives
Bab	(Hu)	Bean
Babat	(Indo)	Tripe
Babi	(Indo)	Pork
Bacalao	(Mex)	Salt cod
Bacalhau	(Por)	Cod
Baccalyaros	(Gr)	Salt cod
Badem	(Tu)	Almond
Badendjel	(Mor)	Aubergine
Badinjan	(Ira)	Aubergines
Bagel	(Is)	Small bread, with hole in middle
Baigan	(Ind)	Aubergine
Baigan ka bharta	(Ind)	Smoked mashed aubergines
Baigan masalewala	(Ind)	Stuffed aubergine
Bakla	(Tu)	Bean
Bamya	(Tu)	Okra
Bamyes	(Gr)	Okra
Baranek	(Pol)	Lamb
Barashek	(Rus)	Lamb
Barbunya	(Tu)	Red mullet
Barrah	(Ira)	Lamb
Bartogal	(Mor)	Orange
Basbousa	(Is)	Semolina cake
Bassal	(Eg)	Onion
Batata	(Mor, Br/P)	Potato
Bawang	(Indo)	Onion
Bawang putih	(Indo)	Garlic
Bayd bi zaitun	(Mor)	Olive omelette
Bazant	(Pol)	Pheasant
Bazin	(Mor)	Semolina dough
Bebek	(Indo)	Duck
Beets	(US)	Beetroot
Beid	(Eg)	Eggs
Beignet	(Fr)	Fritter
Belanak	(Indo)	Mullet
Belegte Brot	(Aus)	Sandwich
Beras ketan	(Indo)	Glutinous rice
Berenjena	(Lat/Am)	Aubergine
Betingan	(Eg)	Aubergine
Betterave	(Bel)	Beetroot
Betzim	(Is)	Eggs
Beurre	(Fr)	Butter
Bhindi	(Ind)	Okra

Bhugia	(Ind)	Vegetable dish cooked without water
Biber	(Tu)	Green peppers
Bij	(Du)	With
Bino	(Rus)	Wine
Birka pörkölt	(Hu)	Stewed mutton
Bisato	(It)	Eel
Biscuits	(US)	Scones
Bissara	(Mor)	Bean purée
Blini	(Rus)	Buckwheat pancakes
Blirgonya	(Hu)	Potato
Blœmkool	(Du)	Cauliflower
Blomkål	(Da)	Cauliflower
Blueberry	(US)	Small blue fruit, related to bilberry
Bob	(Pol)	Bean
Bœrenkool	(Du)	Potato and cabbage purée
Bœuf	(Fr)	Beef
Bœuf en daube	(Fr)	Braised beef
Bolillos	(Mex)	Bread rolls
Bolo	(Por)	Cake
Boniato	(Lat/Am)	White sweet potato
Bønne	(Da)	Beans
Boon	(Du)	Bean
Boqueron	(Sp)	Anchovy
Borek	(Tu)	Stuffed pastries
Borrego	(Por)	Lamb
Bortsch	(Rus)	Beetroot soup
Boter	(Du)	Butter
Botsai	(Ch)	Spinach
Boudin	(Bel)	Black pudding (blood sausage)
Bouillé	(Fr)	Boiled
Bouillon	(Fr)	Stock
Bradj	(Alg)	Semolina cakes filled with dates
Braisé	(Fr)	Braised
Bratapfel	(Aus/Ger)	Baked apple
Bratens	(Aus/Ger)	Roast meat
Bratkartoffeln	(Aus/Ger)	Fried potatoes
Bratwurst	(Aus/Ger)	Fried sausage
Brinjal	(Mal)	Aubergine
Briouat	(Mor)	Stuffed pastry
Brisola	(Gr)	Chop
Brød	(Da)	Bread
Brodo	(It)	Broth
Broil	(US)	Grill
Brood	(Du)	Bread
Brouklou	(Alg)	Cauliflower
Bruschetta	(It)	Garlic toast
Bsal	(Alg)	Onion
Buah-buah	(Indo)	Desserts
Buntjis	(Indo)	Beans
Burak	(Pol)	Beetroot
Burghul	(Eg)	Bulgur wheat
Burro	(It)	Butter
Buterbrody	(Rus)	Open sandwich
Ca	(Viet)	Fish
Cabrito	(Por)	Kid
Cacerola	(Sp)	Casserole
Cachorro	(Por)	Hot dog
Café solo	(Sp)	Black coffee
Calabacitas	(Mex)	Courgettes
Calabaza	(Lat/Am)	Pumpkin
Calamares	(Sp)	Squid
Calamari	(It)	Squid
Camarão	(Br/P)	Prawns

Camarãos	(Por)	Shrimps
Camarones	(Lat/Am)	Prawns
Camote	(Mex)	Sweet potato
Canadian bacon	(US)	Smoked sweet cured back bacon
Canard	(Fr)	Duck
Capperi	(It)	Capers
Carapau	(Por)	Mackerel
Carapulcra	(Lat/Am)	Chicken, pork and potatoes cooked in a peanut sauce
Carabonada en zapollo	(Lat/Am)	A veal stew with fruit baked in a pumpkin
Carellet	(Fr)	Plaice
Carne	(Mex)	Beef
Carne	(Sp)	Meat
Carne	(It)	Meat
Carne crudo	(Sp)	Raw meat
Carne seca	(Lat/Am)	Dried salt beef
Carneiro	(Por)	Mutton
Carnero	(Mex)	Lamb
Caroti	(It)	Carrot
Carotte	(Fr)	Carrot
Carpetbagger steak	(A)	Steak stuffed with oysters
Carpione	(It)	Carp
Casseruola	(It)	Casserole
Castanhas	(Por)	Chestnuts
Castanhas de caju	(Br/P)	Cashew nuts
Catsup	(US)	Tomato ketchup
Cavolfiore	(It)	Cauliflower
Cavolo	(It)	Cabbage
Cay ca chua	(Viet)	Tomato
Cay hanh	(Viet)	Onion
Cebola	(Por)	Onion
Cebolla	(Sp)	Onion
Cebula	(Pol)	Onion
Cenoura	(Por)	Carrot
Cerdo	(Sp)	Pork
Cerveza	(Sp)	Beer
Cha	(Ch)	Deep frying
Cha wan tzu	(Ch)	Deep fried meatballs
Chai	(Rus)	Tea
Chakchouka	(Alg)	A dish of peppers, tomatoes and courgettes, usually mixed with beaten eggs
Chalda	(Mor)	Salad
Chaldra brouklou	(Mor)	Raw cauliflower salad
Champignons	(Fr)	Mushrooms
Channas	(Ind)	Chickpeas
Chancho	(Lat/Am)	Pork
Cheng	(Ch)	Steaming
Che sa di formaggio	(It)	Cheesy
Chevreuil	(Fr)	Venison
Chi	(Ch)	Chicken
Chi ma chiang	(Ch)	Hot sesame seed sauce
Chiang tou fu	(Ch)	Fermented bean curd
Chiao-tzu	(Ch)	Sealed filled dumplings
Chicons	(Bel)	Chicory
Chilaw	(Ira)	Rice
Chiles	(Mex)	Peppers
Chiles rellenos	(Lat/Am)	Stuffed peppers
Chingjiau	(Ch)	Peppers
Chintsai	(Ch)	Celery
Chipotle	(Lat/Am)	Very hot dried pepper
Chirmole de puerco	(Mex)	A pork stew with peppers and greengage plums

Chleb	(Pol/Cz)	Bread
Cholent	(Is)	Shabbat stew, with meat and potatoes
Chorbat	(Mor)	Soups
Chorizo	(Sp)	Spicy sausage
Chou	(Fr)	Cabbage
Choufleur	(Fr)	Cauliflower
Chouriço	(Br/P)	Spiced smoked pork sausage
Chuleta	(Sp)	Chop, cutlet
Chupe	(Lat/Am)	Savoury stew
Ch'ao	(Ch)	Stir-frying
Ch'ieh	(Ch)	Tomato
Ch'un-chuan	(Ch)	Spring rolls
Cilantro	(Mex)	Coriander
Cipolle	(It)	Onions
Citron	(Fr,Da)	Lemon
Cocer a fuego lento en una vasija	(Sp)	Braise
Cocer al horno	(Sp)	Bake
Coco	(Lat/Am)	Coconut
Coelho	(Por)	Rabbit
Coentro	(Por)	Coriander
Colin	(Fr)	Hake
Composta di frutta	(It)	Stewed fruit
Compota	(Sp)	Fruit sauce
Compota de frutas	(Sp)	Stewed fruit
Compote	(Fr)	Stewed fruit
Con	(It)	With
Con	(Sp)	With
Con bo	(Viet)	Beef
Concombre	(Fr)	Cucumber
Condimento	(It)	Seasoning
Conejo	(Sp)	Rabbit
Congrio	(Lat/Am)	A large fish found in Chilean waters
Coniglio	(It)	Rabbit
Contorno	(It)	Garnished
Coquilles	(Fr)	Scallops
Coração	(Br/P)	Ox heart
Corado	(Por)	Roasted
Corbasi	(Tu)	Soup
Corbullon mantuano	(Lat/Am)	Striped bass in sweet pepper sauce
Cordero	(Sp)	Lamb
Costleta	(Por)	Chop
Coteletli	(Swi)	Chops
Côtes	(Fr)	Chops
Couve	(Br/P)	Kale
Couve	(Por)	Cabbage
Cozido	(Br/P)	Stew
Crayfish	(US)	Lobster
Crema	(Sp)	Sweet sauce
Cresson	(Bel)	Watercress
Crevettes	(Fr)	Shrimps
Croutes Ostendaises	(Bel)	Shrimps on toast
Cru	(Fr)	Raw
Crudo	(It)	Raw
Crudo	(Sp)	Raw
Cseresznye leves	(Hu)	(Cold) Morello cherry soup
Csirke	(Hu)	Chicken
Csirke paprikas	(Hu)	Chicken flavoured with paprika
Cuisses de grenouille	(Fr)	Frogs' legs
Cuit	(Fr)	Baked
Cuit à la casserole	(Fr)	Casseroled
Cytryna	(Pol)	Lemon
Dadar	(Indo)	Omelette

D'affumicato	(It)	Smoked
Dag	(Is)	Fish
Daging	(Indo)	Meat
Dahsuahn	(Ch)	Garlic
Dan	(Ch)	Egg
Dana	(Tu)	Veal
Das purée	(Aus/Ger)	Purée
Das ragout	(Aus/Ger)	Stew
Das riechfläschen	(Aus/Ger)	Vinaigrette
Dendê	(Lat/Am)	Palm oil
Der obstsalat	(Aus/Ger)	Fruit salad
Dhal	(Ind)	Split black peas
Dhania	(Ind)	Coriander
Die farce	(Aus/Ger)	Stuffing
Die garnierung	(Aus/Ger)	Garnish
Die sauce	(Aus/Ger)	Sauce
Die schmmorpfanne	(Aus/Ger)	Casserole
Die vinaigrette	(Aus/Ger)	Vinaigrette
Dinde	(Fr)	Turkey
Disznohus	(Hu)	Pork
Djagung	(Indo)	Sweet corn
Djane	(Indo)	Ginger
Djari byad	(Alg)	Thick chicken soup
Djej	(Mor)	Chicken
Djintan	(Indo)	Cumin
Dolci	(It)	Desserts
Dolmasi	(Tu)	Stuffed
Dolmathes	(Gr)	Stuffed vine leaves
Domat	(Bul)	Tomatoes
Domata	(Gr)	Tomato
Domates	(Tu)	Tomato
Douhchyy	(Ch)	Black bean sauce
Eau-de-vie	(Fr)	Brandy
Ecrevisse	(Fr)	Crayfish
Eend	(Du)	Duck
Eggplant	(US)	Aubergine
Ei	(Du)	Eggs
Eierspeise	(Aus)	Scrambled eggs
Eiros	(Por)	Eels
'Eish	(Eg)	Bread
Ekmek	(Tu)	Bread
Elies	(Gr)	Olives
Empadhinas	(Br/P)	Little savoury pies
En brochette	(Fr)	Kebabs
Enguia	(Por)	Eels
En marinade	(Fr)	Marinaded
En papillote	(Fr)	Cooked in foil, or in paper
En ragoût	(Fr)	Stewed
Ensalada	(Sp)	Salad
En sauce	(Fr)	In sauce
Entremeses	(Sp)	Hors d'oeuvres
Épicé	(Fr)	Spiced
Erik tatlisi	(Tu)	Plum desserts
Erizos	(Lat/Am)	Sea urchins
Escalfado	(Sp)	Poached egg
Espadarte	(Por)	Swordfish
Espinacas	(Sp)	Spinach
Espinafres	(Por)	Spinach
Et	(Tu)	Meat
Etli	(Tu)	With meat
Fagioli	(It)	Haricot beans
Fagiolini	(It)	French beans
Faisan	(Fr)	Pheasant

Faisão	(Por)	Pheasant
Fan	(Ch)	Rice
Farce	(Du)	Stuffing
Farci	(Fr)	Stuffed
Farcite	(It)	Stuffed
Fars	(Da)	Stuffed
Faschiertes	(Aus)	Minced meat
Fasol	(Rus)	Haricot bean
Fasola	(Pol)	French beans
Fassolia	(Gr)	French beans
Favas	(Por)	Broad beans
Feijão verde	(Por)	French beans
Feijoada completa	(Br/P)	Black beans and meats
Fiambre	(Por)	Ham
Filete	(Sp)	Fillet, escalope
Filete	(Por)	Fillet
Fisk	(Da)	Fish
Fisolen	(Aus)	Green beans
Flambé	(Fr)	Flamed
Flamiche aux chicons	(Bel)	Chicory and cream cheese flan
Flor de calabaza	(Mex)	Pumpkin flowers
Flummery	(Eng)	Stiff, slightly acid jelly made from cereal
Foie	(Fr)	Liver
Fool	(Eg)	Beans
Forel	(Da,Du)	Trout
Forelle	(Aus)	Trout
Formaggio	(It)	Cheese
Frango	(Por)	Chicken
Frankfurter	(Aus)	Small, Viennese sausage
Frijol negro	(Mex)	Black beans
Frijoles	(Mex)	Beans
Frit	(Fr)	Fried
Fritada	(Sp)	Fried fish
Frito	(Sp,Por)	Fried
Fritos variados	(Sp)	Mixed grill
Frittata	(It)	Omelette
Fromage	(Fr)	Cheese
Fruits de mer	(Fr)	Seafood
Fruta	(Sp)	Fruit
Frutta	(It)	Fruit
Frutta cotta	(It)	Stewed fruit
Fumé	(Fr)	Smoked
Gala	(Tu)	Milk
Gallina	(Lat/Am)	Chicken
Gao	(Viet)	Rice
Garbanzos	(Mex)	Chickpeas
Garbanzos compuestos	(Mex)	Toasted chickpeas
Garithes	(Gr)	Prawns
Garni	(Fr)	Garnished
Garniert	(Swi)	Garnished
Gâteau	(Fr)	Cake; open tart
Gâteau d'oie	(Bel)	Goose pâté en croute
Gaufres	(Fr)	Waffles
Gebraden	(Du)	Roasted
Gebraten	(Aus/Ger)	Roasted/baked
Gefilte helzel	(Is)	Stuffed neck
gekochtes obst	(Aus/Ger)	Stewed fruit
Gekruid	(Du)	Spicy
Gelati	(It)	Ice cream
Gelbe Rüben	(Aus)	Carrots
Gerookte paling	(Du)	Smoked eel
Geröstete Erdäpfel	(Aus)	Fried potatoes

Geselchtes	(Aus)	Salted, smoked meat
Gewürzig	(Aus/Ger)	Spicy
Ghoriba dial jeljlane	(Mor)	Sesame seed cake
Ghoriba Mughrabi	(Mor)	Pastry balls
Giba	(Bul)	Mushrooms
Gibier	(Fr)	Game
Gibna	(Eg)	Cheese
Glace	(Fr)	Ice cream
Glupiec	(Pol)	Cod
Gobi	(Ind)	Cauliflower
Gollatschen	(Aus)	Shortcrust pastries
Golubstry	(Rus)	Stuffed cabbage
Goreng	(Indo)	Fried
Govyadina	(Rus)	Beef
Grammeln	(Aus)	Crackling
Granita	(It)	Water ice
Grelhado	(Por)	Grilled
Grenouilles	(Fr)	Frogs
Grib	(Rus)	Mushroom
Griddle cakes	(US)	Scotch pancakes
Grillé	(Fr)	Grilled
Grives	(Bel)	Thrushes
Gu	(Ch)	Mushroom
Guisado	(Por)	Stewed
Guisante	(Sp)	Pea
Guiso	(Lat/Am)	Stew
Gulai	(Indo)	Curry
Gulyas	(Hu)	Meat soup with vegetables and paprika
Hal	(Hu)	Fish
Halaszle	(Hu)	Fish soup
Haldi	(Ind)	Turmeric
Halib	(Mor)	Milk
Haloua rhifa	(Mor)	Wedding honey cake
Haloumi	(Cy)	Sheep's milk cheese
Hao yu	(Ch)	Oyster sauce
Hareng	(Fr)	Herring
Haricots verts	(Fr)	French beans
Hati	(Indo)	Liver
Häuptlsalat	(Aus)	Lettuce
Havuc	(Tu)	Carrot
Helado	(Sp)	Ice cream
Herdopfel	(Swi)	Potato
Heurige Erdäpfel	(Aus)	New potatoes
Himass	(Mor)	Chickpeas
Hiromeri	(Cy)	Leg of pork, marinated in wine for 40 days, and smoked
Ho jay	(Mal)	Oysters
Hochepot	(Bel)	Stew, hot pot
Homard	(Fr)	Lobster
Hønsekød	(Da)	Chicken
Hovedsalat	(Da)	Lettuce
Hsia	(Ch)	Prawns
Huhn	(Aus)	Chicken
Huidlog	(Da)	Garlic
Huitres	(Fr)	Oysters
I ovn	(Da)	Baked
Iathi	(Gr)	Oil
Indyk	(Pol)	Turkey
Insalata	(It)	Salad
Iskembe	(Tu)	Tripe
Jablko	(Pol)	Apple
Jamón	(Sp)	Ham

Jarret	(Bel)	Shin
Jitomate	(Mex)	Tomatoes
Jajko	(Pol)	Eggs
Jokai bableves	(Hu)	Bean soup with knuckle of ham
Ju	(Ch)	Pork
Judia verde	(Sp)	Green bean
Juger	(Ch)	Broccoli
Jujah	(Ira)	Chicken
Kaas	(Du)	Cheese
Kaasachtig	(Du)	Cheesy
Kabak	(Tu)	Marrow
Kabeljauw	(Du)	Cod
Kaczka	(Pol)	Duck
Kage	(Da)	Cake
Kaiserfleisch	(Aus)	Pork spare rib (slightly cured)
Kaju	(Ind)	Cashew nuts
Kal	(Da)	Cabbage
Kalafior	(Pol)	Cauliflower
Kalkoen	(Du)	Turkey
Kalya	(Tu)	Vegetable stew
Kambing	(Indo)	Lamb
Kamoun	(Mor)	Cumin
Kan	(Ch)	Liver
Kanin	(Da)	Rabbit
Kaninchen	(Aus)	Rabbit
Kaposzta	(Hu)	Cabbage
Kapusta	(Rus,Pol)	Cabbage
Karafs	(Eg)	Celery
Karfiol	(Aus)	Cauliflower
Karotte	(Da)	Carrot
Karp	(Pol)	Carp
Kartofel	(Rus,Pol)	Potato
Kartoffel	(Da)	Potato
Käse	(Aus)	Cheese
Käsig	(Aus/Ger)	Cheesy
Kastrol	(Du)	Casserole
Katjang tanah	(Indo)	Peanut
Kaymak	(Tu)	Clotted cream
Kdra	(Mor)	Cooked with fat or butter
Kedeleh	(Indo)	Soy bean
Kelapa	(Indo)	Coconut
Keledek	(Mal)	Sweet potatoes
Kelem	(Tu)	Cabbage
Kembong	(Indo)	Mackerel
Kentang	(Indo)	Potato
Kenyer	(Hu)	Bread
Kepiting	(Indo)	Crab
Kerouiya	(Mor)	Caraway
Kerrie	(Du)	Curry
Kesksou	(Mor)	Couscous
Ketam birui	(Mal)	Crab
Ketjap	(Indo)	Soy sauce
Khat mithi gobi	(Ind)	Sweet and sour cabbage
Khazilim	(Is)	Aubergine
Khirino	(Gr)	Pork
Khleb	(Rus)	Bread
Khli	(Mor)	Dried meat
Khoai	(Viet)	Potato
Khobz el-aid	(Mor)	Festive bread
Khurma	(Ira)	Dates
Kielbasa	(Pol)	Boiling ring sausage
Kiliç	(Tu)	Swordfish
Kimas	(Gr)	Minced meat

Kipferl	(Aus)	Croissant
Kiselo mlyako	(Bul)	Yoghurt
Kismis	(Indo)	Sultanas
Knoflook	(Du)	Garlic
Knöpfli	(Swi)	Dumplings
Kobis	(Mal)	Cabbage
Kød	(Da)	Meat
Kofi	(Rus)	Coffee
Kofte	(Tu)	Meat balls
Kogt	(Da)	Boiled
Kolbasa	(Rus)	Sausage
Kolbasz	(Hu)	Sausage
Kolokythia	(Gr)	Courgettes
Kolozsvari rakottkaposzta	(Hu)	Dish of layered cabbage from Kolozsvar
Komkommer	(Du)	Cucumber
Kompott	(Aus)	Stewed fruit
Konijn	(Du)	Rabbit
Kool	(Du)	Cabbage
Korma	(Indo)	Date
Kotelet	(Da)	Chop
Kotopoulo	(Gr)	Chicken
Kounoupithi	(Gr)	Cauliflower
Krassi	(Tu)	Wine
Krem	(Pol)	Cream
Kren	(Aus)	Horseradish
Krolik	(Rus,Pol)	Rabbit
Kruiderij	(Du)	Seasoning
Kruidig	(Du)	Spicy
Kryddersild	(Da)	Pickled herring
Ku lao ju	(Ch)	Sweet and sour pork
Kugel	(Is)	Savoury pudding
Kuiken	(Du)	Chicken
Kulebyaka	(Rus)	Fish pie, with grain and egg
Kurczę	(Pol)	Chicken
Kure	(Cz)	Chicken
Kurnik	(Rus)	Chicken pie
Kuru fasulya	(Tu)	Haricot beans
Kuzu	(Tu)	Lamb
Kverpostej	(Da)	Liver paste
La yu	(Ch)	Hot sauce
Lah	(Ch)	Hot (spicy)
Lahana	(Tu)	Cabbage
Lahma	(Eg)	Meat
Lakoumi	(Cy)	'Turkish Delight'
Laks	(Da)	Salmon
Lammbi	(Swi)	Lamb
Lammekød	(Da)	Lamb
Lammfleisch	(Aus)	Lamb
Lamsvlees	(Du)	Lamb
Langostino	(Sp)	Large Mediterranean prawn
Langoustine	(Fr)	Prawn
Lard	(Fr)	Bacon
Lardy cake	(Ir)	Cake made of bread dough, topped with lard, currants and sugar
Lebre	(Por)	Hare
Leche	(Sp)	Milk
Lechuga	(Sp)	Lettuce
Lecso	(Hu)	Dish of tomatoes, onions and green paprika
Légumes	(Fr)	Vegetables
Leite de côco	(Br/P)	Coconut milk
Lever	(Da,Du)	Liver

Leves	(Hu)	Soup
Lima	(Mex)	Lime
Limão	(Br/P)	Lime
Limon	(Sp)	Lemon
Limone	(It)	Lemon
Locro	(Lat/Am)	Thick potato and cheese soup
Løg	(Da)	Onion
Lokshen kugel	(Is)	Baked noodles with raisins and nuts
Lokum	(Tu)	'Turkish Delight'
Lombo	(Por)	Fillet
Lombok	(Indo)	Chili
Lomo	(Lat/Am)	Pork loin
Lountza	(Cy)	Smoked pork
Louvia	(Cy)	Blackeyed beans
Luk	(Rus)	Onion
L'aigre-doux	(Bel)	Sweet-sour sauce
L'hoot-be-louz	(Mor)	Fish stuffed with almond paste
Maçã	(Por)	Apple
Maguda	(Alg)	Omelette
Maiale	(It)	Pork
Malabaria jhinga	(Ind)	Grilled prawns
Mani	(Lat/Am)	Peanuts
Mantega	(Indo)	Butter
Mantequilla	(Sp)	Butter
Manzana	(Sp)	Apple
Maquereaux	(Fr)	Mackerel
Marak	(Is)	Soup
Marak adashim	(Is)	Lentil soup
Marchew	(Pol)	Carrot
Marha nyelv katona	(Hu)	Ox tongue in savoury sauce
Marhahus	(Hu)	Beef
Marisco	(Sp)	Shellfish
Marron	(Fr)	Chestnut
Maslo	(Rus,Pol)	Butter
Maso	(Cz)	Meat
Matambre	(Lat/Am)	Stuffed rolled goose flank steak
Mee hoon	(Indo)	Noodle
Mejillon	(Sp)	Mussel
Mel	(Por)	Honey
Melintzanosalata	(Cy)	Roasted pulp of aubergines with garlic and lemon
Melitzanes	(Gr)	Aubergine
Melk	(Du)	Milk
Mercimek	(Tu)	Lentil
Mergues	(Mor)	Hot, spicy sausage
Merlan	(Fr)	Whiting
Merlano	(It)	Whiting
Meslalla	(Mor)	Olive salad
Meslalla	(Alg)	Crushed olives
Met	(Du)	With
Met kaas	(Du)	With cheese
Mezedhes	(Cy)	Hors d'œuvres
Midye	(Tu)	Mussels
Miel	(Fr)	Honey
Mięsiwo	(Pol)	Meat
Minestra	(It)	Soup
Minestra	(Aus)	Vegetable soup
Mit	(Ger)	With
Mleko	(Pol)	Milk
Mlokhia	(Mor)	Okra
Mock turtle soup	(Eng)	Broth made from calf's head
Mœlk	(Da)	Milk
Môlho	(Br/P)	Sauce

Moloko	(Rus)	Chocolate
Mondongo serrano	(Mex)	Tripe, mountain style
Moqueca	(Br/P)	Stew
Morita	(Lat/Am)	Very hot dried pepper
Morkov	(Rus)	Carrot
Morue	(Fr)	Cod
Moskhari	(Gr)	Beef
Moules	(Fr)	Mussels
Moungra	(Cy)	Pickled cauliflower
Mouton	(Fr)	Mutton
Mqualli	(Mor)	Cooked with olive oil or peanut oil
Mshosh	(Rus)	Salad of walnuts and haricot beans
Mugem	(Por)	Grey mullet
Mulato	(Lat/Am)	Medium hot dried pepper
Muy picante con muchas especias	(Sp)	Lightly seasoned
Myaso	(Rus)	Meat
M'hadjeb	(Alg)	Pancakes filled with onion and tomato
Nan khatai	(Ind)	Coconut biscuits
Narangi	(Ira)	Oranges
Naranja	(Sp)	Orange
Na'na'	(Eg)	Mint
Nata	(Sp)	Cream
Nata batida	(Sp)	Whipped cream
Nemas	(Indo)	Pineapple
Nero	(Gr)	Water
Nier	(Du)	Kidney
Niu-ju	(Ch)	Beef
No forno	(Por)	Baked
Nopal	(Lat/Am)	Prickly pear cactus
Nukhud	(Ira)	Chickpeas
Nuoc cham	(Viet)	Sauce
Obers	(Aus)	Cream
Obst	(Aus)	Fruit
Octapothi	(Gr)	Octopus
Oeufs	(Fr)	Eggs
Oeufs pochés Gambrinus	(Bel)	Eggs poached in beer
Oeufs sur le plat	(Fr)	Fried eggs
Ogorek	(Pol)	Cucumber
Oie	(Fr)	Goose
Oie à l'instar de visé	(Bel)	Goose, boiled, then fried, in garlic sauce
Oignon	(Fr)	Onion
Okorok	(Rus)	Ham
Oksekød	(Da)	Beef
Olio	(It)	Oil
Oliwa	(Pol)	Oil
Omelette norvégienne	(Fr)	Baked alaska
Ortikia	(Gr)	Quail
Osbane es'smid	(Alg)	Semolina balls in lamb soup
Ost	(Da)	Cheese
Ovos	(Por)	Eggs
Ovos	(Lat/Am)	Eggs
Pabellon caraqueno	(Lat/Am)	Goose steak with rice, black beans and plantains
Pain	(Fr)	Bread
Pain d'épices	(Bel)	Sweet spiced bread
Palmito	(Lat/Am)	Heart of palm
Pan	(Sp)	Bread
Pan dressed fish	(US)	Cleaned and filleted fish
Pane	(It)	Bread

Pantott csirke	(Hu)	Chicken croquettes
Panuchos	(Mex)	Fried stuffed tortillas
Pan-broiled	(US)	Fried
Pão	(Por)	Bread
Papas	(Lat/Am)	Potatoes
Paprikahuhn	(Aus)	Chicken in paprika sauce
Paradeiser	(Aus)	Tomatoes
Paradicsom	(Hu)	Tomato
Pargo	(Por)	Bream
Partan bree	(Sc)	Crab soup
Pasas	(Lat/Am)	Raisins
Pashtet	(Rus)	Pâté
Pasilla	(Lat/Am)	Very hot dried pepper
Pasteis fritos	(Br/P)	Fried turnovers
Pastel de nata	(Sp)	Cake
Patata	(Sp)	Potato
Patatas fritas	(Sp)	Chips
Patate	(It)	Potatoes
Patate fritte	(It)	Fried potatoes
Patates	(Tu)	Potatoes
Pâté de foie gras	(Fr)	Goose liver pâté
Patitas de cerdo	(Mex)	Pig's trotters
Patladzhan	(Bul)	Aubergine
Patlican	(Tu)	Aubergine
Pato	(Por)	Duck
Pavo	(Mex)	Turkey
Peber	(Da)	Pepper
Pechenyi	(Rus)	Baked
Peen	(Du)	Carrot
Peixe	(Br/P)	Nuts
Pepe	(It)	Pepper
Peperoni	(It)	Sweet peppers
Perdiz	(Por)	Partridge
Perdrix	(Fr)	Partridge
Pernice	(It)	Partridge
Pescada	(Por)	Hake
Pescado	(Sp)	Fish
Pesce	(It)	Fish
Pesca	(It)	Peach
Pescado frito	(Sp)	Fried fish
Petjel	(Indo)	Salad
Petti di pollo	(It)	Chicken breasts
Phirni	(Ind)	Blancmange
Picante	(Sp)	Spicy
Piccante	(It)	Spicy
Pieprz	(Pol)	Pepper
Pikant	(Du)	Spicy
Pile	(Bul)	Chicken
Pimiento	(Sp)	Pepper
Piperies	(Gr)	Green peppers
Pirasa	(Tu)	Leek
Pirzola	(Tu)	Grilled chops
Pisang	(Indo)	Banana
Piselli	(It)	Peas
Pivo	(Rus)	Beer
Piyaz	(Ira)	Onion
Platano	(Mex)	Green banana
Poché	(Fr)	Poached
Podlivka	(Rus)	Sauce
Poireaux	(Fr)	Leeks
Poisson	(Fr)	Fish
Poisson grillé	(Fr)	Grilled fish
Poivre	(Fr)	Pepper

Poivron	(Fr)	Capiscum
Polevka	(Cz)	Soup
Polish links	(US)	Frankfurter-type sausages
Pollo	(It,Sp)	Chicken
Polpi	(It)	Octopus
Pølse	(Da)	Sausage
Polvo	(Por)	Octopus
Pomidor	(Rus,Pol)	Tomato
Pommes de terre	(Fr)	Potatoes
Pomodoro	(It)	Tomato
Porc	(Fr)	Pork
Porco	(Por)	Pork
Porgy	(US)	Sea bream
Porotos Granados	(Lat/Am)	Cranberry beans with corn and pumpkin
Porri	(It)	Leeks
Postre	(Sp)	Dessert
Potage	(Fr)	Soup
Potée	(Bel)	Soup-cum-stew
Potiron	(Bel)	Pumpkin
Pot-au-feu	(Fr)	Meat and vegetable stew
Powsowdie	(Sc)	Vegetable broth made with sheep's head
Prasso	(Gr)	Leek
Prato	(Por)	Course, dish
Presunto	(Por)	Smoked ham
Prezzemolo	(It)	Parsley
Pryanik	(Rus)	Spice cake
Psaria	(Gr)	Fish
Psito	(Gr)	Roast
Psomi	(Gr)	Bread
Pstrąg	(Pol)	Trout
Pudig	(Swi)	Pudding
Puerco	(Mex)	Pork
Pullao	(Ind)	Rice and meat dish
Pulpo	(Sp)	Octopus
Pulyka	(Hu)	Turkey
Purée de marrons	(Fr)	Chestnut purée
Purée de pommes de terre	(Fr)	Mashed or purée'd potatoes
Pyaz	(Ind)	Onion
Pye gwut	(Mal)	Spare ribs
Qua trung	(Viet)	Egg
Queijo	(Lat/Am)	Cheese
Queijo	(Por)	Cheese
Quesadillas de flor de calabaza	(Mex)	Pumpkin flower turnovers
Queso	(Sp)	Cheese
Queso ralla do	(Sp)	Grated cheese
Quibebe	(Lat/Am)	Pumpkin soup
Quindes de yaya	(Br/P)	Coconut cupcake dessert
Quotban	(Mor)	Lamb kebab
Ragoût	(Fr)	Stew
Ragù	(It)	Meat sauce, esp. served with pasta
Raie	(Fr)	Skate
Raisins	(Fr)	Grapes
Rajce	(Cz)	Tomato
Rauw	(Du)	Raw
Rebung	(Indo)	Bamboo shoot
Recheado	(Br/P)	Stuffed
Recheio	(Lat/Am)	Filling
Reh	(Swi)	Venison
Rejse	(Da)	Prawns

Relleno	(Sp)	Stuffing
Requesón	(Sp)	Cream cheese
Retes	(Hu)	Strudels
Revythia	(Gr)	Chickpeas
Ribisl	(Aus)	Redcurrants
Rijst	(Du)	Rice
Rijstpap	(Bel)	Saffron-flavoured rice pudding
Rindfleisch	(Aus)	Beef
Ringlotten	(Aus)	Greengages
Ris	(Da)	Rice
Ris	(Rus)	Rice
Risipisi	(Aus)	Rice with peas
Riso	(It)	Rice
Riz	(Fr)	Rice
Rizi	(Gr)	Rice
Robalo	(Por)	Bass
Rognone	(It)	Kidneys
Rognons	(Fr)	Kidneys
Roh	(Aus/Ger)	Raw
Rohes Fleisch	(Aus/Ger)	Raw meat
Romaine	(US)	Cos lettuce
Rosbif	(It)	Roast beef
Rostbraten	(Aus)	Beef (including ribs) roasted with onions
Rôti	(Fr)	Roast
Rou	(Ch)	Meat
Roulades d'asperges à l'Ardennaise	(Bel)	Asparagus and Ardennes ham rolls
Roupa velha	(Br/P)	Casserole of goose skirt, cooked and shredded
Roz	(Alg,Eg)	Rice
Rundvlees	(Du)	Beef
Ryba	(Cz)	Fish
Ryba	(Pol)	Fish
Ryba	(Rus)	Fish
Ryz	(Pol)	Rice
Sabroso	(Sp)	Spicy
Sajt	(Hu)	Cheese
Salade	(Fr)	Salad, lettuce
Salade Liégeoise	(Bel)	Warm cooked salad of green beans, potatoes and bacon
Salat	(Rus)	Salad
Salat Benoosach Hakibbutz	(Is)	An array of vegetable salads
Salata	(Gr)	Salad
Salata	(Pol)	Lettuce
Salcicce	(It)	Pork sausage
Sale	(It)	Salt
Salmonete	(Por)	Red mullet
Salsa	(It,Sp)	Sauce
Salsa di pomodoro	(It)	Tomato sauce
Salsicha	(Por)	Sausage
Saltsa	(Gr)	Sauce
Samak	(Eg)	Fish
Sambutes	(Mex)	Stuffed miniature tortillas
Same	(Ind)	Green beans
Sanguinante	(It)	Raw, of meat
Santan	(Indo)	Coconut milk
Şarab	(Tu)	Wine
Sarde	(It)	Sardine
Sardina	(Sp)	Sardine
Sargarepa	(Hu)	Carrots
Saucijs	(Du)	Sausage

Saucisse	(Fr)	(Fresh) sausage
Saucisson	(Fr)	(Dry) sausage
Sauerkraut	(Ger)	Pickled cabbage
Saus	(Du)	Sauce
Sauté	(Fr)	Saute
Sauté de (veau)	(Fr)	Saute of (veal, etc)
Sazonado	(Sp)	Seasoned
Scallion	(US)	Spring onion
Scapece	(It)	Skate
Schmarrn	(Aus)	Sweet pancake
Schöpsernes	(Aus)	Mutton stew
Schwammerin	(Aus)	Mushrooms
Schwarzbrot	(Aus)	Brown bread
Schwenefleisch	(Aus)	Pork
Seco de carne	(Lat/Am)	Beef stew
Sel	(Fr)	Salt
Sennep	(Da)	Mustard
Ser	(Pol)	Cheese
Serdine	(Alg)	Sardines
Sfenaj	(Alg)	Raisin doughnuts
Sgombri	(It)	Mackerel
Shao	(Ch)	Stew
Shao-mai	(Ch)	Open filled dumplings
Shchi	(Rus)	Vegetable soup with sauerkraut
Sheftalia	(Cy)	Sausage
Shieh	(Ch)	Crab
Shorba	(Eg)	Soup
Sikoti	(Gr)	Liver
Sild	(Da)	Herring
Sinea	(Is)	Baked minced meat
Siri	(Br/P)	Crabs
Skara	(Gr)	Grill
Skinke	(Da)	Ham
Skortho	(Gr)	Garlic
Smid	(Mor)	Semolina
Smør	(Da)	Butter
Snow peas	(US)	Mangetout peas
Sobras	(Por)	Offal
Soep	(Du)	Soup
Soffrito	(Gr)	Stewed steak
Sogan	(Tu)	Onion
Sogliole	(It)	Sole
Sol	(Pol)	Salt
Solha	(Por)	Plaice
Sop	(Indo)	Soup
Sopa	(Sp)	Soup
Sopa de almejas	(Lat/Am)	Clam soup
Sopas	(Por)	Soups
Sornle	(Swi)	Trout
Sos	(Pol)	Sauce
Soupa	(Gr)	Soup
Soupe à la bière douce	(Bel)	Sweet brown ale soup
Soupe tchantchès	(Bel)	Vegetable soup
Souvlakia	(Cy)	Lamb kebab
Sovs	(Da)	Sauce
Spaanse peper	(Du)	Chilli
Spanako	(Gr)	Spinach
Speculoos	(Bel)	A light biscuit
Spegesild	(Da)	Salt herring
Spiegeleier, setzeier	(Aus/Ger)	Fried eggs
Spinat	(Da)	Spinach
Spinazie	(Du)	Spinach
Sprossenkohl	(Aus)	Brussels sprouts

Stark gebraten	(Aus/Ger)	Well done
Steak sauce	(US)	Piquant sauce
Stegt	(Da)	Fried
Steurgarnaal	(Du)	Prawns
Stifado	(Cy)	Beef stew
Sto fourno	(Gr)	Baked
Stoofschotel	(Du)	Stew
Subbe	(Swi)	Soup
Sup	(Rus)	Soup
Suppe	(Da)	Soup
Süt	(Tu)	Milk
Sutlaç şarapli	(Tu)	Rice in wine syrup
Svinekød	(Da)	Pork
Svinska meso	(Bul)	Pork
Swun	(Ch)	Bamboo shoot
Syr	(Rus)	Cheese
Szpinak	(Pol)	Spinach
Szynka	(Pol)	Ham
Tacchino	(It)	Turkey
Tali	(Ind)	Fried
Tamatar	(Ind)	Tomato
Tamban	(Indo)	Pilchards
Tansy	(Eng)	Sweet pancake
Tarhonya	(Hu)	Dried noodles
Tartink	(Rus)	Hot titbits on white bread
Tatlilar	(Tu)	Desserts
Tauge	(Indo)	Bean sprouts
Tava	(Cy)	Lamb stew
Tavşan	(Tu)	Rabbit
Tavugu	(Tu)	Chicken
Tavuklar	(Tu)	Poultry
Taze fasulya	(Tu)	French beans
Tbikha foul wa karnoune	(Alg)	Artichoke and bean stew
Tejfeles tökfözelek	(Hu)	Vegetable marrow with sour cream
Tejszin	(Hu)	Cream
Teke	(Tu)	Shrimp
Telor	(Indo)	Egg
Ternera	(Sp)	Veal
Terung	(Indo)	Aubergine
Thit lon	(Viet)	Pork
Thon	(Fr)	Tuna
Tiab l'sane	(Mor)	Meat tajine(qv) with cumin and coriander
Tiganita	(Gr)	Fried
Tipsy Laird	(Sc)	Trifle
Tiram	(Indo)	Oyster
Tiri	(Tu)	Cheese
Tjuka	(Indo)	Vinegar
Tmar	(Mor)	Dates
Tojas	(Hu)	Eggs
Tomaat	(Du)	Tomato
Tomate	(Fr,Sp)	Tomato
Tomatich	(Mor)	Tomato
Tome	(Eg)	Garlic
Tongkol	(Indo)	Bonito
Tonno	(It)	Tuna
Torsk	(Da)	Cod
Torta	(It)	Cake
Torta de castanhas-do-pará	(Br/P)	Brazil nut cake
Torte	(Ger)	Cake, or tart
Tou-ya	(Ch)	Beansprouts

Trote	(It)	Trout
Trübel	(Swi)	Grapes
Trucha	(Sp)	Trout
Truffles	(Fr)	Truffles
Truite	(Fr)	Trout
Truta	(Por)	Trout
Tsyplenok	(Rus)	Chicken
Tukhm	(Ira)	Egg
Tumis	(Indo)	Sauté
Turshi	(Ira)	Pickles
T'ang	(Ch)	Soup
Ubi	(Indo)	Sweet potato
Udang	(Indo)	Prawns
Ui	(Du)	Onion
Ukha	(Rus)	Fish soup
Unda	(Ind)	Egg
Uova	(It)	Egg
Uova in camicia/uova affogate	(It)	Poached eggs
Uskumru	(Tu)	Mackerel
Vaca	(Por)	Beef
Variety meat	(US)	Offal
Varkensvlees	(Du)	Pork
Vatapa de galinha	(Br/P)	Chicken in shrimp and almond sauce
Veau	(Fr)	Veal
Vejce	(Cz)	Egg
Verduras	(Sp)	Vegetables
Vereshchaka	(Rus)	Casserole of pork and beetroot
Verlorenes Ei	(Aus/Ger)	Poached egg
Viande	(Fr)	Meat
Vinagré	(Sp)	Vinegar
Vinaigrette	(Fr)	French dressing
Vino	(It)	Wine
Vis	(Du)	Fish
Vitello	(It)	Veal
Vlees	(Du)	Meat
Volaille	(Fr)	Poultry; chichen
Vöröshagyma	(Hu)	Onions
Vrasto	(Gr)	Boiled
Vutiro	(Tu)	Butter
Watroba	(Pol)	Liver
Wenig gebraten	(Aus/Ger)	Underdone
Wienerbrød	(Da)	Danish pastry
Wieprzowina	(Pol)	Pork
Wild	(Aus)	Game
Wolowina	(Pol)	Beef
Wortel	(Indo)	Carrot
Wurst	(Aus)	Sausage
Xiphias	(Cy)	Swordfish
Yabloko	(Rus)	Apple
Yadz	(Ch)	Duck
Yangbaitsai	(Ch)	Cabbage
Yaourti	(Tu)	Yoghurt
Yaprak	(Tu)	Vine leaves
Yemista	(Gr)	Stuffed
Yu	(Ch)	Fish
Yu cha huang tou	(Ch)	Fried soybeans
Yu pao hsia	(Ch)	Fried shrimps
Yuh'mi	(Ch)	Corn
Zalm	(Du)	Salmon
Zelka	(Bul)	Cabbage
Zeytin	(Tu)	Olive
Zeytinyagi	(Tu)	Olive oil

Zhulien	(Rus)	Baked mushrooms
Zout	(Du)	Salt
Zu sehr gebraten	(Aus/Ger)	Overdone
Zucchini	(It,US)	Courgettes
Zupa	(Pol)	Soup
Zwiebel	(Aus)	Onion

THE MENU DICTIONARY

ABALONE *(American/Oriental)*
A large univalve sea mollusc with a flattened, opalescent shell. Eaten fresh in American west coast cooking, usually sautéed. Also eaten fresh and dried in Chinese and Japanese cuisine. Only the central muscle is considered fit for eating, and it must be pounded long and hard to tenderise the tough meat. Abalone steak must not be overcooked, or it will toughen again.

ABBACCHIO *(Italian)*
An exceptionally fine speciality of the Latium region (around Rome) – young, milk-fed lamb which has never tasted grass, roasted whole in an oven or on a spit, basted with oil and rosemary, or with an anchovy, garlic and oil and vinegar sauce – *alla cacciatora*. It is also served braised with an egg, lemon and parsley sauce – *abbaccio brodettato*.

ABSINTHE *(French)*
A strong, bitter cordial made primarily from wormwood, the aromatic herb, but also containing extracts of fennel, anise, parsley and marjoram. Light green in colour, and 50–70 per cent alcohol, it became popular in mid 19th century France, but later became a social scourge, causing brain-damage in *belle époque* alcoholics. It was banned in France and most other countries, though a less potent version is still available in Spain.

ACACIA *(French)*
There are about 500 species of acacia, widely scattered in the warmer regions of the world. Originally a native of Africa, it has maintained its popularity both as a decorative tree and as a food source, since its yellow blossoms are often used, particularly in southwestern France, for making puffy deep-fried fritters and a liqueur.

ACHAR *(Indian/Pakistani)*
Pickles – usually pickled fruit, such as mango, lemon or limes or pickled vegetables such as aubergine. There is also a diced prawn pickle – *jhinga achar* – which has a particularly hot bite.

ACKEE *(Caribbean)*
A fruit now found in various parts of the Caribbean, but a speciality of Jamaica, where it was first brought by the Captain of the *Bounty* before harder times. It is a brilliant red, with large, deep black seeds. When ripe it splits into three, exposing its yellow, rather 'gooey' bland flesh. It is usually served with salt fish, salt cod which is shredded, and then combined with the fruit together with garlic, onions and peppers. It can be served hot or cold.

AFRICAINE, a l' *(French)*
In the African style. A wide-ranging description, used for soup, main courses and a garnish. *Consommé a*

l'Africaine is based on chicken, flavoured with curry spice and completed by the addition of rice. As a main entrée, a dish served a *l'Africaine* will usually contain curried chicken, rice and/or horseradish. The garnish of the same name comprises a selection of aubergines, tomatoes, mushrooms and potatoes, all sautéed in oil.

AGAR-AGAR *(Japanese/Health-Food)*

A gelatine derived from gelidium seaweed, used in the far east and in health-food recipes as a substitute for commercial meat-derived gelatines. It can be used in any dish that calls for ordinary gelatine – as in jams, jellies, aspics, and mousses – being semi-transparent, tasteless and odourless. It has a high mineral and vitamin content. (See also *Carragheen*.)

AGNES SOREL *(French)*

Crème Agnès Sorel is a delicate cream of chicken soup, garnished with julienne-cut chicken, mushrooms and ox tongue. An entrée *à l'Agnés Sorel* is decorated with mounds of chicken mousse, whole baby mushrooms and slivers of ox tongue. The lady herself was the mistress of the French King Charles VII. A short-lived career as she died aged about 28.

AGNOLINI (ANOLINI) *(Italian)*

Small pasta squares or 'peaked caps' filled with chicken, cheese and spices and served in a chicken stock.

AGNOLOTTI *(Italian)*

Small crescent-shaped pasta or pasta rectangles which are filled with a meat mixture (*alla genovese* – brains and liver, or chicken, ham, cheese, spinach and egg yolk; or *alla piedmontese* – with beef and vegetables), usually served with melted butter or a meat sauce. The name means 'little fat lambs'. *Agnolotti* are really ravioli filled with meat; strictly speaking only vegetable or cheese-filled pasta should be called ravioli.

AGRODOLCE *(Italian)*

A sweet-and-sour sauce much favoured in Italian cookery – particularly for vegetables and meat (primarily duck and hare). It is originally from the region around Rome and has indisputable antecedents in the sauces of the ancient Romans. The modern versions include sugar and vinegar, as well as possibly raisins, tomatoes, pine nuts, wine and honey.

AIGO BOUIDO *(French)*

A Provençal broth heavily flavoured with garlic and thickened with oil and eggs, served over slices of fried or toasted bread. This is a traditional Christmas Eve dish and is also served at weddings.

AIOLI *(French)*

A mayonnaise-like sauce, made of garlic, pounded to a paste with egg yolk and emulsified with olive oil. It is served mainly with fish and cooked vegetables. *Aioli garni* is a Provençal dish consisting of a selection of fresh lightly-boiled vegetables, unskinned potatoes, hard-boiled eggs, and sometimes fish, served with the

sauce. There are special *aioli* festivals held in the south
of France when the garlic is harvested.

AJA BLANCO, SOPADE (*Spanish*)

Also called 'white gazpacho', this garlic and almond
soup was the gift of the Moors over 1,000 years ago. It
is made of soaked and pulverised bread, olive oil,
garlic, vinegar, iced water or broth and ground
almonds. The sophisticated Malaguenan version is
garnished with grapes while the Castilian version omits
the ground almonds and substitutes beaten eggs.

AKKRA (*Jamaican*)

Red bean fritters, deep-fried and served with a hot
tomato dipping sauce. This recipe is also found on the
West Coast of Africa.

AKOORI (EKURI) (*Indian*)

A Parsi dish of eggs scrambled with chilis, ginger,
cumin and fresh coriander. It is served with *parathas* or
chapatis (qv).

ALASKA, BAKED (*American*)

A spectacular dessert, if well executed. A sponge cake
base is piled high with ice cream, and then the whole
covered in meringue. The Alaska is then toasted in a
hot oven until the meringue browns at the tips, but the
ice cream remains firm.

ALBONDIGAS (*Spanish*)

A popular *tapas* – or *hors d'oeuvres* made to be eaten
with sherry – these are meatballs of minced pork and
herbs, cooked in a tomato and coriander sauce and
served hot.

ALEVINS (*French*)

Three-year-old baby eels, a delicacy of the south and
southwest of France. The baby eels come from their
cradle in the Sargasso Sea and make their way up the
mouth of the rivers where they are caught by special
nets. Today many alevins served in France actually
come from the west of England. They are thin and
slimy, but when washed and deep-fried have a nutty
flavour somewhat like whitebait. See also *Elvers*.

ALIGOT (*French*)

A speciality of the Auvergne and the Rouergue which
makes something wonderful out of the simplest ingredients. A purée of potatoes, garlic butter and cheese, it
should be at the same time light and substantial, the
perfect winter warmer. The classic cheese used is also
called *tompre d'Aligot*, a fresh curd cheese similar to
mozzarella, but slightly more sour. Leftover Aligot can
be formed into cakes and pan-fried.

ALLSPICE (*Spices*)

Originally called Jamaican pepper, and still called this
in Spanish, German and sometimes in French, this is
the green berry of the *Piper Nigium* dried – and usually
ground – to make the spice. Though the name almost
implies the presence of more than one ingredient, it
refers to the flavour, since the spice is said to contain
varying hints of cinnamon, nutmeg, and cloves. It does
duty in many dishes in which one or all of these spices

are required and is used in many fish, poultry and sweet dishes of the Caribbean and particularly Jamaica, where it is still primarily grown.

(See *Herbs and Spices* chart for translations.)

✕ *ALLSPICE*
Allspice has the unique reputation of tasting like three things at once. Namely cloves, cinnamon and nutmeg, although some experts (as experts always do), disagree. Jamaica is the main supplier to the world at large, and most countries have a use for it either in cakes, curries or pickles. In appearence it is very like the three-leaved shamrock Ireland's St. Patrick used to explain the Divine Trinity and although the Irish found his story quite digestible, there's no record of any culinary use for that diminutive piece of greenery.

✕ *ALMOND*
This loveliest of nuts with its profuse white blossom has inspired a charming legend in Portugal's Algarve, where it is said a Moorish prince took for his wife a Scandinavian princess who longed, in that temperate climate, for the sight of her homeland's snow. He enterprisingly ordered the whole coast to be planted with almond trees, which each Spring carpeted the landscape with snow-like petals.

AMERICAINE, à l' *(French)*
Sauce usually served with lobster and other crustaceans, combining white wine, brandy, garlic, shallots and fresh tomato sauce. The fish meat is sautéed in oil, cooked with the sauce and usually served with rice. Originated in Brittany, the 'land of the Aimorici', the designation has become confused with dishes *à l'Americaine*. Today the term is usually used interchangeably with the latter to mean fish dishes cooked in a wine and tomato sauce.

ANCHOIADE *(French)*
A paste made of pounded anchovies, oil and garlic, sometimes enriched with fresh figs, which is served as a dip with raw vegetables, or spread on warm toast, as an *hors d'oeuvre.*

ANDA KARI *(Indian)*
A hard-boiled egg curry, dressed with spiced tomato and onion sauce.

ANDOUILLE, ANDOUILLETTE *(French)*
Types of pork sausage made from the pig's intestine (large intestine – andouille, small intestine – andouill-ette) stuffed with a combination of meat, chitterlings and stomach. Both are highly flavoured (described by some as 'tasting of the barnyard') and are an acquired taste. Andouilles are usually cooked and served cold; the smaller sausages are served grilled with strong mustard and an accompaniment of apples and/or potatoes.

✕ *ANGELICA*
Angelica, to most people is nothing more than some green stuff used with chopped peel for cake making and usually with glacé cherries for outside decoration. Well what exactly

*is it? It's actually the candied stem of a giant plant which
grows to several feet in height in Scandinavian and other
far northern countries, who know it as a vegetable. Its name
comes from the legend that the Archangel Raphael
appeared to a holy hermit and advised him that the plant
was a sure cure for the plague! This, I think, is mythological history's most serious recommendation to 'Eat your
greens'!*

ANGEL FOOD CAKE *(American)*
An extremely light cake, slightly dry in texture, which
became an American favourite in the twenties. It
derives its airiness from the combination of American
flour, which is softer than many European types, and
the multitude of egg whites required for its manufacture. It is usually baked in a traditional high tin with a
hole in the centre, which also assists in maintaining
lightness.

ANGUILLES *(French/Belgian)*
Eels can be found in restaurants throughout France,
but they are particularly appreciated in the area around
Bordeaux and the Charente. Fished from the mouths of
the Dordogne, Garonne and Gironde, they are prepared
in many ways, including *aux pruneaux* – stewed with
prunes and red wine, also known as a *Bouilliture*; *à la
bordelaise* – with garlic, shallots, parsley and red wine,
and *au verjus* – marinated in fresh grape juice, then
grilled. *Anguilles en gelée* are sometimes seen in the
Limosin (see also *Eels, Elvers* and *Alevins*). In Belgium,
eels are almost a 'national dish' in spring and summer.
The classic Belgian dish is *anguilles au vert*, in which
pieces of tender young eels are sautéed and then
simmered with sorrel, mint, sage, parsley and other
herbs, as well as white wine. The stew is then thickened
with egg yolk before serving.

ANITRA *(Italian)*
Duck. *Anitra arrosto* is simple roast duck, a popular
North Italian dish, simply dressed with marsala and
sage. Other indigenous treatments include *Anitra agrodolce* – with sweet and sour sauce (see *agrodolce*) – and
Anitra farcita alla movarese – boned duck stuffed with a
farci of veal, rice and pork sausage, roasted.

ANJOVISLADA *(Swedish)*
A kind of omelette, made with potatoes and *ansjovis*,
the special sprats of the area. It is baked flat like a cake,
rather than folded, and served cut into wedges hot or
cold.

ANNA, POMMES *(French)*
Potatoes sliced very thinly and layered with butter,
baked until golden on top. The dish is reputed to have
been named after a naughty lady of the 19th century.

ANTIPASTO *(Italian)*
An assortment of small nibbles which are served either
in separate dishes or as an individual serving (usually at
a restaurant) as a first course or *hors d'oeuvres*. The
selection depends on the imagination of the cook and on

seasonal availability. Some dishes, such as *caponata* (qv), stuffed eggs or aubergines, or small mixed salads, may need preparation, but many are simply presented – slices of ham, sardines, raw vegetables, canned marinated artichoke hearts or peppers, olives, tuna, salami and other appetisers. *Antipasto alla genovese* (*hors d'oeuvres* in Genoa style) are young fava or broad beans served cold with sausage and cheese sliced and mixed in.

✖ APPLE
We all know what an apple is, although for commercial convenience few of us are familiar with more than half a dozen of the several thousands of varieties which actually exist and, not suprisingly, a wealth of stories surround this 'King of all fruits'. Most famous of all is Adam and Eve's illicit encounter in the garden of Eden, which has been repeated religiously from generation to generation, but in fact the apple is not actually named as the corrupting influence. The Bible simply refers to the 'Forbidden Fruit' from the 'Tree of Knowledge'. The world of art is to blame. For it was those early painters and sculptors who 'put the finger' on this innocent representative of the fruit family by choosing it as the principle accessory to the crime. Other traditions name pomegranate and quince.

APPELFORMAR (*Scandinavian*)
Filled muffins made with sweet dough and filled with a mixture of apples, apricot preserve and almonds before cooking. They are a traditional breakfast muffin.

APFELSTRUDEL (*Austrian/German*)
A mixture of sliced apples, raisins or sultanas, sugar and cinnamon wrapped in sheets of fine, almost transparent dough, that bakes to a crisp delicacy. The dessert is baked in a long cylinder, and afterwards dusted with sugar. It is served sliced into individual pieces.

APPENZELL (*Swiss*)
A type of Gruyère, a cow's cheese, made in the eastern canton of the same name. It is rich and fruity, with a pleasant sharpness; some of its flavour is due to the regular washing its rind receives, in brine flavoured with white wine or cider. It has a firm consistency with no holes and an ivory to pale yellow paste. It should not be dry or cracked. It is made in both farmhouse and pasteurised versions, but is not much seen outside Switzerland and France.

ARBROATH SMOKIES (*Scottish*)
Smokies are small haddock which have been beheaded, but not split, and then hot-smoked. They are copper-skinned and always sold tied at the tail in pairs. Since the fish are already cooked by the process, they may be eaten cold, but they are best grilled, boned and smeared inside with butter. The smokies are named after Arbroath, near Montrose, on the

Scottish east coast, where this kiln-smoked fish is produced.

ARROZ *(Spanish)*

The generic term for rice, *arroz* is the basis of much Spanish cooking, particularly around Valencia, the rice-producing area of the country. It is short-grained rice and lends a special texture to the recipes which contain it. Most of the *arroz* recipes are meals in themselves – containing meat or fish and vegetables.

Arroz con pollo is rice and chicken (with peppers and saffron), *Arroz a la Catalana* contains *butifarra* (qv), rabbit or chicken, pork ribs, ham, mange tout and pimento; *Arroz negro*, squid and squid ink, together with garlic, chilis and tomato. *Arroz con bacalao* (salt cod, pimentoes, chili, potato, onions and tomato) and *Arroz con Cordero* (lamb, garlic, chick peas and *morcilla* (qv)) are two more classics.

ARROZ CON LECHE *(Spanish)*

Perhaps Spain's most famous dessert – a cold sweet rice eaten all over the country. It is made from round-grained rice, milk, vanilla, egg yolks, castor sugar, cinnamon, lemon peel and cream.

ARTER MED FLASK *(Swedish)*

See *Gule aerter*.

ARTICHOKE, CHINESE *(Chinese/Japanese/French)*

This is a close relative of the Jerusalem artichoke, but with an even more delicate nutty flavour. They look like little spiral shells, with a pale, smooth, creamy exterior – and interior. Called *crosne* in France, they are extremely popular in *nouvelle cuisine* cookery – simply blanched then sautéed in butter. In China they are used in stir-fries and vegetable mixtures. They are known as *Kon loh* there, and are also valued in homeopathic medicine.

ATAYEF *(Lebanese)*

Small dessert pancakes are formed into a cone around clotted cream, flavoured with rose water and honey syrup, and dusted with crushed walnuts or pistachios.

ATHOL BROSE *(Scottish)*

A warmer – now treated as a dessert – made by pouring hot milk over oatmeal and stirring until it thickens. When the pudding has cooled to room temperature, stir in a shot or two of whisky. Double cream and chopped nuts give it dinner party status.

AVGOLEMONO *(Greek)*

The most common Greek soup, a chicken broth base with beaten eggs and lemon juice stirred in at the last minute to thicken it.

✗ *AVOCADO*

The best way to eat an avocado in my opinion is simply with lemon juice, salt and black pepper or, if the calories don't count, with a good French dressing, although many restaurants seem to delight in overstuffing them with various shellfish and a blanket of mayonnaise-based sauce, which overpowers the natural taste. There's a great American public relations story set in the 1920s when the avocado growers issued a stout public denial of any truth in the rumour that their product possessed aphrodisiac qualities. Naturally sales immediately rocketed!

AWABI GOMA ZU (*Japanese*)
Raw abalone sliced into paper-thin pieces combined with cucumber and dressed with toasted sesame seed, sugar and vinegar.

AYAM (*Indonesian*)
Chicken. In most Indonesian recipes it is either grilled, fried or braised. Familiar dishes include:
Ayam goreng Jawa and *Ayam goreng asam* are two styles of fried chicken: the first cooked in a sauce of coconut milk, coconut, candle nuts and many spices until the sauce has almost evaporated onto the chicken, which is then deep-fried; the second version is marinated in spices and tamarind liquid, then shallow-fried. *Singgang ayam* splits and flattens a whole chicken, which is marinated in coconut milk and spices, simmered in the marinade and then barbecued or grilled. *Ayam petis* is curried chicken bits in shrimp sauce; and *Ayam Bali* is chicken pieces simmered in a puréed mixture of soy sauce, chilis, garlic, coconut milk and candle nuts. *Ayam Panggang* is an exception in that it is basically a roast chicken which is finished off over coals until the skin is black-brown and crisp. In *Ayam Panggang Bumbu Rujak* the whole chicken is rubbed with a paste of coconut milk, shrimp paste and spices then barbecued. It is served with a coconut and tamarind sambal.

BABA GHANNOG (*Egyptian*)
One of the most traditional Egyptian dishes, a purée of peeled and baked aubergines and *tahini* or sesame paste, which has a dressing of olive oil, lemon juice and crushed garlic trickled over it. *Moutabel* or *Mutabel* are the Levantine versions.

BABAS AU RHUM (*French*)
Plump yeast dough cylinders or circles baked in a mould, then unmoulded, while still warm, into a sugar and dark rum syrup. They are traditionally served with glacé cherries and *Crème Chantilly*.

BACKHENDEL (*Austrian*)
A traditional Viennese speciality. Young spring chicken is halved or quartered, flattened and dipped into egg, flour and breadcrumbs before deep-frying.

BAGELS (*American*)
A contribution of New York Jewish cooking to American cuisine, bagels have been enthusiastically taken up all over the United States and further afield. Basically, bagels are bread rolls with a hole in the centre, made from unleavened bread which is first boiled then baked. This gives bagels a close texture and their traditional glazed appearance. The tops can be embellished with

sesame seeds, poppy seeds or onions. Bagels are often served with *Lox* (qv).

BAGNA CAUDA *(Italian)*
A speciality of the Piedmont; a hot dip composed of oil, garlic and anchovies into which raw vegetables are dipped, rather in the order of a *fondue* (qv). While all kinds of vegetables can be dipped, *cardoons* (qv) are a particular favourite of the region.

BAHB (BAP) *(Korean)*
Rice, either steamed or fried.

BAKLAVA *(Middle Eastern/North African/Greek or Turkish)*
The most popular dessert – certainly the most well-known to Westerners – of the near eastern repertoire. Light, thin *fillo* (qv) pastry is interleaved with spices and pistachio nuts, walnuts, and almonds, baked until crisp and then soaked in a sugar and honey syrup. It can be made as separate small pastries or as one large piece cut into diamond-shaped servings.

BAKMIE GORENG *(Indonesian)*
See *Mie Goreng*.

✕ *BANANA*
According to the Koran this was the forbidden fruit of the tree of knowledge and the first Hindi Christians thought so as well. To the French and Italians the banana was first known as 'Adam's Fig' and certainly the banana leaf would have made a much more sensible covering for the guilty pair in the Garden of Eden. The first public display of bananas in London took place on the 10th of April 1633, but regular importation from the Canary Islands didn't occur until well over two hundred years later, (1884) and about a year later to the USA by the Boston Fruit Company. The banana leaf, apart from possibly helping out Adam and Eve, has also served as a roofing material, food wrapping and, especially in India, as a table mat.

BANGERS AND MASH *(English)*
A popular pub lunch and high tea dish, this consists of large fried sausages accompanied by mounds of mashed potatoes. Sometimes onion sauce is an addition.

BANKMI CHEEN TOM *(Vietnamese)*
Shrimp toasts. Made with shrimp paste (*Tom bam*) spread onto thin bread and then deep-fried.

BANNOCKS *(Scottish)*
Oatcakes are known as 'bannocks' in Scotland and were the usual 'bread' of ordinary folk in days past. They are traditionally made with bacon dripping, and were eaten at breakfast dinner and supper, with fish, soup or meat. Cooked on an ungreased griddle, they were once 'finished' on a toasting stone, but today it is more usual to use a heavy frying pan. Known as *Bara Ceirch* (qv) in Welsh.

BANON *(French)*
One of the most distinctive of French cheeses, identifiable by the chestnut leaf wrapping over the small

round cheese. A Provençal product, it is available both in farmhouse (unpasteurised) and *laitier* (dairy-pasteurised) forms, and is usually made of cow's milk today, although it was originally made of goat's or ewe's milk. The goat's milk version is best in summer and autumn, the ewe's in spring and summer; the cow's version is much the same all the year round. It has a sharp clean taste when young (about 2 weeks old), left later it becomes higher in flavour. The leaves are often soaked in eau-de-vie before wrapping, which lends an even more complex flavour.

BAO *(Chinese)*
This word in a Chinese recipe title means rapidly fried – even faster than stir frying. Very high heat is used to seal the ingredients. (Literally means 'to explode').

BARA CEIRCH *(Welsh)*
The Welsh version of bannocks or Scottish oatcakes. Unlike the latter, they do not contain bacon dripping, and they are somewhat thinner. Customarily, they are also given a glaze of milk, sugar and egg, which makes them less porous than the Scottish variety. See also *Bannocks*.

BARFI *(Indian/Pakistani)*
A condensed milk sweet, flavoured and thickened with ground almonds, pistachio nuts and cardamom, and reduced and cooled until it can be cut into bars. It is often decorated with silver leaf or *Vark*.

✕ BARLEY
Since prehistoric times Barley has been the friend of man, providing bread, beer and whisky. Today over half the world's crop is used for animal feed, so unless you're a teetotal vegetarian it's likely that you're enjoying its benefit although even if you don't use alcohol and meat you probably take it in some other way.

BARSZCZ *(Polish)*
The Polish version of *Borscht* (qv), a soup based on vegetable stock, beetroot, mushrooms and any meat to hand. Mild beer may also be added. It is traditionally served on Christmas Eve (when no meat is allowed in it, since it is a day of abstinence) and at Easter.

✕ BASIL
From the Greek word for 'kingly', and if you've never eaten finely shredded fresh basil leaves scattered over sliced ripe tomatoes then I urge you to do so at the earliest opportunity. For even greater enjoyment add a tablespoon of oil, some salt and a dollop of cream cheese. Forget about dried basil though, it is nothing like the fresh leaf. History is full of 'Basilmania'. It was sacred in India, the Egyptians offered it to the Gods, for the Romans it was the emblem of lovers and Saint Helena, after a dream, found the true cross beneath a bed of basil. The Italians particularly and justly appreciate its qualities (see PESTO qv), although in

Morocco, Spain and Greece they grow it just to keep the flies away.

BASTELA *(Morroccan)*
Layers of thin, crispy pancake, filled with pigeon, eggs, almonds and spices.

BATH CHAP *(English)*
Still a favourite among the burghers of Bath and found in many of the butchers, Bath Chaps are made from the cheek pieces of the pig, salted and smoked like hams. After the initial dry salting, the cheeks are pickled in brine for about two weeks. Then they should be smoked, according to the traditional recipe, although many people today prefer them unsmoked. Normally they are sold cooked and covered in breadcrumbs. They are eaten hot with parsley sauce and pease pudding, or cold with piccalilli and potato salad.

BATH OLIVER *(English)*
Invented by Dr W Oliver, around 1750, these dry biscuits still bear his impressed portrait. Dr Oliver was the founder of the Bath Mineral Water Hospital, and his biscuits were deliberately bland in flavour to counteract the richness of the fashionable 18th century table and to complement the therapeutic and diuretic properties of the waters. They are still made to the old recipe, from flour, butter, yeast and milk, and are picked all over with a fork before baking, which gives them their distinctive pock-marked appearance.

✕ *BAY LEAF: (SWEET LAUREL)*
The stout supporter of many a casserole or stew, whose strength requires only a leaf or two to accomplish its valuable task. Greek athletes were crowned with the leaves after sporting success and the Romans followed suit when victorious in battle. Julius Caesar was particularly fond of wearing a bay wreath and, when chided for overdoing the practice, his friends explained on his behalf that the poor man was simply trying to conceal his bald pate. Another Roman emperor, Tiberius, wore a bay wreath whenever a thunderstorm threatened, following the belief that lightening never struck a laurel tree, and Culpepper, writing in the 17th century, attested to the same life saving protection. Mountain laurel on the other hand, is highly poisonous to man and the Delaware Indians used its leaves to brew up a suicidal cuppa!

BEAN CURD *(Vegetable derivative)*
See *Tofu*.

BEARNAISE *(French)*
A thick creamy sauce made from melted butter combined with white wine, vinegar, tarragon and shallots, thickened with egg yolks. It originated in the province of Bearsin, where that early gourmet, Henry IV, was born. Variations include Béarnaise Brune – with meat

juices added – and Béarnaise Tomate – a rich rose colour.

BEAUFORT ***(French)***
A particularly rich flavourful type of gruyère, made in the mountains of the Savoie. An *appellation d'origine* cheese, it is made from summer cow's milk of particular areas around Beaufort. It is cooked, pressed into large wheels and aged six months until it develops its fruity taste and aroma and hard but buttery texture. There is also a *laitier* (dairy factory) version made in winter. It is one of the smoothest of the gruyères, with few or no holes.

BECHAMEL SAUCE ***(French)***
One of the cornerstone sauces of classic cuisine, it consists of a roux of butter and flour, stirred with milk, cream and seasoning. It forms the base for many other sauces, and is often used on its own with vegetables and fish.

✕ *BEEF*
The world's most popular meat, despite religious (India) and economic restrictions. The 'Roast Beef of Old England' is legendary, although America has consumed more beef per head than anyone else ever since the 19th century. Japan, according to some, produces the world's finest beef. I've not yet had the chance to test this, but as their top cattle are massaged daily with gin to distribute their fat they must certainly be the happiest!

✕ *BEET*
Not a favourite vegetable of mine, but Napoleon had good reason to be grateful to the sugar beet variety, for when England blockaded France's sugar cane supply, Bonaparte greatly encouraged the fledgling industry by having 70,000 acres planted. The cash for the refinery was put up by one Benjamin Delessert, who was made a Baron for his trouble and still today the Boulevard Delessert exists in his memory, although not many people in Paris know this!

BEGGAR'S CHICKEN ***(Chinese)***
See *Har Yee Kai*.

BEGOS ***(Polish)***
The great national dish, this 'Hunter's stew' is even better the second day. Its basis is sauerkraut and a variety of meats – smoked pork, beef, sausages and bacon – cubed and baked for a long time, together with herbs, spices, stock and wine. It is usually served with sour cream.

BEI JING NGAP ***(Chinese)***
'Peking Duck', *the* Chinese classic. Actually a three-course meal designed around the duck, though the third course (duck soup) cannot really be served at the same sitting since it requires long simmering. What is commonly meant by 'Peking Duck' is really the first course – the honey roasted skin of the air-dried duck. The skin is torn off the duck, and served together with

a plate of shredded spring onions and cucumber, small saucers of *hoisin* sauce, and a pile of delicate *mandarin* pancakes. The diner takes a pancake, paints it with some hoisin sauce, adds a helping of skin, tops it with the shredded vegetables, rolls it up and eats it. After all the pancakes and skin are finished, the duck meat is brought out, to be eaten with other dishes.

BEL PAESE *(Italian)*

A smooth buttery cow's cheese, pale yellow with a golden rind, was developed in the 1920s by Edidio Galbani, a Lombard cheese-maker. It is today made there and in the USA and Brazil. It is an uncooked cheese, pressed into a large round mould (or small individual serving moulds), and it ripens quickly. It is creamy, spreads easily and is delicately flavoured. The name means 'beautiful country' and was the name of a book written by a friend of the family, Abbot Antonio Stoppani. His portrait appears on the wrapping.

BENEDICT, EGGS *(American)*

This is an elegant way to serve eggs – equally good as a breakfast dish, brunch entrée or late night supper. A toasted buttered English muffin is covered with a slice of Canadian bacon (or ham), and this topped with a poached egg. Warm Hollandaise is ladled over the whole.

BHAJI *(Indian/Pakistani)*

A vegetable dish, lightly spiced and in a dryish sauce. The usual vegetables may be *sag* (spinach), *bhindi* (ladies' fingers or okra), *brinjal* (aubergine) or *same* (green beans). This style of vegetable cooking is used particularly in Bengal, and is characterised by adding cooked and fried spices to the cooked vegetable just before serving.

BHAJRIA *(Indian)*

Round or flat deep-fried fritters made of flour, spices and a vegetable, usually onions, aubergines or spinach. Other more exotic fillings may also be used. They are usually eaten as a *chat* (qv) or snack between meals, and can be bought on the street.

BHINDI *(Indian)*

Okra or ladies' fingers. They are most usually found in *bhajis* (qv), a spicy fried curry, or as a *kari* (curry) a more saucy, moister preparation, usually in a base of yogurt or coconut milk.

BHUNA GOSHT *(Indian/Pakistani)*

A 'dry' meat curry from the North of India, made with lamb or beef and several spices, cooked until the sauce has thickened and reduced.

BIGOLI *(Italian)*

A speciality of the Venetian region, bigoli is a thick spaghetti, homemade rather than manufactured, and often made from buckwheat. Sauces include duck and giblet *(con l'anatra)* and in *salsa* (with onions and anchovies).

BILTONG *(South African)*

Thin strips of beef or ostrich meat, seasoned, pounded and hung to air dry until tough as leather. Eaten raw, it was a traditional provision to take on the Boer treks in the wilderness, though today it is more popular as a cocktail accompaniment.

BINTATOK (BINDAI DUK) *(Korean)*

Mung dhal (dried mung beans) ground together with pork mince, onions, garlic, eggs, bean sprouts, cabbage and spices, formed into 'pancakes' or a kind of flat pizza by frying on a hot griddle. They can be served hot or cold.

BIRD'S NEST SOUP *(Chinese)*

See *Ghuy yoong yien wan*.

BIRIANI *(Indian/Pakistani)*

A *biriani* is an especially well-produced *pilau* (qv), the rice usually layered or studded with a spicy mutton (lamb) or chicken mixture (sometimes prawns as well), and steamed together so that the subtle flavours blend. *Birianis* are particularly characteristic of Pakistan and the neighbouring north-western provinces of India. Lamb is the usual meat of both areas, and dishes tend to be subtly spiced without extreme hotness.

BITTER GOURD *(Indian/West Indian/Malaysian/Thai)*

See *Karela*.

BLACK PUDDING *(English)*

A large sausage (or sausages) made from pork fat and pigs' blood thickened with oatmeal and stuffed into casing. It is a close relative of *boudin noir* (qv). It is served cut into slices and fried.

BLINTZES *(Russian/Jewish)*

Pancakes filled with a mixture of sugar and curd cheese (and sometimes raisins) and folded into a packet. They are served especially during *Shavuot*, the feast of weeks.

BO NUONG DAM *(Vietnamese)*

A table-top prepared dish, in which thin fillets of pork or beef are pounded and macerated in oil, then barbecued on a strange inverted copper bowl, under which a fire burns. Rice paper is soaked until pliable, and then the barbecued meat – together with sprigs of coriander, mint and slivers of cucumber, onion and lettuce – are assembled on the rice paper, which is folded over them, dipped in *Nuvo Cham* or *Nuoo Leo* sauces, and eaten.

BOBOTIE *(South African)*

A Boer stew or casserole based on minced beef flavoured with curry powder, lemon, sugar, and almonds, thickened just before serving with beaten eggs.

BOEUF *(French)*

Certain types of French beef are quite highly prized, for instance that of the Charolais. Recipes with the word 'boeuf' in them usually use cuts of meat equivalent to topside and rolled sirloin, which is either stewed or boiled with vegetables.

Boeuf en daube is a layered casserole of beef, onion, and carrots supported by garlic, juniper berries and a calf's foot. The beef and vegetables are usually marinated for several hours in wine before long slow-cooking. It can be served hot or cold.

Boeuf à la mode is a braised pot roast of beef, traditionally larded and marinated in red wine for twenty-four hours before cooking. Carrots and baby onions, veal knuckles and calves' feet provide the typical character and consistency. It is served with the vegetables arranged around the meat or attractively moulded in aspic, chilled and served *en gelé*.

Boeuf bourguignon is a stew in which the beef is first marinated with the onions, carrots, herbs and red wine, then stewed with garlic, baby onions, and mushrooms. That's one version but this dish, once every hostess's delight, has been so messed about with by various persons that it really ought to be renamed 'pot luck bourguignon'. In its simplest and probably best form the ingredients are: beef cubes, salt pork, small onions, bouquet garni, lard, flour, seasoning and a bottle of burgundy.

Boeuf à la ficelle is beef boiled together with vegetables including celery, carrots and onions. The broth is then served as a bouillon poured over slices of toasted bread and the meat and vegetables follow as the main course, accompanied by a tomato sauce. The title of this dish comes from the tradition of tying the meat up with string (*ficelle*) attached to the handles of the stewpot so that it can't actually touch the bottom during cooking.

BOLLITO MISTO (*Italian*)

A speciality of Piedmonte, Lombardy and Emilia-Romagna in Northern Italy, this is a combination of several boiled meats which may include beef, tongue, veal *zampone* (qv), and possibly chicken or turkey. It may be served from a special trolley and carved at the table. The meats are accompanied by *salsa verde*, a combination of parsley, anchovies, garlic oil and pine nuts.

BOLOGNESE, alla (*Italian*)

In the Bolognese style. This usually refers to the *ragu* or sauce served with pasta, risotto, or meat dishes. It should be made with beef and pork, finely minced; *prosciutto* (qv), mushrooms, tomatoes, vegetables, garlic and herbs. For the 'real thing' dry white wine, milk, nutmeg and 3½–5 hours cooking time are required. It can also refer to meat or poultry egg-dipped, breaded and fried, with ham and cheese. See also *Crescentina*, *Lasagna* and *Stecchini*.

BOMBAY DUCK (*Indian*)

Hardly feathered, Bombay duck is no bird but a fish. Resembling the herring, it is caught in vast numbers along the southern east coast of India. It is cleaned and gutted, heavily salted, then strung up on lines to dry in the sun. After drying it is fried in *ghee* (qv) and deep-fried before serving. It will keep for weeks in an airtight container. It is eaten as an appetiser by Westerners, but the Indians eat it crumbled over rice, or eaten in small bites to accompany rice or other dishes.

BORCK (*Turkish*)

Small packages or envelopes of fillo (qv), pastry – either triangular or cigar shaped – containing a cheese, spinach or meat mixture. Most usually served as a first course,

large versions with more substantial fillings are also
served as a main course.

BORSCHT *(Russian/Jewish)*
A traditional peasant soup with the rich colour and
flavour of beetroot, combined with meat broth, carrots,
and sometimes potatoes and/or cabbage. It is served hot
in the winter with a garnish of sour cream, and cold in
the summer.

BOSTON BAKED BEANS *(American)*
A Puritan dish which has become synonymous with
Boston, 'home of the bean'. It was originally baked on
Saturday to be reheated and eaten on Sunday, when the
strictly observed Sabbath allowed no work. The basic
recipe uses navy (haricot) beans or other small white
beans, salt pork, mustard, brown sugar and molasses all
baked in a low oven for several hours, until the pork
shreds easily and the beans are engulfed in a thick
brown syrupy sauce. Variations include using maple
syrup instead of sugar, and the addition of tomato paste
and cloves.

BOTI KEBAB *(Indian/Pakistani)*
A small snack kebab of lamb pieces, first marinated,
then grilled and served with lime or lemon to squeeze
over.

BOUDIN BLANC *(French)*
A white pudding in a sausage case, made from pork (or
sometimes chicken) onion, eggs, cream and occasionally *foie gras* or truffles for a special touch. It is poached
in butter and apple slices added at the last minute,
before serving.

BOUDIN NOIR *(French)*
The Gallic version of English *Black Pudding* (qv),
omitting the cereal content, consisting primarily of
seasoned concentrated pork blood and fat. It can be
made into small sausages, but is more usually sold by
French butchers in custom-cut sections from a long
coil.

BOUILLABAISSE *(French)*
The great thick soup or stew of Provence, which has
near relatives throughout the Mediterranean. It
includes several kinds of fish, which for authenticity
should include rascasse, gurnard, John Dory and eel, as
well as optional extras like monkfish, red mullet and sea
bass, crab, mussels and other shellfish. Additional
necessary ingredients are onion, saffron, tomato, garlic,
wine and olive oil. After cooking, the fish are often
removed and served separately while the broth alone is
poured over croutons of bread. In either case the soup
is served with *aioli* (qv). See also *epinard*.

BOXTY *(Irish)*
A kind of potato bread, floury in texture, made of
mixed mashed and grated potatoes, together with butter or bacon fat. It is baked in round cakes in the
oven, and divided into quarters, or *farls*, when
served.

BRAMBOROVA POLEVKA *(Czeck)*
Potato and mushroom soup, flavoured with celery, parsley and marjoram.

BRANDADE DE MORUE *(French)*
A salt cod dish, popular in Provence and Languedoc, and traditionally served there on Good Friday. It consists of pre-soaked and poached salt cod, pounded with garlic and olive oil, then stirred with additional oil and cream, until it is smooth and fluffy, like mashed potatoes. Some less strictly orthodox cooks mash potatoes in with the cod. (See also *bacalão*).

BRATWURST *(German)*
A large pork sausage found throughout Germany and Austria, usually served fried or grilled. Together with *frankfurters* and sometimes *Debrecziner sausage* (qv) they are offered in street kiosks, *Würstchenstands*, together with a serving of *senf* (mustard) and brown bread.

BRAWN *(Scottish/English/Irish)*
Traditionally made from pork trimmings, although sometimes other meats are used. The meat from the head and trotters is chopped, seasoned and spiced, cooked and allowed to set in the jelly from the reduced stock. It is always eaten sliced and cold.

BREAD AND BUTTER PUDDING *(English)*
Slices of bread, sprinkled with currants, raisins, cinnamon and sugar, then covered with an egg and milk custard and baked. It has been a nursery favourite – equally popular with adults – for generations.

BREAD SAUCE *(English)*
This typically English sauce is served with almost all poultry and game birds. An onion stuck with cloves is steeped in milk, and then flavoured and thickened with butter, spices and breadcrumbs. It is simmered until it is of a fairly stiff gluey consistency.

BRESAOLA *(Italian)*
Air-dried and cured beef fillet, served in thin, dark slices as a first course. It is usually moistened with olive oil and lemon.

BRIE *(French)*
'The King of Cheeses' – so elected by the members of the Congress of Vienna in 1814 – brie has long been a favourite of gourmets, including most of the kings and queens of France. The best farmhouse brie is still made in the Ile de France from unpasteurised cow's milk, and includes the types *Brie de Meaux* (the most famous) and *Brie de Melum Affine*, both of which are *appellation d'origine*. The latter has a darker brown rind and a more pungent smell and lactic flavour than the former, though the rind of *Brie de Meaux* is still darker than that of a laitier Brie. All bries are soft unpressed cheese, made in large flat wheels, from 3lb to 7lb in weight, with a white, floury rind with some browning. The interior texture should be smooth and glossy, without excessive runniness or chalkiness. There are several variations of the pasteurised cheese around today – studded with pepper, blue-veined, and other pastes –

but they are distracting additions to an already excellent cheese.

BRIK à l'OEUF *(Tunisian)*

One of the best dishes in Tunisian cookery. The *brik* or packet contains a raw egg – and perhaps cheese and onion, or a vegetable mixture – wrapped in fillo pastry. The packet is then deep-fried quickly, so that the egg is just coddled. When bitten into, the soft-cooked egg should mix with the other steaming filling to produce delightful combinations of taste and texture. Make sure the egg doesn't run down your chin!

BRINJAL *(Indian/Pakistani)*

Aubergine. A favourite vegetable of the subcontinent, aubergine is found mixed with yogurt (*Dahi* (qv) or in a dry curry known as a *Bhaji* (qv)). Indians use both the large aubergine familiar to Europeans and Americans, and the smaller round aubergines.

BRODETTO *(Italian)*

An Adriatic fish soup, with innumerable variations. White fish are mixed with shellfish, squid and sometimes eel. The broth is usually made separately with fish heads, while the fish, tomatoes and onions are sautéed in garlic and oil. The broth and stewed fish are combined to simmer, then separated again for serving. Well-known versions include those from Ravenno, Anconetana and Venice. The broth is usually made with fish trimmings while the fish pieces are sautéed separately in oil, garlic and often tomatoes. In Ravenna-style (*alla ravennate*) the squid, eel, red mullet and other fish are added for the last few minutes, then served separately from the broth; in the Venetian-style (*alla veneziano*) the grey mullet, monkfish, etc., are kept in large pieces and served with fried bread.

BROODJE *(Dutch)*

Sandwich. The usual lunchtime snack all over Holland in bars and cafes. Often 'open-faced' – with sliced cheese (Gouda or Edam) topped with cold meat and garnish.

BROWNIE *(American)*

A cake-like confection with a crumbly consistency, made of flour, butter, chocolate and nuts. It is a favourite sweet snack and dessert, and is either frosted (with chocolate icing) or served with ice cream.

B'STILLA (PASTILA) *(Moroccan)*

This is considered to be the jewel in the crown of Moroccan cuisine. It takes time and patience to make, while the thinness of the pastry is a true test of a cook's skill. Semi-transparent fillo pastry (qv) is filled with slices of pigeon (sometimes combined with, or replaced by, chicken in less affluent households), beaten eggs and pistachio nuts, the pastry in alternating layers with the filling. The whole pie is enclosed in a final covering of pastry, baked, and served dusted with cinnamon and sugar, cut into wedge-shaped slices. Alternatively

B'stilla can be made in small envelopes as finger food at larger gatherings.

BUBBLE & SQUEAK (*English*)
Today bubble and squeak is made with left-over cabbage and mashed potatoes, mixed together. Sometimes it is further fried in cakes. In earlier times the name referred to a mixture of salt-beef and cabbage, sometimes extended with potatoes.

BUCATINI (*Italian*)
A commercially-produced pasta, in the form of long, spaghetti-length macaroni.

BUCCELLATO (*Italian*)
A Tuscan dessert speciality baked in a ring-shaped mould. It is made of flour, sugar, vanilla, raisins, and aniseed, and is usually served with strawberries marinated in sweet wine.

BUCK RAREBIT (*English/Welsh*)
Welsh rarebit with a poached or fried egg on top. See *Welsh Rarebit*.

BULBUL YUVASI (*Turkish*)
A Turkish dessert. Fillo (qv), pastry is shaped into a small circle, baked and then filled with egg custard and dusted with cinnamon.

BULGALBI (*Korean*)
See *Bulgogi*.

BULGOGI (*Korean*)
Thin cut fillets of steak pounded very thin and cut into squares are marinated in a mixture of soy, garlic, ginger, sugar, spring onions, pepper and sesame seeds for several hours. They are then grilled briefly over charcoal and served with a sweet/sour hot sauce called *Yangnum Kanjang*. A similar treatment and sauce are used for beef short ribs, *Bulgalbi*. Pork versions of *Bulgogi* (*Dwagi Bulgogi*) and chicken versions (*Dak Bulgogi*) are often available in British Korean restaurants, although they are not actually authentic.

BUNDI (*Indian/Pakistani*)
Rice and wheat flour batter in a mixture like that used to make *Jalebi* (qv), but passed through a sieve to take the shape of tiny rice-shaped droplets. These are deep-fried, then soaked in sweet syrup, then allowed to dry until the syrup congeals and hardens.

BUNUEOLOS (*Mexican*)
A sweet dessert or treat popular all over Mexico, made in both North and South, though in different guises. In the south they are deep-fried as large, crisp wheat tortillas, with hot muscovado sugar syrup, cream and nuts on top; in the north they are cut into segments, deep-fried, and then tossed in sugar and cinnamon after frying.

BURGHUL (*Lebanese/Middle Eastern*)
Cracked wheat. (See *Tabbouleh* and *Kibbeh*).

BURGOO (*American*)
A thick southern stew, whose main ingredients are beef and chicken, was once based on squirrel and rabbit. Other traditional constituents are potatoes, okra, corn,

tomatoes, beans, red pepper and brown sugar. It is still made in gargantuan quantities for church suppers and political rallies, and it is *the* traditional dish on Kentucky Derby Day.

BURRITOS *(Mexican)*
A soft wheat *tortilla* (qv) is filled with a pre-cooked hot stuffing – refried beans, and cheese, or eggs scrambled with chili peppers – and then folded and eaten, often in the hands.

BUTIFARRA *(Spanish)*
A white sausage, flavoured with cinnamon, nutmeg, cloves and other spices. Originally from Catalonia, it is used extensively in Catalan and southern cooking. It is a particularly characteristic component of *Butifarra con setas* (Catalan baked sausage and mushrooms) and *Cazuleas* (Catalan casseroles). It is also used ground and skinned in certain recipes.

BUTTERFLY PRAWNS *(Chinese)*
See *Woo Dip Har.*

✘ *CABBAGE*
History is rather vague about the exact origin of the cabbage, which includes in its family broccoli, Brussels sprouts and cauliflower. To the Romans it was an expensive and highly prized luxury, and the Roman Senate, under Emperor Claudius, voted the combination of Salt Beef and Cabbage the finest in the world. Mind you, the Emperor was a big fan of the dish, so what else could they do? Regarding red cabbage, there comes from France the story of the kindly Bishop of Perigueux, who befriended a young unwed mother-to-be, as she carried a large cabbage through a jeering throng. Taking the vegetable from her he wrapped it in his episcopal mantle and escorted her to her door. When he handed the cabbage back it had miraculously changed its colour to that of the Bishop's robe.

CA CHIEN MUOI XA *(Vietnamese)*
Fish rubbed with oil and spices – including lemon grass, chilis and garlic – then grilled or sautéed.

CABOC *(Scottish)*
A pale full-cream cow's milk cheese which is unpressed, and simply moulded into logs or cylinders which are coated in oatmeal. The flavour complemented by the coating is mild with a slight nutty overtone.

CACCIATORA, alla *(Italian)*
Literally 'Hunter's style'. Meat or poultry cooked in a thick sauce of mushrooms, onions, tomatoes and herbs in white wine. The most usual main ingredient is chicken or veal.

CACIK *(Turkish)*
Chopped cucumber in a garlic and mint flavoured sauce made of thick strained yogurt. It is usually decorated with a swirl of olive oil or a sprinkling of paprika.

CACCUICCO *(Italian)*
A thick fish soup or stew, whose best-known version comes from Livorno (alla Livornese). It contains an

assortment of fish, including cod and mackerel, perhaps halibut and various shellfish, such as scallop and shrimp, as well as white wine, tomatoes and numerous spices. It is a close relation to Marseilles' famous *Bouillabaisse* (qv) and is usually served as a main course.

CAERPHILLY *(Welsh/English)*

The whitest, sourest of the British cheeses. A granular semi-hard cow's milk cheese which is aged only two to four weeks, it was once known only as 'new cheese' because of its quick maturation. Though first developed and made in farmhouses in Wales, today it is made in England, both as a creamery and farmhouse cheese. It has a clean, buttermilk-like flavour, and is easily digestible. It was the original cheese used in *Welsh Rarebit* (qv).

CAESAR SALAD *(American)*

The invention of a renowned New York chef at the turn of the century, Caesar salad is an original concept. It should be made with cos (Romaine) lettuce leaves torn into pieces and tossed in a large bowl with a dressing made of anchovies, oil and lemon juice. At the last moment, a coddled egg is broken in, a large sprinkling of parmesan cheese and garlic croutons added, and the whole tossed briefly again before serving.

CALABRESE, alla *(Italian)*

In the style of Calabria, the 'toe' of Italy. It is used in relation to several classic dishes, notably *ravioli*, *triglie* (red mullet), *sgombro* (mackerel) and other fish. It usually indicates a sauce containing herbs (oregano, or marjoram and parsley), olives, capers and/or anchovies.

CALALOO (CALALOU) *(Caribbean)*

The most famous soup of the Caribbean, named after the leaves of the tare plant, called *calaloo* by the native peoples. It is particularly common to Trinidad and Tobago, but it is found in varying forms throughout the islands. It is a thick soup, a form of gumbo, containing salt pork, crab or conch, tomatoes, onions, okra, aubergine or marrow, spices and herbs and coconut milk. The true *calaloo* is quite hot, with pepper sauce stirred in.

CALAMARES *(Greek/Spanish/French)*

Squid, cleaned and sliced into rings is used in dishes all over the Mediterranean. Particularly popular is *Calamares fritos* or deep-fried, battered squid, served with a slice of lemon as a first or a main course. Calamares also form a main part of most seafood salads, or *insalata de mare*.

CALLOS *(Spanish)*

The Spaniards are great lovers of tripe. The two most favoured recipes are for *Callos à la Andaluzo* and *Callos à la Madrilena*. The latter, from the capital city, combines the tripe with white wine, tomatoes, chorizo, ham, onion, garlic, many herbs and a pig's foot. It should be served in traditional earthenware bowls. The former, from the Southwest, substitutes calf's foot for the pig's foot and inclues chick peas, peppers and saffron.

CALZONE *(Italian)*

A speciality of Naples, this is an envelope made of pizza dough stuffed with ham and mozzarella. Another version, from the heel of Italy (Basilicata) has a stuffing of onions, olives, anchovies, capers and cheese. Smaller versions – often open-faced – are called *Calzoni* or *pazerotti*.

CAMEMBERT *(French)*

An *appellation d'origine* cheese, Camembert is probably the best-known of French cheese, widely exported from France and also imitated by many countries in the world. While most is made from pasteurised cow's milk in large and small dairies, and some indeed are good cheese with a full mellow lactic flavour and creamy texture, they cannot compare with the true unpasteurised farm Camembert, with its slightly brown rind and tangier, richer flavour. These farm cheeses come in a chipboard box and should be imprinted *lait esu, non pasteurisée* or *fromage fermier*, and the letters VCN – *veritable camembert de Normandie*. That from the Auge is deemed best of all. Although the Camembert type of cheese goes back to the Middle Ages, it was not until the 1790s that Mme Harel 'perfected' the recipe. Camembert is chiefly eaten as a dessert or savoury cheese (it goes particularly well with grapes), though it is often deep-fried as a first course.

CANNELLONI *(Italian)*

A Piedmontese speciality, these large filled tubes of pasta originated in the Catalonia region of Spain, and passed over to Italy several hundred years ago. The tubes are either manufactured, or made from rolling flat sheets of egg pasta. The usual filling is a ragout of beef and tomato, the rolls then covered with *Béchamel* sauce; or the filling can be a mixture of spinach, eggs, cream and cheese, covered in a tomato sauce; or cheese and ham, covered in tomato and basil sauce. All of these combinations – and several more – can be presented in a restaurant simply under the title 'cannelloni'.

CANNOLI *(Italian)*

A speciality of Sicily, these are puff-pastry horns piped full of sweetened Ricotta, cocoa, nuts and candied peel.

CANTAL *(French)*

This Auvergne cow's milk cheese claims to be the oldest in France, made since the days of the Gauls in mountain huts, or *burons*. The centre for the true unpasteurised version is around Salers; this cheese is notable for its heavier rougher texture. Those *fermier* (farmhouse) products labelled 'Haute Montagne' denote that it is made from the milk of cows who have fed on Alpine herbs and flowers. Smaller *Cantalet* or *Cantalon*, are made at the end of summer and are particularly high on butterfat. The commercial *laitier* version has a creamier texture and a less assertive flavour. The yellow paste of all Cantals is close-textured and tastes rather like a medium-to-mild Cheddar. For this reason it is not much beloved by Cheddar-loving gourmets who find it rather dull. But it is a subtle cheese and is much used in French soufflés and other dishes.

CANTALOUPE (*American/British*)
The most popular of the orange rock-melons, with a rough, webbed skin, pitted all over. It has a bright orange flesh, and when ripe is succulent and pungent. It is much favoured in the US for both first courses and desserts, and is a prime ingredient in fancy fruit salads. It lacks the finesse of the *Charantais* (qv), but is hardier and fast gaining ground.

CAPONATA (*Italian*)
This Sicilian dish is usually served at room temperature and made some time ahead to allow the flavours to blend. It is a sauté of peeled and diced aubergines and onions, simmered afterwards in a tomato, vinegar and sugar sauce, and then mixed with chopped capers, olives, celery and anchovies. Oil is dribbled over the top and it can be served with tuna or other fish scattered over the top.

CAPPELLETTI (*Italian*)
Small stuffed pasta shaped like small peaked caps – the meaning of the name. The stuffing is usually a mixture of meat – sausage, chicken and pork – spiced and filled out with cheese. It is traditionally floated in chicken or capon broth at Christmas in the Umbria, Marche and Emilia-Romagna.

CAPPOR MAGRO (*Italian*)
An elegant salad of white fish – usually sea bass, monkfish, etc. – and shellfish – crayfish, shrimp, etc. – piled on a base of croutons or dried bread, together with mixed vegetables. The whole edifice is covered with a veil of garlic, anchovy, caper and mayonnaise sauce. So rich and large, it is usually served as a summer main course. A speciality of Liguria and Rome.

CAPRA, CAPRETTO (*Italian*)
Goat meat is eaten throughout Italy, and *Capretto* – kid or baby goat – is a highly regarded delicacy. It is particularly popular at Easter, when it is roasted with olive oil, carrots, onions, rosemary, and white wine. This is *Capretto alla pasqualina*.

CARAPULCRA (*Latin American*)
Chicken pork and potatoes in a peanut sauce.

CARACOLES (*Spanish*)
Snails – a speciality of Barcelona and Catalonia. Instead of serving a dozen or half dozen on a plate, as in France, the snails are simmered in their shells in a thick sauce of tomatoes, garlic, onions and wine. Because they are small snails, servings may include up to twenty.

CARAWAY (*Herb*)
A relative of dill and fennel, caraway grows wild in many parts of Europe, and is commercially grown in many other spots. It was once an important ingredient

of English cooking, much found in Medieval through to Victorian recipes, principally in breads, cakes and desserts. It is today more associated with Austro/German and Middle European cookery, its partnership with dill especially notable in pickles and fish, and in *sauerkraut*, breads and soups.

(See the *Herbs and Spices* chart for translations.)

CARBONARA, SPAGHETTI alla *(Italian)*

Spaghetti is usually the pasta teamed with Carbonara sauce. Butter and bacon are sautéed together, then the hot, strained spaghetti tossed with it. Beaten eggs are then added, the whole tossed again, and finally mixed with parmesan cheese. The heat of the pasta cooks the eggs.

CARBONNADE *(Belgian)*

Together with *Waterzooi* (qv), this is probably the best-known national dish. It is a beef stew, but a special one, in which the meat is simmered in brown beer together with brown sugar, onions and herbs. The term originally meant 'half burned' or 'grilled' and probably refers to the very dark colours of the stew – when finally cooked. It may also refer to the topping of mustard-spread bread slices which are traditionally added to the dish and then grilled until bubbling and brown before serving.

CARCIOFI *(Italian)*

Artichokes are a particularly important vegetable in Italian cuisine – baby artichokes or artichoke hearts appear in everything from antipasto, spicily marinated, to omelettes, deep-fried (*alla guidia*) or stuffed. Stuffing can include garlic and breadcrumbs, with the artichokes braised in oil, or stuffed with fish and cheese, or garlic and capers and baked.

CARDAMOM *(Spice)*

A necessary spice in curries and in many dishes from India and Pakistan. The dried seed pod – usually green or bleached white – contains small black seeds with a strong, pungent smell. The pod is split and used whole in Middle Eastern and Far Eastern cooking, while only the seeds tend to be used in European pickles, mulled wine and pastries (the last particularly in Sweden and Scandinavia). It is a distinctive spice, whose absence when required, cannot easily be disguised.

(See the *Herbs and Spices* chart for translations).

CARDOON *(English and French)*

Known as *cardons* in French, where they are a vegetable staple, cardoons can be found in some speciality green-grocers in England. The plant of which they form the stalk leaves resembles the globe artichoke, and some varieties can grow to eight feet. The stalks of the inner leaves are bleached in sunlight until white, and are cooked until just tender-crisp.

✕ CARP

This freshwater fish, for long a collector's delight, is now being more widely bred for the table and apart from the

*claimed fact that it can live up to the remarkable age of 150
years, has two other notable points of interest. Firstly, it
actually chews its food before swallowing, (most fish simply
swallow it whole) and should the water in which it is living
become short of oxygen, for example in a hot summer, it
simply pops its head out of the water for a gulp of life saving
fresh air!*

CARPACCIO (*Italian*)

A speciality of the Venetian region, now much loved by
the *novelle cucina* school. It consists of thin, paper-like
slices of raw lean beef fillet, dressed with an oil and
lemon sauce, or a mustard sauce. Thin shavings of
Parmesan are often scattered over the top.

CARRAGHEEN (*Irish*)

Also known as Irish Moss, carragheen is a small edible
seaweed found in colder waters. It is washed, bleached
in the sun on the beach, and dried then sold commercially for use in cooking and in clarifying malt beverages. It is much used in Gaelic and Celtic cooking for
making a milk jelly dessert and for a ginger jelly.

✖ CARROT

*Claimed to be Britain's second most popular vegetable,
(after the potato) carrots are a good source of Vitamin A,
which probably accounts for the old belief in their benefit to
the eyesight. Containing more sugar than any other vegetable except sugar beet, it's good to see that carrot cake
seems to be making a popular comeback. That famous
nation of sweet talkers, the Irish, are credited with the
description of carrots as 'underground honey'.*

✖ CASHEW

*Ever wondered why you never see cashew nuts in the shell?
Quite simply because this relative of poison ivy contains in
its shell a dangerous oil, which must be removed by heat,
and carefully washed for safety. This unpleasant factor
however doesn't prevent it from being the world's second
most popular nut, after the almond.*

CASINO, OYSTERS OR CLAMS (*American*)

Oysters or clams on the half shell, covered with a
topping of minced green pepper, seasoning and bacon,
and broiled (grilled) over rock salt.

CASSAVA (*African/Caribbean*)

A white, stodgy, starchy vegetable, usually served as a
solid lump. It is the pounded and boiled root of the
manioc or yucca, and is the 'bread of life' to numerous
tribes in Africa.

CASSOULET (*French*)

The most famous dish of the Languedoc region, a
combination of white haricot beans, garlic, onions,
sausages and various meats and/or preserved fowl,
according to the town from which it comes. The dish,
when cooked authentically, needs several days, and
when ready, will have a thick crust which can be

cracked with a spoon. The main centre famed for its cassoulet is Toulouse, where the dish originated.

✗ CAULIFLOWER

When Mark Twain wrote in jocular mood that "Cauliflower is nothing but a cabbage with a college education", he wasn't too far out since, as explained elsewhere, they are of the same family. Madame du Barry, the mistress of Louis XV, had a cauliflower dish named after her, which is why to this day if you find a menu item featuring the term 'du Barry' it denotes the presence of the vegetable in its composition.

✗ CAVIAR

Incredible as it may seem this most expensive of luxury foods used to be given away free in American Saloon Bars to promote the sale of beer. This was in the days when the sturgeon was a plentiful fish which sadly found itself unable to cope with modern industrial pollution. The most sought after caviar of all, principally for its colour is 'Golden Caviar' from a rare species called Sterlet. The yearly total supply is only a little over 40 pounds and in the days of the Czar all the take from his territories went to him. It's interesting to note that Stalin, that great champion of fair shares for all, regularly helped himself to two fifths of the annual supply.

CAYENNE *(Spice)*

See also *Chilis*. Originally, the chilis for use in Cayenne were from the coast of South America, although today they come from all over. Cayenne is used in a number of Creole American dishes, as well as those of the Caribbean and oriental dishes. It is the dried and ground pods of chili peppers, and bears a relationship to chili powder, though it is more finely ground.

CELERI-RAVE *(French)*

See *Celeriac*.

CELERIAC *(French/Italian/British)*

A 'turnip-rooted' vegetable found throughout the Mediterranean, though most closely associated with France, where it is called *céleri-rave* and features in every *traiteur* (delicatessen) as *céleri remoulade*, a mayonnaise-bound salad of shredded celeriac. In fact, it is not a root but a type of celery with a knobbly bulbous stem covered in a rough, dark skin. When the skin is peeled off, a white flesh is revealed which smells of celery. The raw flesh can be grated and served as salad, or the vegetable can be cut into pieces and lightly boiled, to be either served with butter or puréed. It has a texture and flavour which is a fine complement to game and pork dishes.

CENCI *(Italian)*

Deep-fried pastry knots or twists made from flour, eggs and rum. When fried they puff up and are dusted with icing sugar. They are particularly popular in the Florence region.

CÈPE (French)

The late summer and autumn mushroom *Boletus*, brown-capped with a thick stem and spongy underside, a speciality of Southwestern France, though found throughout the country *and* many others. In the region of Perigord it is usually sautéed in oil, garlic and parsley and served on its own, as a side dish with meats, poultry (especially the famous *confit*), or in omelettes.

CERKEZ TAVRIGU (Turkish)

Often called 'Circassian chicken' even in ethnically correct restaurants, this is a dish of chopped or shredded chicken covered with a sauce of crushed garlic, walnuts, paprika and chicken stock. It is usually served as a first course.

CEVAPCICI (Yugoslavian)

A mixture of ground lamb and beef, flavoured with paprika, onion and garlic, which is made into small rolls and skewered. The kebabs are traditionally grilled over charcoal, but they can be cooked on an oven grill. They are served with chopped onions and pickled hot peppers.

CEVICHE (SEVICHE) (Mexican)

Raw white, non-oily fish (halibut, snapper, salmon) or shellfish (usually scallops, sometimes conch) marinated in a mixture of lime juice, dried or fresh chili pepper, onion, tomato, salt and oregano, sometimes with a dash of olive oil. A well-known, and now much imitated speciality of the coast near Acapulco and Puerto Vilarta.

CHA CHU KUEN (Chinese)

Pork and bean sprout stuffed spring roll, deep-fried and served as *dim sum*.

CHA GEO (Vietnamese)

Spring rolls made with rice paper and stuffed with pork mince, crab meat, noodles, Chinese mushrooms, onion, garlic and beansprouts or other greens. They are then deep-fried and drained. Served wrapped in a lettuce leaf, with sprigs of mint and coriander, dipped in *Nuoc Cham*.

CHA YIP DAHN (Chinese)

Marbled eggs. They are made by just coddling the eggs, then gently cracking the shells all over and hard-boiling them in tea and five-spice powder. Served as an appetiser.

CHABICHOU (French)

One of the more well-known goat cheeses or *chèvres*, made in Poitou and instantly recognisable by its truncated cone shape. The cheese has a chalky-white interior and a white bloomy rind if made from pasteurised milk at a *latier*; a bluish-white, red-streaked rind if made of unpasteurised milk at a *fermier*. Both have a strong barnyard smell and a very 'goaty' flavour. The average age of a cheese is two weeks, but some are eaten as a fresh cheese in the Poitou-Charente region. The *cendre* version has a cinder-covered, black exterior to inhibit mould growth. It tends to have a slightly fresher, lighter flavour.

CHALEYSA (*Mexican*)

Literally 'boats'. Named after the flat boats used in old Mexico City. They are cooked similarly to a flat tortilla, except that the edges are pinched all around to hold the sauce, which is usually a combination of hot enchilada sauce, dried chili sauce (*salsa adobado*) or a spicy tomato sauce. This is topped with crumbled white Mexican cheese and onions. It is usually eaten as an appetiser with drinks or as a snack.

CHAMP (*Irish*)

A dish of the northern counties, based on potatoes mashed with milk or cream, then mixed with spring onions, chives or nettles. A well is normally made in the centre when serving, and filled with butter or it can be filled with scrambled egg or sausage for a more substantial supper dish.

CHANG CHA HSUING YA (*Chinese*)

Duck smoked over tea and camphor leaves, after being marinated in a paste of salt, pepper, rice wine and *hoisin* sauce. After smoking the duck is then deep-fried, cut into small pieces, reshaped and served. This is a Chengdu dish, from the west of China.

CHAN PEI FUN GAI (*Chinese*)

Tangerine smoked chicken. The chicken is first rubbed all over with soy sauce, salt, Chinese wine and sugar, then steamed. It is finally smoked over grated dried tangerine skin and star anise, pounded together to make a powder.

CHANNA (*Indian/Pakistani*)

Boiled chick peas spiced with turmeric, cumin and chili, cooled and used as a snack before drinks or as a small separate snack. They are often allowed to dry slightly and are mixed with *ki dhal* and *sev* as Bombay mix.

CHANNA KI DHAL (*Indian/Pakistani*)

Deep-fried split peas, spiced with *garam masala* and chili. They can be served on their own as a snack or titbit with drinks, or mixed with *sev*, *channa* and spiced nuts to make Bombay mix, as it is popularly known in the West.

CHANTILLY, à la (*French*)

In the style of Chantilly, a town above Paris in the north, and the elegant centre of French racing. It usually implies the addition of cream.

Crème chantilly is cream whipped with sugar and vanilla, used to accompany desserts.

CHAO (*Chinese*)

This word in a Chinese recipe title means stir-fried, traditionally done in a wok over a specially constructed platform with a fire underneath.

CHAO HAAH LOOK (*Chinese*)

A favourite of Western diners, stir-fried shrimp with spring onions, in a sweet-and-sour sauce. The prawns are marinated in egg white and cornflour before being deep-fried, then stir-fried in the sauce. This is a Shandong dish, from the North.

CHAO SHAO PAO (*Chinese*)
Steamed white yeast pastry dumplings stuffed with barbecued pork, served as *dim sum* (qv).

CHAO TOM (*Vietnamese*)
Balls of shrimp paste, mixed with egg white and oil, skewered on sugar cane sticks and barbecued or grilled. The balls are then removed into a moistened rice pancake and dipped into *Nuoc Mam* (qv) before eating.

CHAP CHE (*Korean*)
A stir-fried mixture of vegetables cut into thin strips (spring onion, Chinese cabbage, carrots, cucumber, spinach, bamboo shoots), rice vermicelli and fillet beef. All ingredients should be stir-fried separately, then mixed together on a platter and seasoned with soy, sugar and pepper.

CHAPATI (*Indian/Pakistani*)
The *chapati* is a flat disc of wholewheat bread traditionally cooked on a griddle. It has a slightly sour flavour and a chewy texture. Chapatis are eaten with a curry and pieces are torn off to be used like a spoon to mop up rice, sauce or meat.

CHARENTAIS (*French*)
A round smallish melon with a light greenish pitted, grooved skin, and bright orange flesh with a juicy texture and very sweet flavour. In appearance it is somewhat like the *cantaloupe* (qv), although it is more delicate and sweeter in flavour and its skin is not so webbed. Charentais melons are traditionally served in the Charente and Dordogne with the deseeded centre filled with port, or so I have been told, although in several visits to the region I've never seen it done and personally I much prefer to enjoy my melon and port separately. However, Madame Jeanne Moorsom, a native of La Rochelle, the delightful capital of the Charente-Maritime, introduced me to the practice of sprinkling a little salt over the fruit which dramatically enhances its lovely flavour and this has become a custom I follow gratefully and enthusiastically recommend.

CHARLOTTE (*French*)
One of two types of dessert, both moulded with a dry lining. In the first the mould or dish is lined with toasted bread and then filled with fruit (such as apples or peaches), baked and served hot. In the other variation, the dish is lined with sponge fingers or biscuits, and filled with a cream mixture, chilled to set, and served cold. The word seems to be a corruption of the old English 'charlyt' or custard.

CHASSEUR, à la (*French*)
In hunter's style. A garnish or sauce incorporating mushrooms and shallots; in the case of the sauce,

reduced with white wine to a dark brown, rich coating.

CHAT *(Indian)*
A generic term for snacks. The word 'chat' also some-times appears in the title of a dish, such as *also chat* (dry spiced potato slices) or *murgh chat* (small pieces of chicken cooked in spices). Other types of *chat* include *Bhajiia*, *pakoras*, *samosas*, *channa*, *sev* and *pani puri* (qv).

CHATEAUBRIAND *(French)*
This meltingly tender middle cut of beefsteak is named for the Viscount Francois Auguste Chateaubriand, who was born in 1768 and died in 1848. He was renowned as an author and gourmand, and this double fillet was a personal favourite. It is usually served with *Chateau-briand* sauce – made with butter, shallots, herbs and dry white wine – or a classic *Béarnaise* (qv).

CHATNI *(Indian/Pakistani)*
Chutney – the origin of our own English word. *Chatnis* take a variety of forms, from the sweet to the sour, from those made with fresh ingredients (the real Indian version) to the preserved kind, like the famous sweet mango chutney, which were products of the Raj. Frequently encountered *chatnis* include *dhania* chutney (with fresh coriander), *Podina chatni* (with fresh mint and *Nariyal chatni* (made with desiccated coconut and spices, often served with a *Dahi* (qv).
(See also *Achar*).

CHAUMER *(French)*
A washed-rind semi-soft cow's milk cheese which is becoming more popular abroad. It is a pasteurised cheese, but boasts a nutty, pleasant flavour and a springy texture, rather like a mild *Reblochon* (qv).

CHAWAN MUSHI *(Japanese)*
The only Japanese main dish to require a spoon, this savoury egg custard is actually classed as a soup. Mushrooms and prawns or fish cake are flavoured with *mirin* or soy sauce, then covered with beaten egg in a special chawan mushi cup. The cups are covered and placed in boiling water to steam.

CHAYOTE *(Caribbean/Indonesian and Malaysian/South American)*
See *cho-cho*.

CHEDDAR *(English)*
Sister cheese of Cheshire, in location and in style of flavour, Cheddar is more golden, firmer and even richer in flavour. It is available in farmhouse and creamery versions, and though the true Cheddar still comes from Somerset, the type is now made in Ireland, Scotland, America and as far afield as Japan. The commercial version ranges from mild (almost flavourless) to 'sharp' or 'mature', but the real West Country version, made to traditional methods and standards, has an inimitable depth of flavour and denseness of texture, without waxiness, and can be aged up to two years. It is

produced in truckles (small 9–11lb cheeses) and great wheels of up to 60lb.

CHELO (Iranian)
Boiled and steamed rice prepared in the Persian manner. The rice is first soaked then boiled normally. But then it is steamed in a good deal of butter, covered by a cloth. The result is elegant; separate grains on a bed of crisped, brown rice that has formed a crust at the bottom of the pan. This crust is considered a delicacy and is offered to the guests.

CHEMISE, en (French)
Baked or roasted in oiled greaseproof paper or envelope. This treatment is in the classic tradition and is used for fish, meat, poultry and occasionally crustaceans like lobster and crab. (See also en papillote). The term can also be used for food wrapped in pastry or batter, or in the case of potatoes – Pommes en chemise – in their jacket. (See also Negresse en chemise).

✗ CHERRY
You remember the famous story of George Washington as a lad, being let off punishment after chopping down his father's cherry tree, for admitting his guilt with the immortal line, "I cannot tell a lie"? Well, its totally untrue! (Made up in fact by one Parson Weems).

CHESHIRE (English)
The oldest British cheese; semi-hard, somewhat salty and crumbly. A cow's milk cheese, it took its name from the county in which it is still made; it is sometimes also called Chester, which was its original town of production. It is available in the natural pale state and in an annatto-coloured version which is more commercially popular. There are still a respectable number of farmhouse makers, who age their cheeses longer than the one to two months allowed the creamery cheeses. It is an excellent eating and cooking cheese, melting easily and imparting a mellow sharpness.

CHICKEN à la KING (American)
A now classic combination of sautéed mushrooms, cooked chopped chicken, and pimentoes in an egg-thickened, sherry-flavoured cream sauce.

CHICORY (Vegetable)
A member of the dandelion family, the root is used as a coffee substitute or additive, and the leaves as a salad. The green leaves are serrated and it resembles a ragged lettuce; the taste is somewhat bitter. Although called chicory in the US and chicorée in France, it is more commonly known as 'curly endive' in the UK. The root is white and fleshy, but when roasted it has a taste akin to coffee and no caffeine. Another variation of chicory is *escarole*, its broad-leaved, wavy cousin. See also *Endive, Belgian*.

CHILI (South America, Mexico, Africa, Middle and Far East)

A profusion of chilis are available all over the world. They come in varieties of colours – red, orange, green, yellowish, almost black. The smaller varieties are usually the hottest, but there are exceptions like the bonnet chili and others of Mexico, Central and South America. It is also true that the red and green are the hottest, those which are fresh are more pungent and assertive than the dried version, though some pickled versions are roof-raisers. Milder forms, in Mexico, for example, are stuffed with cheese and/or meat. See *Chilis Rellanos*. The hot versions are pulverised for chili sauces, in the Far East, Middle East (see *Harissa*), the Caribbean and Louisiana.

CHILI CON CARNE (*Mexican/American*)

A popular peasant dish of the states along the Mexican/American border, it consists of a mixture of kidney beans, shredded or minced beef, tomatoes, spices and chili powder and peppers. The use of the two last is a hotly debated subject, and there are numerous recipes for fiery super-chilis.

CHILI SAUCE, HOT (*Chinese*)

See *La Jiao Jiang*.

CHILIS RELLENOS (*Mexican*)

Mild yellow or green chili peppers stuffed with cream cheese, *picadillo* (qv) or beans and onions. The chilis are usually *poblanos*, and are grilled and peeled before being filled with the stuffing and baked. It is served as a main course with rice and beans or can form a side dish.

CHINESE GOOSEBERRY (*Chinese/New Zealand*)

See *Kiwi Fruit*.

CHIRINABE (*Japanese*)

A version of *sukiyaki* made with fish and vegetables, rather than beef and vegetables. The fish and baby corn cobs, spring onions, mushrooms, rice noodles and bean curd, are simmered in a delicate fish stock, then dipped in a selection of sauces, including soy sauce and *wasabi*.

CHITTERLINGS (*British/American*)

The cleaned and boiled intestines of oxen, pigs or calves. The term is also used for sausages made from the above. See also *Andouilles/Andouillettes*.

CHIVICHANGA (*Mexican*)

A flour tortilla, wrapped around a filling – either spiced chicken or a chilied meat sauce or *picadillo*, partnered with grated cheese and onion – then deep-fried. Before serving the *Chivichanga* is topped with puréed avocado (See *Guacamole*) and sour cream. It may be a Tex-Mex invention, but it is popular Sonora way.

CHLODNIK (*Polish*)

A cold, summer variation of *Barszcz* (qv), this soup is a bright, fluorescent pink – a combination of beetroot, vinegar, chicken stock, cucumber, spring onions, radishes and dill, puréed and thickened with sour cream. It is garnished with thin slices of cucumber radish, and snips of chives and dill.

CHO-CHO (CHOW-CHOW) (*Caribbean/Indonesian/Malaysian/South American*)

The *chayote*, a light green marrow-like vegetable with a pear-shaped, knobbly skin and a single large seed. It is peeled and plainly boiled and served as a vegetable in the Caribbean and South America. It is also found in the Far East, but is less ubiquitous to the cuisine. This writer awards it the distinction of being, for him, the world's most uninteresting vegetable.

CHOLENT (*Jewish*)

The traditional Sabbath meal, put in the oven before sundown on Friday and consumed on the evening of Saturday, the Sabbath. It thus complies with the Torah's injunction against working on the Sabbath. It is therefore a very slow-cooked casserole of beef brisket, partnered with potatoes, butter beans and barley.

CHOP SUEY (*American*)

A thick, stew-like concoction with oriental overtones, actually invented to satisfy the western palate. Its probable birthplace was San Francisco's Chinatown in the early days of this century (although New York has also been suggested). Its principal ingredients are bean sprouts, mushrooms, bamboo shoots and rice, combined with pieces of chicken, meat or shellfish and topped with deep-fried crispy noodles.

CHORIZO (*Spanish*)

A fairly hot Spanish sausage, heavily impregnated with garlic and paprika. It is fried or eaten cold on its own. When cooked it may be combined with other ingredients in stews and casseroles – this is usually the moister, less cured version. Drier chorizos tend to be eaten cold.

CHOUCROUTE GARNI (*French*)

A speciality of Alsace, this is a huge platter groaning with sauerkraut and piled high with ham, sausages, pork and sometimes fresh or smoked goose. There is usually a garnish of potatoes as well. The sauerkraut has been cooked in stock and white wine, with carrot, onion, celery and juniper berries as flavouring, and the meats added at various stages.

CHOW MEIN (*Chinese*)

More popular in the West than in China, Chow Mein – 'fried noodles' – is a combination of shredded pork or chicken, mixed with rice wine, sugar and cornstarch, stir-fried with Chinese cabbage, bamboo shoots and egg noodles. It is from *Giangxe*, an Eastern province.

CHOWDER (*American*)

A thick soup, heavy with ingredients and usually containing salt pork as a flavouring. It is a speciality of the northeast as a winter warmer, and the most famous chowder is *Clam Chowder*. It is traditionally eaten while the clambake is still cooking, and contains chopped clams, onions, potatoes and seasoned clam juice. The classic is *Boston Clam Chowder* with milk added, while *Manhattan Clam Chowder* has tomatoes and garlic. *Corn Chowder* substitutes corn for the clams, together with potatoes, tomatoes and, often, cheese.

CHU HAU JEUNG MUNGAI *(Chinese)*

Chicken cut into small dice and stir-fried with barbe-cued oysters.

CHUAN (CHUEN) *(Chinese)*

This word means rapidly-boiled over high heat – as in certain fresh vegetable soups.

CHURRASCO *(Brazilian/Spanish)*

Pieces of beefsteak or skewered cubes of beef grilled over an open fire until charred on the outside and served with a thin tomato and onion sauce. A speciality of Brazilian cowboy country near the Argentinian border, and of Cordoba in Spain.

CHURROS *(Spanish)*

Churros are a fried batter of flour and water, dipped in sugar and shaped into loops. They are a staple of the Spanish breakfast, and are traditionally dipped into hot chocolate before eating. *Churrerias* are small sit-down cafes or stalls which sell nothing but these breakfast specials.

CINNAMON *(Spice)*

Cinnamon is a spice which has been around since the days of the ancient Egyptians. The name does service for two members of the genus *Cinnamomum*: cinnamon proper – the more delicate thinner, flaky bark of the tree, with a sweeter, milder taste – and cassia, a stronger, more bitter bark from China. The best *true* cinnamon (as opposed to cassia) comes from Sri Lanka. The bark is carefully peeled off the culled shoots of young trees grown either wild or in 'orchards'. Only the valuable inner bark is used; the outer is thrown away. Cinnamon has been a popular spice in Europe since the Crusades, and it features in the cooking of most Western countries, notable among them Austria (and its many desserts), the biscuits and pies of England and the stews and desserts of Spain, Mexico and Portugal. (See *Herbs and Spices* chart for translations.)

CIRCASSIAN CHICKEN *(Turkish)*

See *Cerkez tavrigu.*

CIVET *(French)*

The French version of *jugging* as in *Jugged Hare* or Venison. It is a rich combination of either hare (*lièvre*), venison (*chevreuil*) or rabbit (*lapin*), stewed with wine, onions, garlic, carrots and other vegetables, and thick-ened with its own blood. *Civet de lièvre à la Perigordine* or *à la Landais*, adds ceps and more garlic; *farci en cabessal*, a speciality of the Auvergne, bones and stuffs the carcass with bread and vegetables, then simmers it in local red wine and its own blood. Civets are tradi-tionally served with croutons spread with *ail*.

Civet is also used to describe various fish stews, although the term is not strictly accurate since no blood is involved. Such dishes are classically of shellfish or crayfish/lobster (*Civet de langouste* or *Civet de pecheur*), although *nouvelle cuisine* has introduced several other fish into the repertoire.

CLAFOUTI(S) (*French*)

A speciality of the Perigord and the Auvergne, this is a simple batter pudding of egg, flour, sugar and milk poured over fresh fruit and baked. The classic fruit is cherries, but plums, grapes and other soft fruits are all used.

✗ *CLAM*

This tight lipped shellfish has a significant role to play in Japanese wedding celebrations where clam soup is traditionally served. No sensory stimulation is intended here though, it merely symbolises the steadfast closeness of the clamshell halves, as representative of the newly wed couple's attachment to each other.

CLAPSHOT (*Scottish*)

See *Haggis*.

CLOUD EARS (*Chinese*)

See *Wun Yee*.

✗ *CLOVE*

In 1972 Zanzibar, the world's chief supplier of this valuable spice, made it a capital crime to smuggle cloves out of the island which led, in that year alone, to the death sentence for 15 persons!

CLOVES (*Spice*)

Familiar in a number of regional cuisines all over the world, most cloves come from Zanzibar and Indonesia, where they are picked still pinky-green and tender, and then dried. Cloves are the unopened flower buds of a type of tropical myrtle, and in its dried state it resembles a nail with round head. Its colloquial name in many languages 'clou' (French), 'ting-liang' (China), 'nelki' (German) and 'nekhah' (Persian) refers to this resemblance. Cloves have a long history in medicine, used as a mild anaesthetic and in China as an aid to longevity. They are also an important constituent of *paan* (qv), and, with pepper and cinnamon, form the basis of many Eastern dishes.

(See *Herbs and Spices* chart for translations).

CLUB SANDWICH (*American*)

Like the hamburger, the club sandwich is a truly American gift to the world's lunch tables. It is the perfect sandwich – or *should* be. Three freshly toasted slices of bread are liberally spread on one side with mayonnaise. Cooked chicken or turkey breast is piled on that, seasoned, covered with another slice of bread, and that piece topped with sliced tomato and grilled bacon. The final slice of bread covers it. Serve the sliced sandwich with pickles and olives.

COCIDO MADRILENO (*Spanish*)

One of the great classic Spanish stews – or cocido – this one native to Madrid. It is cooked in a large earthenware pot, and consists of a staggering mixture of beef, chicken, ham or bacon, sausages, pigs trotters, chick peas and many vegetables. When all the constituents are cooked, the meat and poultry are served with the chick peas and the sausages with the remaining vegetables. The broth is thickened with cooked rice and served as a first course, to be followed by the other two.

COCK-A-LEEKIE (Scottish)

There are a number of versions of the origins of this soup. One claim is that it was served after a cockfight, using the defeated cock as its base. Another says it was made from the oldest cock in the barnyard, and served as a kind of funeral celebration feast in honour of its long life. Whatever the truth, it was well-established by Victorian days. Traditionally the bird should be served in the soup, but today there are usually a few pieces of chicken floating in a broth containing leeks and prunes.

COLCANNON (Irish)

An Irish country dish, a mixture of chopped, cooked (usually leftover) cabbage or kale and mashed potatoes, often enriched with mashed carrots and turnips.

COM CHAY (Vietnamese)

Stir-fried vegetables – usually Chinese cabbage, mushrooms, onions, mustard greens, celery and lettuce, flavoured with ginger, soy sauce and other spices. It is usually served with plain boiled rice.

CONCH (CONCHA) (Caribbean)

Probably the most common fish dish served in the Caribbean. Conch is the meat of a large univalve shellfish. It must be pounded and marinated to tenderise it. Most commonly used in chowders or chopped and mixed with flour and egg and deep-fried as fritters, it can also be marinated in lime and lemon juice, spiced with coriander and chili, and served raw in a ceviche (qv).

CONFIT (French)

Preserved in fat. This is a treatment for geese and duck particularly associated with the Perigord, although it is practised throughout southwestern France. Confit d'oie (goose) and confit de canard (duck) are occasionally joined by confits of chicken and turkey. The tradition of confit began with the necessity of preserving the flesh of the poultry that were killed by the dozen for their enlarged livers – foie gras. The fat of the plump birds was rendered down and together with the cooked meat, bottled and preserved, sometimes for years. It soon became an end in itself, and has become a regional speciality.

CORBEILLE (French)

A basket. Often a large basket of fresh fruit – oranges, pears, peaches, bananas, grapes, etc. – is offered at the end of a meal instead of a dessert, usually at family-run or less expensive restaurants.

CORIANDER (Herb)

Both the seeds and leaves of this plant are used in cooking, in the Near and Middle East and the Orient, and in Mexico and Central America. The dried seed (*dhania*) is the basis of many commercial curry powders, and the leaves (*dhania sabz*) are used in green *masalas* (qv) and many Indian dishes. In Greece and Turkey it is used in salads, in cooking and as a garnish; in the Far East its special flavour is found in soups, garnishes and in sauces. (Chinese; *yuen sai*, Thai: *pak chee*, Burmese: *nannam*). In Mexico, the Caribbean and Central America it is known as *cilantro*, and is included in stews and hot sauces. It is characterised by a peculiar sweet-tart flavour and almost 'fetid' aroma. (See *Herbs and Spices* chart.)

CORN OYSTERS (*American*)
A kind of fritter. Corn kernels are combined with egg and seasoned flour, and fried until golden in butter. Usually served with ham and maple syrup.

CORNICHONS (*French*)
These are tiny gherkins, very sour to the taste, which are pickled with dill, whole peppercorns and carda-mom. They are traditionally served in a crock to accompany pâté, and with *jambon, saucissons* and other cold meats.

CORNISH PASTY (*English*)
Originated in Cornwall, the pastry 'meal in one' has now become a widespread snack and lunch dish, particularly in pubs. In the old days, the pasty was wrapped in a handkerchief and taken to the fields in a pocket. The traditional Cornish pasty is made of short-bread pastry, torpedo-shaped, or semi-circular, pin-ched along its length, and filled with a combination of chopped meat, potatoes and onions, sometimes with turnip, carrot and parsnip as well. The traditional meat was mutton, but today beef has replaced it in popular-ity. After baking the pasty can be served warm or cold.

COUSCOUS (*Moroccan*)
This is cooked in a special implement – a kind of double boiler – known as a *couscousier*. The meat (either lamb or chicken) and vegetables – usually carrots, courgettes and celery – are cooked in a broth in the lower section; the semolina or fine wheatgrain is steamed in the sieve-like upper half, this acquiring the flavouring of the stew. The semolina is piled on a plate and the stew is piled on top. The broth is served separately, to be added as desired, and a hot sauce – *harissa* (qv) – is also offered.

✕ *CRANBERRIES*
Ever since the early 18th century American Cranberries have been imported to the UK and where would our Christmas turkey be without this traditional British accom-paniment? Surprising then to learn that the Red Indians were making cranberry sauce before Columbus set sail.

CRECY, POTAGE OR CREME (*French*)
A soup whose base is the rich carrot harvest of Crecy. It is usually served as a smooth purée made from chicken

stock, carrots, cream and seasoning. It was supposedly served to the English troops at the Battle of the same name in 1346, and as such has been claimed as a British, rather than French, culinary triumph. Other variations include Crecy à la Chantilly (purée of carrots and lentils) and Consommé à la Crecy (garnished with julienne of carrot).

CREMA CATALANA *(Spanish)*
Catalan custard, a kind of *crème brulée*, which is particularly popular around Barcelona.

CRÈME BRULÉE AND CRÈME CARAMEL *(French)*
These two custard-based desserts are close relatives. The former custard is topped by a thick crust of brown sugar which is glazed until hard. It is then cracked with a spoon before serving together with the creamy pudding underneath. Crème Caramel is a more liquid variant of the former, in which the soft caramel forms a pool around the custard when it is turned out of its baking dish.

CRÈME CHANTILLY *(French)*
The French version of whipped cream; sweetened with sugar and flavoured with vanilla.

CREOLE *(French/American)*
A descriptive adjective applied to many dishes of which rice – or a combination of tomato and rice – form a large part. Examples include pear and apricot creole (rice) and shrimp creole (rice and tomato).

CREPINETTE *(French)*
A small flat patty of minced pork (or sometimes veal or lamb), often with a sliver of truffle on top, wrapped in a thin coating of lamb's caul. It can be grilled or fried. It is a traditional dish in winter and early spring.

CRESCENTINA *(Italian)*
A broad flat bread, baked in wood-fired ovens. The dough is mixed with chopped bacon before being formed into loaves. A speciality of Bologna and Emilia-Romana.

CRESPOLINI *(Italian)*
Rather cannelloni-like pancakes stuffed with a mixture of spinach, ricotta, egg, chicken livers and cheese (Parmesan and/or pecorino), covered with béchamel and baked. Served as a pasta course.

✕ CRESS
In the 13th century Louis IX, out hunting one summer's day, called for some liquid refreshment. There being none available he was given instead a bunch of watercress. So delighted was he by its refreshing quality that he decided immediately to honour the area and so today the city of Vernon still displays the Royal Symbol and three bunches of watercress on its heraldic coat of arms.

CROMESGEIS *(Russian/Polish)*
Croquettes of minced chicken, meat or fish, dipped into batter and deep-fried in fat.

CROQUE-MONSIEUR *(French)*
A pavement café snack, now unhappily commercialised to a mere shadow of its former self. The true Croque Monsieur depends on the freshest ingredients: two crustless slices of bread with a slice of tangy Gruyère and a slice of *Jambon blanc* between. It is then liberally dotted or spread with butter on both outer sides and gently grilled or baked. The *Croque Madame* is the same with the addition of a fried or poached egg.

CROSNE *(Chinese/Japanese/French)*
See *Artichoke, Chinese*.

CROSTATA DI RICOTTA *(Italian)*
A sweet rich cheesecake, a speciality of Rome, which has been part of the culinary repertoire since the days of the early Romans. The pastry is a shortcrust with butter, egg yolks and sugar, and marsala adding a special flavour. The ricotta filling is enhanced with orange rind, sultanas, candied peel, pine kernels or almonds, and nuts.

CROSTINI *(Italian)*
Small pieces of fried bread served as an appetiser. *Crostini napoletani* is the most common, topped with mozzarella cheese, anchovies and tomato.

CRUDITÉS *(French)*
A choice of raw crisp vegetables served on a platter as a first course. It may include radishes, celery sticks, carrot slices, pepper slices, spring onions, cauliflower and others. They are usually accompanied by dips made from mayonnaise and garlic, blue cheese or other possibilities.

✘ CUCUMBER
"A cucumber should be well sliced, dressed with pepper and vinegar, and then thrown out as good for nothing" Dr. Johnson.

CUMBERLAND HERRINGS *(English)*
A method of preparing these fish in which they are stuffed with their roes, chopped and mixed with onions, breadcrumbs and served with a mustard sauce.

CUMIN *(Spice)*
A main crop of North Africa (particularly Morocco and Tunisia) as well as the Middle East, India and Italy. It is a dominant flavouring in those countries (bar Italy) as well as in Mexico, where with cinnamon, it is much used in sauces and stews (such as the Tex-Mex *chili con carne*). There is also much confusion between cumin and caraway, because of their appearance, and also because of translations into other languages – in France caraway is often called 'cumin'. (For correct translations see *Herbs and Spices* chart.) They can be easily distinguished by their idiosyncratic flavours: while cumin is distinctly spicy, with a slightly peppery aftertaste, caraway is milder, with the reminiscent

flavour of pickle, since it is much used with dill in pickles and cabbage (sauerkraut) dishes.

CUSCUZ PAULESTA (*Brazil*)

A speciality of the southern interior near Sao Paulo. It is a combination of steamed corn and manioc meal topped with cooked meat (usually beef and pork) and vegetables. A seafood version is also sometimes encountered.

CUSTARD APPLE (*Caribbean/South American/Southeast Asian*)

Also commonly called the sweetsap, this is a large, strawberry-shaped fruit, with overlapping fleshy scales. When ripe the scales split open, allowing easy access to the creamy flesh, with its sweet, custardy bouquet. Something of the same name which is probably related to the West Indian custard apple, Cherimoya is produced on the tiny fertile island of Madeira

CYUU-SASHIMI (*Japanese*)

The Japanese version of steak tartare; the meat is very thinly sliced fillet, served with garlic and *wasabe* (qv).

DAHI (*Indian/Pakistani*)

Yogurt or curd. That used by the Indians/Pakistanis has a naturally sour flavour and is thickened. A reasonable substitute is strained Greek or goats'-milk yogurt. A *Dahi Raita* is yogurt with vegetables – often cucumber or onions – chopped into it.

DAHL (DAL) (*Indian/Pakistani*)

The Hindi generic term for all pulses, also used to describe dishes made from a variety of lentils, the most common pulse in India. North Indian and Pakistani *dahls* tend to be quite thick, those from vegetarian Southern and Western India tend to be more soupy in nature, to be used as a kind of gravy for rice and *chapatis* (qv). The most usual dahls are:
Masur dahl: red lentils, from Masur or Mysore; *Murg or moong dahl*: split mung bean, said to be the most nourishing; *Arhar* or *Tur dahl*: pigeon peas from the area around Madras, used in hot sweet-sour dishes; and *urd ki dahl*: black beans.
Chana dahl is probably the most flavourful; made from lentils which resemble yellow split peas. It is available from Indian shops and is also the dahl most featured in Indian restaurants. The lentils are cooked slowly, covered, until tender, and then mixed with several spices and fried in *ghee* (qv).
(See also *Sambar*.)

DAIKON (*Japanese/Chinese/Indonesian/Malaysian/Indian*)

One of the most common of Japanese vegetables, used as an accompaniment to *sushi* (qv) in soups, as a garnish for various dishes and grated as a pickle. It can be served raw, or soaked then cooked quickly. It is also much loved in India, pickled or added to curries or stuffed breads. In all oriental countries it is respected for its curative and diuretic properties.

DAK HIM *(Korean)*
Pieces of chicken marinated with sesame oil, soy, garlic and cayenne, then fried with green peppers, spring onions, mushrooms or ginko nuts. It is served with *Bahb* (qv).

DAMPER BREAD *(Australian)*
A flat unleavened bread made with buttermilk and eggs.

DANABLU *(Danish)*
Once called Danish Roquefort, although it has always been made with cow's milk. It has a salty character and should be quite creamy to offset the saltiness. The most often used cheese in blue-cheese dressings and other cookery uses in substitution for Roquefort. The colour should be toward white rather than yellowish, with strong blue (not green) veins.

DASHEEN *(Southeast Asian/African/Caribbean)*
See *Eddol*.

DASHI *(Japanese)*
The basic cooking stock of Japanese cuisine, used for everything from soups and sauces to *shabu shabu* (qv) and Japanese 'stews'. It is very light and delicately flavoured, made from boiled kelp and the shavings of dried bonito fish.

DASHIMAKI TAMAGO *(Japanese)*
A rolled omelette. One omelette is cooked in a rectangular pan, then gently rolled to the back of the pan, a second and third omelette are then cooked, and each rolled around the earlier omelettes. The completed three-roll omelette is then turned onto a bamboo mat, and rolled up firmly. It is served garnished with parsley and sliced into thick rounds.

DAUBE DE BOEUF *(French)*
See *Boeuf*.

DAUPHINE, POMMES *(French)*
These are croquettes of mashed potato combined with a *choux* of flour, eggs and cream, breaded and deep-fried. They are named for the region of the country in the Alps, bordering the Savoie and Provence.

DAUPHINOISE, POMMES *(French)*
One of the world's great potato dishes. The potatoes are thinly sliced, seasoned, lightly sprinkled with chopped garlic, covered with milk or cream, (or a mixture of both) dotted with butter flecks and slowly baked until cooked and brown on top. Grated gruyère cheese is sometimes added on top which is nice but not really necessary.

DEBRECZINER *(Hungarian/Austrian)*
A very spicy sausage, thin and usually sold in pairs, often from a *würst* stand in city centres of Austria and Hungary. The meat used is pork and the main flavouring is paprika.

DENDENG *(Indonesian)*
A kind of oven-baked spicy jerky made from beef, numerous spices, soy sauce, peanut oil and tamarind liquid. The thinly sliced meat is first fried in the mixture

until it has almost evaporated, then quickly sautéed in sugar, then dried in a low oven until it is dark brown and absolutely dry. Stored in an airtight tin it can be eaten like *Bombay Duck* (qv), or as an accompaniment to rice, vegetables and sambal.

DENVER SANDWICH (*American*)

A diner special, this should be served with the egg slightly underdone so that it soaks into the bread. Two slices of bread contain an omelette made with sautéed onions, green pepper and ham, stirred with seasoning and cayenne pepper.

DERBY (*English*)

A hard, pale, slightly crumbly cow's milk cheese, with a character akin to Cheddar, though moister and less sharp. It has been factory-produced since 1870 and is aged between one to three months. A version with sage marbling is more popular, although the flavour is an acquired taste.

DHANSAK (*Indian*)

A Parsi dish from the western state of Gujarat. It is traditionally served every Sunday in Parsi homes and is a usual festival dish. The basic recipe combines meat or chicken, lentils, vegetables, including potato, spinach and aubergine, and a wet and a dry *masala* (See *Garam Masala*). It has a special, spicy sour flavour and, served with rice, is a complete meal.

DIEPPOISE, à la (*French*)

In the style of Dieppe, a seaport on the Normandy coast. Thus, it is fish which is served this way, typically with a white wine and cream sauce. Mushrooms may also enrich the sauce, while *Sole Dieppoise* is decorated with mussels and peeled crayfish before being surrounded with the usual sauce.

DILL (*Herb*)

Popular in Middle European cookery, which makes use of both the seeds and the feathery leaves, dill has a distinctive sweet sour flavour. It is used in pickling, in fish dishes and in sauces. It also has a place in Laotian and Sri Lankan cooking, where it is used in fish and meat dishes. (Laos: *phank si*, Sri Lanka: *enduree*). (See also *Herbs and Spices chart*.)

DIM SUM (*Chinese*)

This means, literally 'dot on the heart' – and these little titbits are both heart *and* tummy pleasing. They are usually served in Chinese restaurants from lunch through tea-time, presented in a succession of steaming baskets from carts pushed round the tables. Familiar *dim sum* include: *Chao Chao* dumplings (qv), prawn dumplings, chicken and glutinous rice in lotus leaves, savoury and sweet stuffed pancakes, spring rolls, *shaomai* dumplings (qv), and paper-wrapped prawns.

DIVAN, TURKEY OR CHICKEN (*Turkish*)

This is really a dish claimed by international cuisine – created by a French chef in an Istanbul hotel and usually known by its anglicised name. It consists of turkey cutlets beaten flat and baked with broccoli spears and a cheese and cream sauce.

DOBOSTORTE (Austrian)

A relic of the Austro-Hungarian Empire, this *torte* was a favourite of the Emperor Franz Joseph and his court. Named after the Hungarian town of Dobos, wafer-thin round cakes, usually seven, are layered with a chocolate cream filling and stacked on top of each other with further chocolate cream spread around the outside and the whole is topped with a glaze of caramel.

DOLCELATTE (Italian)

A blue-veined cow's cheese, milder, creamier and more delicate than *Gorgonzola* (qv). It is unlike the latter in that it is factory made.

DOLMADES (Greek)

Vine leaves rolled and stuffed with onions, rice, mint and dill, sometimes with the addition of minced meat. They can be served warm or cold, after being braised in water.

DONBURI (Japanese)

Named after the utensil in which it is served, an earthenware bowl, the term covers the food served in it, boiled rice covered with an egg mixture sometimes enlivened with other ingredients such as vegetables, poultry or fish. A popular version is *Dyako Donburi* – 'Parent and Child' Donburi, the rice covered with scrambled eggs and chicken. Another is *Kitsune Donburi* made with fried bean curd. It is usually served with *Dashi* (qv).

DONER KEBAB (Turkish)

Slices of lamb marinated in herbs and oil are packed tightly with minced lamb and pieces of fat onto an upright spit. The result looks like one large three foot hunk of meat which is then slowly turned before a vertical grill, and the meat sliced off as the outside layers cook. Served with rice and salad or as a filling for pitta bread. See also *Shawarma*.

DONG GWOO LAP CHEONG JING GU YOOK (Chinese)

The longer name for *Kay Jee Ghuy* ('Draughtsmen's Chicken') enumerating ingredients – mushrooms, pork and chicken breast – minced with ginger, Chinese rice wine, soy sauce and garlic and stuffed into sausage casing. The sausage is roasted, then cut into slices to serve.

DOPIAZA (Indian/Pakistani)

A lamb or chicken dish, of medium curry hotness, which has a creamy consistency and is distinguished by its rich use of onions. The name literally means 'two onions' which may mean that both raw and fried onions are used in its preparation or simply that it has more than the usual curry.

DOSAI (Indian/Pakistani)

A ground lentil and rice bread which is flat as a pancake. It is much favoured by Southern Indian and vegetarian Indian restaurants, often filled with a spicy mixture of potatoes, garlic, lentils and many spices. In this form it is called *Masala Dosai*. (Also called *Thosai*.)

DOUBLE GLOUCESTER *(English)*

A hard cow's milk cheese, with a mellow rich flavour, lacking in sharpness. It is made in both the natural pale yellow form and also coloured deep orange by annatto, and is available in both farmhouse and creamery versions. It requires some four months to mature, and is even better if left longer. A smaller, less well-matured type, known as Single Gloucester, is in the process of being revived.

DOW FOO *(Chinese)*

See *Tofu*.

DRAGEE *(French)*

Sugared almonds, covered in pastel coating of white, pink or blue, traditionally given out to guests at a christening. They are a speciality of Verdun in the Meure, made there since the 13th century. Modern versions may also include an undercoating of chocolate, marzipan or nougatine.

DRUNKEN CHICKEN *(Chinese)*

See *Tsui ghuy*.

DUCHESSE, POMMES *(French)*

In the style of the duchess. Refers to puréed or mashed potatoes mixed with egg yolks and piped or moulded into shapes. They are then either baked or dipped into egg and breadcrumbs and deep-fried when the name then changes to Pommes Croquettes.

DUELOR Y QUEBRANTOS *(Spanish)*

See *Revueltos*.

DUNG GU *(Chinese)*

Fried or pickled mushrooms, of which there are two main types: the straw mushroom, cultivated on straw, with a long thin stalk and brown cap (*Volvariella volvacea*) and the winter mushroom, a type of tree mushroom (*Lentinus edodes*). (See also *Tsao gu*).

DURIAN *(Malaysian/Caribbean/South American)*

A yellowish or olive-green prickly fruit, it is large and oval. The inside divides into three or five segments, with large brown seeds. The flesh is soft and pulpy and possesses a very distinctive smell. *Aficionados* call it pungent, but those less impressed use less kind words. It is definitely an acquired taste, although Indonesians and Malaysians seem to have acquired it enthusiastically. Some idea of its powerful smell may be realised by the information that it is forbidden to carry or otherwise transport durian on commercial aircraft. Also called *erizo de arbal* in the Caribbean.

EDAM *(Dutch)*

The famous red ball of wax conceals the yellow, smooth, cow's milk cheese of the Netherlands, one of the world's best known cheeses. In its native country it is called *Edammer* and is sold without the wax seal. It is factory made and is usually sold young, after about three months, when the texture is still supple and the flavour mild and slightly soapy. There is also a growing international market for cheeses over a year old, which are drier and saltier, as well as annatto-coloured, deep orange Edam, which is sold in France as *Mimolette*.

EDDOE (DASHEEN) (*Southeast Asian/African/ Caribbean*)

A starchy vegetable, a member of the taro family. The dasheen is a larger, more elongated version of the eddoe – both have white or yellow flesh and a rough brown outer skin. The smaller eddoe, the shape and size of a new cyprus potato, if barkier, has a sweeter, nuttier flavour, the larger dasheen is heavier and starchier, without the delicacy of flavour. The eddoe is now seen in many UK supermarkets; it can be used as a sweet potato or yam. The many national names for these vegetables are too numerous to mention, but eddoe – dasheen are commonly understood in many places.

✘ EDIBLE OILS

Jane Grigson has the most disturbing revelations concerning the production of certain cooking oils, namely crude palm, soya and ground oils. 'First the oils have to be degummed and neutralised. Phosphoric acid is injected into the oil and mixed under pressure to precipitate the gums. Then it is mixed with caustic soda which forms a soap containing gums and colour which can easily be separated from the oil. Next stage is to wash the oil, dry it, bleach it with fuller's earth and filter it. At this point its a fully refined oil but the original taste and smell still remain, making it unacceptable for consumption. The final stage, therefore, is deodorisation, to ensure a bland, odourless oil that won't tinge the flavour of what's cooked in it.' As Mrs Grigson says you will understand why butter, lard and olive oil are the fats she prefers.

EELS (*British*)

Eels have been a part of popular London life since Victorian days. Eel pies are no longer seen, but jellied eels and eels and mash can still be found at a few preserved shops in the capital. For jellied eels, the eels are chopped, cooked in stock and left to cool, forming their own aspic. In eels and mash, the cooked fish are served warm with mashed potatoes and a thin green parsley sauce is poured over all. See also *Alevins, Elvers* and *Anguilles*.

EGUSI BEEF (*East African*)

A dark beef stew made with melon seeds, spinach and dried shrimps. It has a light spiciness to set off the usual accompaniment of stodgy *cassava* (qv).

EKURI (*Indian*)

See *Akoori*.

ELVERS (*English*)

These baby eels were once a delicacy popular throughout the west of England and along the west coast of France. Today, the English have lost their taste for them, and those caught in the Severn make their way to the restaurant pots of Bordeaux. These transparent three-year-old fish are long, slimy and spaghetti-like, and can legally be caught only between the 1st March and the 25th April. They are usually served deep-fried, like whitebait or in an omelette. See also *Alevins*.

EMPANADA *(Spanish/Mexican and Philippino)*
In Mexico and the Philippines, a puff pastry turnover, usually filled with *bacalao* or *picadillo* (qv). It can be eaten for lunch or a snack, and smaller versions are cocktail pastry *hors d'oeuvres*. The Spanish variant is filled with minced pork, fish or *chorizo* (qv).

EMMENTAL *(Swiss/French)*
Named for the valley of the same name in the canton of Berne. Three different bacteria are used as starters, one of which is responsible for the characteristic eyes. The enormous wheels of cow's cheese can weigh up to 200lb (80kg). The curd is cut, cooked, 'rasped' or cut again and after firming slightly it is placed in a mould for the whey to drip away, and finally pressed. It is aged between three months and a full year. It should have a light yellow body, a smooth rind, evenly distributed holes (not *too* large) and a sweet, mellow flavour. It is very good for both eating and cooking, but should not be overheated because it coagulates and 'threads'.

ENCHILADAS *(Mexican)*
Traditionally *enchiladas* were only stuffed with raw onions and cheese, and then a bubbling tomato and chili sauce poured over them. Today they are made with many fillings, including chicken, beef, cheese and pork, always spiced up with coriander, chilis and onions. Only corn tortillas are used, and garnishes include grated cheese, onion, sour cream or guacamole.

ENDIVE, BELGIAN *(Vegetable)*
Called 'Belgian' endive to differentiate it from the 'curly endive' or chicory plant with its frizzy head. This 'Belgian' endive is a member of the same family, but is made up of long, tightly growing, pale-green, almost white, leaves. The vegetable is grown in the dark to maintain this blanched colour, and has a slightly bitter flavour. It is served raw in salads or braised in butter or with a cheese sauce.

ENTRAMMER *(French)*
See *Port-Salut*.

EPINARD *(French)*
Spinach. This is a favourite vegetable in French cookery, served crisp and fresh in salads or cooked and presented in many dishes *à la Florentine*, the frenchified version of *alla Fiorentina* (qv), which involves eggs or fish on a bed of spinach covered with *béchamel sauce* (qv). Spinach is also the main constituent of *Epinards en bouillabaisse*, a thick soup with potatoes, garlic and saffron suffused with olive oil and poured over croutons. It is then topped with poached eggs. (See also *Bouillabaisse*).

ERIVENTENSOEP *(Dutch)*
A thick pea soup, green and steaming, and enriched by rounds of Dutch smoked sausage. It is a classic winter

warmer, usually served with a rasher of smoked bacon on *pumpernickel* bread.

ESCABECHE *(Portuguese)*

Together with sardines, one of the most frequently encountered fish in the country. It is a type of shad, and is marinated first in olive oil, garlic, herbs and wine, then fried.

ESCARGOTS *(French)*

Like frogs' legs *(cuisses de grenouille)*, snails have long been a curiosity of French cuisine for the foreigner. But as more visit the continent, and France in particular, the taste for these small shelled beasts has spread. The most renowned snails come from Burgundy, where they grow large and fat on the vineyard leaves. The style *à la bourguignonne* is also the most favoured way of serving them – the snail shells stuffed with the cleaned boiled snail, butter, parsley and garlic, and quickly baked in the oven.

Other treatments include that of the region around Bordeaux *(à la bordelais* or *à la vegneronne)*, quickly sautéed in walnut oil, and then sauced with shallots, garlic and white wine; *à la chablisienne* – stuffed with shallots and cooked in garlic, herbs and Chablis; *à la Perigordienne* – stuffed with pâté, butter and bread-crumbs and baked, and the Provençal method – cooked in a soup of garlic, tomatoes, onions, and red or white wine.

Today snails are more often farmed for restaurants, but in the countryside peasants still search the vineyards and fields after a rain for the much-valued creature. It must be starved for twenty-four hours before proceding with a recipe.

ESPAGNOLE, SAUCE AND à l' *(French)*

A standard of French cuisine, one of the four 'mother' sauces used to make most of the classical sauces. It is made with a brown *roux* (qv) and brown stock, together with tomatoes, mushrooms, herbs and ham. It was originally from Spain – hence the name – but has been assimilated into the French tradition. When reduced it is called demi-glace. *A l'Espagnole* means a dish served in the Spanish style, with tomatoes, garlic and onions.

ESROM *(Danish)*

A washed rind cheese, likened to a Danish Port Salut, but with a much more assertive character. A cow's milk cheese, aged about one month, it has a pale yellow paste sprinkled with many small holes. It has a sweetish flavour with a slightly spicy nose. The rind is meant to be eaten.

ESTOFADO *(Spanish/Portuguese)*

A stew. Two of the most notable versions are *estofado de vaca* (beef stew flavoured with garlic and white wine) or *estofado la Catalona* (beef stew with bacon, wine, *butifarra* sasusage (qv) and grated chocolate).

FAAT CHOY *(Chinese)*

A hairy moss-like seaweed unique to the Orient. Dark green in colour it is sold in wads, and when deep-fried

becomes crisp and delicate. In the West dried cabbage
is usually substituted.

FABADA (*Spanish*)

A dish from the northwest of Spain, Asturias, in which
white beans and sausages are stewed together with
garlic and herbs. Another version substitutes cured
beef for the sausage.

FABLOUSH (*Lebanese*)

A salad made from pitta bread which has been grilled
then torn and softened with lemon juice. It is mixed
with cucumbers, tomatoes, onions, mint, pepper and
oregano. *Fattoush* is the Egyptian version.

FAGGOTS (*Welsh/English*)

A favourite of Wales and the North of England, these
were once traditionally made at pig-killing time. Today
they are usually made daily by butchers. Pig livers are
usually used. These are minced together with breadcrumbs, oatmeal, suet, spices and herbs and onions,
and baked in a loaf or patted into balls and baked. They
are served cold with apple sauce, or hot with gravy.

FALAFEL (*Israeli*)

A mixture of minced chick peas, parsley, coriander,
onions and garlic, shaped into balls and deep-fried.
They are eaten hot with *tahine* (qv) as an appetiser or
stuffed into pitta bread as a snack.

FALOODA (FALUDA) (*Indian/Pakistani*)

A sweet drink, taken as a refreshment or with a meal. It
is a combination of rose syrup and cold milk, with a
characteristic cornflour vermicelli floating in it. The
latter is often replaced by tapioca or coloured *agar-agar*
(qv) jellies.

FAROFA (*Brazilian*)

A staple of Brazilian cuisine, ground manioc meal,
mixed with pepper and toasted or browned in oil. Used
as a condiment over many dishes – particularly *Feijoada*
(qv) and as a stuffing for meats and vegetables.

FASCHINGSKRAPFER (*Austrian*)

These are traditionally eaten – in large quantities – at
Fasching, the pre-Lenten carnival time, but they are
also found at other times of the year. They are versions
of a superior doughnut, a yeast dough filled with
apricot jam, deep-fried, and dusted with castor sugar.

FATTOUSH (*Egyptian*)

See *Fabloush*.

FEIJOADA (*Brazilian*)

The national dish of Brazil, a speciality particularly of
Rio and environs. It is a thick dark stew made from
black beans, with beef, pork ribs, sausage and other
meat bits added. It is served with *farofa*, which is
scattered over the top, and white rice.

FEIJAOS (*Portuguese/Brazilian*)

Beans. In Portugal, the most common dishes are *Feijão
guisado* – kidney beans cooked with bacon, then
covered in a tomato sauce; *sopa de feijão* – red bean and
vegetable soup, and *Feijao verde a provinciana* – green
beans sauted with garlic, *chorizo*, onions and tomatoes,

and then topped with an egg which is poached in the vegetables.

FÊN KUO *(Chinese)*
Steamed crab dumpling, served as *dim sum*.

FENNEL *(Herb and Vegetable)*
The stem bases are cooked and served as a vegetable, or eaten raw in salads; the feathery leaves and seeds are used as a herb flavouring in Eastern and Middle European cookery. The herb is called *sonf* in India, *samouk-saba* in Burma, *jintan manis* in Malaya and *adas* in Indonesia. When eaten as a vegetable it can be cooked whole, sliced or stuffed, it can be baked, steamed or fried. The Italians make extensive use of it, as do the French and North Africans. (See also *Herb and Spice* chart).

FETA *(Greek)*
A white, crumbly salty cheese, made from ewe's milk. It is kept fresh in brine, rather like *mozzarella* (qv). It is used frequently in salads and in cooked dishes in its native country, as well as eaten on its own. Much of the product exported to Britain and the rest of Europe today is not from Greece, but is a respectable version produced in Denmark.

FETTUCCINE *(Italian)*
Long, flat strips of egg pasta, slightly broader than *tagliatelle* (qv). It is a speciality of the Liguria, Naples and Rome, where *Fettuccine Alfredo* became famous (the pasta covered with a sauce of butter, cream and parmesan). Other sauces include fresh tomato and basil (*alla marinara*), or *alla ciociara* – with meat sauce.

FILE *(American)*
One of the prime secrets of Creole and Cajun cooking, filé is sassafras, the root of a southern tree used to flavour gumbos and stews. It lends a hot sourness to meats and helps them to 'blacken', the way much Cajun food is preferred.

FILLO *(Greek/Middle Eastern)*
A very fine pastry dough available throughout the Middle East, though particularly associated with Greece, where it is used in both savoury and sweet dishes, in pies (of lamb, cheese and/or spinach) and in individual pastries (*Baklava, galemboureko*, etc.). It is now widely available in the West, sold in packets of sheets, from the cool or frozen section of the supermarket – or delicatessen. The packet will usually bear the title, phyllo or strudel pastry.

FIORENTINA, à alla *(Italian)*
In the Florentine style. When applied to eggs, fish or vegetables it usually means with spinach and cheese – as in the Frenchified *Oeufs Florentine* (in Italian *Uva Fiorentina*). When applied to meat, however (as in *Bistecca alla Fiorentina*), it often means with a herb and tomato sauce.

FIRNI *(Indian/Pakistani)*
Ground rice pudding usually flavoured with cardamom, and often with pistachios or almonds.

✖ *FISH*

England, sadly, seems to be the one country of the British Isles which most neglects the bounty of its coastal waters and where the number of local fishmongers' shops is on the decline. Hopefully the growing consciousness of fish as a 'healthy' food may help to redress this gastronomic imbalance.

Talleyrand, the famous French statesman and noted gourmet, so this story goes, had planned a dinner party for twelve guests having just taken delivery of a magnificent pair of turbot, regarded for centuries as the aristocrat of all fish. Wanting desperately to show them both off even though one alone would suffice for the fish course and at the same time, not wishing to appear ostentatious, he devised the following plan to achieve his aim. The first turbot was presented at the table and received by all with great admiration and applause. Then, as secretly arranged, the waiter slipped and dropped the whole thing on the floor to cries of anguish and distress. At which point Talleyrand with serene calm simply said, "Bring us another turbot".

FISKEPUDDING *(Norwegian/Swedish)*
A fish pudding found throughout Scandinavia composed of flaked white fish fillet and breadcrumbs, bound together with a rich combination of butter, egg and cream, seasoned with nutmeg and other spices and baked in a mould.

FISKESUPPE *(Norwegian/Swedish)*
A thick fish soup made from white fish cooked in fish stock together with parsnips, carrots, leeks, potato, celery, onions and bay leaf. Cream and egg yolks are added at the last minute to enrich and thicken the broth.

FIVE FLOWERED PORK *(Chinese)*
See *Jing ng far nam.*

FIVE SPICE POWDER *(Chinese)*
See *Heung new fun.*

FLAMANDE, la *(French)*
In the Flemish style, or the cooking of northeastern France and Belgium. When used in relation to a garnish, it means baby carrots, turnips, potatoes and peas, mixed with small braised sausages, when applied to sauce, it means a mustard-cream combination.

FLAMICHE *(French)*
A speciality of the north of France – Picardy and Flanders – a flamiche is a type of savoury tart or quiche, served as a first course. It is usually filled with leeks and cream, but less frequently, replaces the leeks with pumpkin purée.

FOFOS *(Portuguese)*
Made from *bacalhau* (see *bacalão*) or salt cod, these are deep-fried fritters, or 'puffins'. They are made simply

of soaked and flaked salt cod, eggs, flour and sharp cheese, and dipped in boiling olive oil.

FOGAS (*Hungarian*)

A traditional fish dish of the lake district of Hungary. The *fogas* is a zander or perch pike, found particularly in Lake Balaton; it is cooked when alive and served with the back arched in *rigor mortis* and the head and tail standing up from the plate.

FOIE GRAS (*French*)

This delicacy is found in many regions of France, but it is most closely associated with the Dordogne and with Strasbourg. *Foie gras* itself is the bloated liver of a goose – or, increasingly, duck – which has been produced by force feeding of corn, known as the *gavage*. The 'ripe' livers are ready in November–February, and are sold whole, to be served fresh, lightly sautéed, or preserved *en bloc*. Smaller pieces are made into *pâté de foie gras*. In the Dordogne, the base of the pâté is pork meat – liver, with slices of the *foie gras* implanted, usually with truffles. In Strasbourg, the pâté is of a rich, creamy consistency, the livers themselves being pulverized and sealed with butter in the distinctive crock. Both are highly valued and expensive, in their home country and abroad.

FONDUE (*Swiss/French*)

There are several versions of fondue, the most famous being that made popular by the Swiss, using gruyère, fontina, emmental and other similar cheese, singly or in combination, together with white wine and kirsch, to form a melted dip kept liquid over a flame. Bread cubes are dipped into the hot melted cheese on long forks, and then eaten.

Fondue Brillat-Savarin is a version from the Franche-Comté across the border in France, and substitutes cream and eggs for the kirsch. This thicker fondue is served over toast.

Fondue Bourguignonne is, despite its Burgundian appellation, an invention of the French region of Switzerland. In this version, cubes of steak are dipped into a special pot containing hot oil, then dipped into a selection of sauces including *mayonnaise, béarnaise* and *remoulade*. *Fondue Chinois* is served much like Fondue Bourguignonne, but consists of thinly sliced pieces of prime beef wrapped around a long fork and cooked in bouillon rather than oil.

FONDUTA (*Italian*)

A north Italian version of fondue, using melted fontina cheese, milk, egg yolks and grated white truffles. Because it is thicker than the Swiss version and coagulates it cannot be kept over a flame, so it should be served in individual earthenware bowls with pieces of toast to dip in.

FONTINA (*Italian*)

One of the best of Italian cheeses. The genuine article comes from the Val d'Oasta high in the French/Swiss Alpine border. It is made of unpasteurised cow's milk from a single milking, and is pressed and cooked. The medium-ripened cheese has a sweet and semi-soft consistency with a light brown skin. The paste is slightly freckled with holes, and the taste is like a sweeter, smoother Gruyère. A winter version is made in factories, but it lacks the rich, subtle flavour of the summer farm cheese. It is the principle constituent of *fonduta*, the more exclusive North Italian version of *fondue* (qv).

FOO YOUNG (*Chinese*)
Stuffed omelettes – or little egg rolls – filled with ground pork mixed with ginger roots and spring onions, and deep-fried. the rolls are then drained and served with a dipping sauce or a sauce of Szechuan pepper and salt mix. A speciality of Peking and of the South.

FRANGIPANE (*French*)
A term used for a number of different culinary devices. It comes from the name of an Italian noble-man who served in the French Court of Catherine de Medici. Frangipane can refer to a mixture of flour, butter, milk and egg-yolks used to bind forcemeat and stuffings for meat, poultry and fish; it is also used to denote an almond cream dessert popular during the 18th and 19th centuries. Today it is more usually used to describe a mixture of butter, eggs and almonds, topped by cake or macaroon crumbs, which forms the filling of small tarts, generally known as Frangipane tarts.

FRIJOLES REFRITOR (*Mexican*)
A 'typical' Mexican dish, these refried beans have a taste and texture all their own. They are made from soaked and simmered pinto or rosecoco beans, which are then mashed with oil and onion into a lumpy purée. They are served as a side dish or used as a filling for *burritos* (qv), *tostadas* (qv) or other dishes.

FRIKADELLA (FRIKADEL) (*Danish/Swedish*)
Meatballs formed from finely minced veal, beef or pork or a combination, rolled into balls and fried in butter. They are eaten hot or cold, often as part of a *Smörgåsbord* (qv). Called *Frikkadel* in Holland.

FRITTATA (*Italian*)
An Italian omelette. These are served all over the country, the ingredients varying according to region and availability. In Genoa, spinach is often mixed with the egg; in the Piedmonte sausage; in the Savoie borders, ham, potatoes and cheese; and in Sicily cheese, onion and basil. It is often served cold, in wedges.

FRITTO MISTO (*Italian*)
A mixed plate of deep-fried fish, usually squid slices, whitebait, mullet, sole and other white fish, shrimp, mussels and other shellfish. It can also refer to a mixed fry of meats, usually including brains, veal, liver and other offal or meats and, sometimes, vegetables.

FUFU *(West African)*
The peeled, pounded, boiled root of the Cassava plant. It is a bland, starchy pulp, used to sop up the juices of stews and soups.

FUL MEDAMES *(Egyptian/Lebanese)*
Boiled *faves* – a type of brown broad bean – dressed with olive oil and lemon juice and flavoured with garlic, a favourite *hors d'oeuvre* in the Middle East.

FUNGHI *(Italian)*
The Italians are mushroom mad, perhaps even more than the French. While all kinds of funghi are foraged in season, it is the *porcini* or boletus mushroom which causes the greatest stir. In the late summer and autumn when these are in season, the hills are alive with local people prodding the leaf-strewn ground in search of them, and the restaurants offer meals in which sometimes every course is a celebration of the *porcini*. Other prized mushrooms include *ovuli* – the imperial agaric – and the spring morel. Field mushrooms are stuffed with breadcrumbs, garlic and parmesan and baked (*Funghi alla parmigiana*), or fried with potatoes, garlic and basil (*alla genovese*). A favourite Roman and Lombardian antipasto is mushrooms sauted with herbs, oils, garlic, wine and lemon juice and served cold (*alla ambrosiana*).

GA XAO XA OT *(Vietnamese)*
A standard Vietnamese dish made from chopped chicken and lemon grass stir-fried in a wok with chilis, peanuts, sugar and fish sauce (*Nuoc mam* (qv)).

GADO-GADO *(Indonesian)*
The name for both the cold cooked vegetable salad so popular in Indonesia and for the spicy peanut sauce with which it is dressed. Peeled potatoes, green beans, carrots and cabbage are boiled and chilled, then combined with scalded bean sprouts, cucumber, watercress and sliced hard-boiled egg. The sauce of peanut oil, chilis, garlic, ground peanut paste, shrimp paste, palm sugar and lemon juice is then poured over.

GAJJAR *(Indian/Pakistani)*
Carrot. A vegetable hardly used in main dish Indian cookery, but which is a popular ingredient for desserts, such as *halva* (qv) and *kheer* (pudding).

GALAKTOBOUREKO *(Greek)*
Flaky fillo pastry encircling a vanilla-flavoured custard centre made with milk, semolina, butter and eggs.

GAMBAS *(Spanish)*
Gambas are large prawns, which are probably the most widely-served shellfish in Spain. They appear as both first courses, main courses and in *tapas* – appetisers – and common methods of preparation include: *al ajillo* – prawns in their shells marinated in olive oil, garlic and parsley, then grilled; *a la plancha* – prawns in their shells, buttered and grilled; and *picantes* – fried prawns in their shells served with a spicy tomato and chili sauce.

GAMMELOST *(Norway)*
A sour skimmed-milk cow's cheese with a crusty brown rind. It is a cooked, pressed and moulded cheese, the

forms with the cheese are then boiled in whey for several hours. Thereafter it is pierced with needles containing the *penicillium* mould, which starts the cheese blueing. The curing period is some four weeks, during which a surface mould also begins to grow. The final cheese is strong and sharp, an 'old socks' cheese which should be sliced using thin Scandinavian cheese-paring implements.

GARAM MASALA *(Indian/Pakistani)*

The Indian cook's time saver. A dry mixture of ground spices which varies from cook to cook, it is usually made in batches and kept in an airtight container to be used, when necessary, for curries and other dishes. The *garam masala* is sometimes added at the frying stage of a recipe, and sometimes in the last few minutes of cooking. Common ingredients, which are pounded to a fine powder together, include coriander seeds, cumin seeds, cinnamon, cloves, nutmeg, cardamom, dried chilis and pepper. Other *masalas* can be wet pastes, including other fresh ingredients like mint leaves, fresh ginger, garlic, coriander leaves and/or fresh chilis.

GARBURE *(French)*

A thick, vegetable and meat rich stew, a speciality of the Béarnaise and other parts of the southwest. It is usually served over chunks of bread. When finished, red wine is poured into the warm bowl and drunk in a single long gulp. This custom is known as *goudale* in the south and *chabror* in the Perigord/Quercy.

GASPACHO *(Portuguese)*

A Portuguese soup, quite a different variation from its similar Spanish namesake. It is cold and does contain a thick peasant bread, but there are several vegetables besides tomatoes and onions in it, and there are large chunks of cumin-flavoured sausage as well.

GAY LIM SOAK MI GAI TONG *(Chinese)*

A thick chicken soup made with puréed chicken breast simmered with creamed corn.

GAZPACHO *(Spanish)*

To qualify as a gazpacho, a soup must have a fair proportion of bread in its makeup. The Andalusian version of gazpacho is the most renowned and is also referred to as a 'liquid salad'. Purists insist that the ingredients should be pressed through a sieve and not blended or processed. The gazpacho contains tomatoes, onions, breadcrumbs, peppers, cucumber, garlic, ice water, vinegar, sugar and spices, strained and/or blended to produce a smooth liquid. It is then garnished with croutons and diced cucumber, pepper, tomato and onion.

GEBACKENE SCHWAMMERL/CHAMPIGNON *(German/Austrian)*

Mushrooms dipped in eggs and breadcrumbs, then deep-fried. They are served as a first course, with a dip of *tartare sauce* (qv).

GENEVOISE, à la (*French*)

In the style of Geneva. *Sauce Genevoise* is a brown sauce, based on fish essence, garlic and red wine or madeira, used chiefly on salmon and trout.

GENOISE, à la (*French*)

In the Genoese style. When applied to sauces, it usually means containing butter and eggs. When it applies to stuffing – as in *tomate à la genoise* – it is with chopped green peppers, anchovies and potatoes. It can also mean simply tomato sauce or even a kind of mayonnaise with herbs, pistachios and almonds. *Genoise* in confectionery denotes a sponge cake, either round and flat, and served with whipped cream; or the mixture used to make several types of cake which are embellished further.

GHEE (*Indian*)

A necessity for much Indian cooking; what gives the distinctive flavour of North Indian cuisine. It is pure butterfat, or clarified butter, having no milk solids. It can thus be heated to much higher temperatures than ordinary butter and will keep far longer without refrigeration. It is sold in packets, tubs, or cans or can be made at home from heated and finely strained ordinary butter.

GHIOTTA, alla (*Italian*)

Literally 'delicious-style'. It is usually in connection with fish stews or thick soups, particularly in the deep south and Sicily. The base is often salt cod or swordfish and additions include onions, tomatoes, olives, peppers, capers, courgettes and potatoes in various combinations.

GHUY-YOONG YIEN WAN (*Chinese*)

'Bird's nest soup'. A speciality of both Hong Kong and Peking, this classic soup cannot be duplicated in the West without the proper ingredients – the 'bird's nests' themselves – really the predigested protein from a certain seaweed which is used by swallows along the coast of China, and an alkali powder to clean and soak the nests. Both of these are necessary to contribute flavour and texture. The other ingredients are simply chicken stock, rice wine and monosodium glutamate.

GINGER (*Spice*)

A rhizome essential to most Asian and Oriental dishes. Called *Adrak* in India, *Gin* in Burmese, *Khing* in Thai, *Jeung* in Chinese, *Shoga* in Japanese and *Jahe* in Indonesian, it has an irregular shape, with knobbly extensions covered in a woody skin. It must be peeled to be used and has a pungent smell and rather fiery flavour. It is usually chopped or minced into marinades, sauces and dishes. It can be pickled and candied but is most useful fresh, and can be preserved over long periods by immersing peeled rhizomes in sherry in a sealed jar. It is used in numerous Chinese dishes and in Japanese dishes, as well as most Indian curries. (See also *Herbs and Spices* chart).

GINGERBREAD (*English/French and German*)

Originally a Christmas festival bread, gingerbread is found in traditional cuisines throughout Europe. It is baked in a loaf as a soft cake-like bread, but even more *folkloregue* are the moulded figures and shapes which have been made at least since the 17th century, and which are harder and drier than the loaves. These flat biscuits are often decorated with dried fruits, icing and in earlier times, with gold and silver leaf which was believed to be good for the heart, hence the saying 'to take the gilt off the gingerbread'.

GJETOST *(Norwegian)*

Made from goat's milk and cow's milk whey. Since it is made from whey, it is not really a 'true' cheese, but it is much beloved of Scandinavians, and is sliced with a special cheese plane. While some cow's milk is allowed in the manufacture of *Gjetost*, it must have at least 10 per cent goat's milk. When it is made from goat's milk alone, it can call itself *Ekte* (real) *Gjetost*, or *Geitmysost*. It is much appreciated with herring and other fish dishes.

GNOCCHI *(Italian)*

Small dumplings, made from a variety of ingredients, served with a simple sauce as a first course in the North of Italy.

Gnocchi di patate are little potato dumplings. They can be served *alla genovese* – with a *pesto* sauce; *alla parmignana* – with a tomato and parmesan sauce; or *alla romana* – also with tomatoes and cheese.

Gnocchi di semolini are probably the second most common form; these can be served simply with butter and cheese, or *alla romana*, as above.

Gnocchi di polenta – made with maize or corn flour – and *gnocchi alla bava* – from the Piedmonte, and made of buckwheat, are two other cereal forms.

Gnocchi verdi are the green dumplings of Tuscany, made with spinach and ricotta, eggs and cheese. They are served with a butter and cheese, or sometimes a tomato sauce. *Gnocchi di ricotta* replaces the spinach with flour, so that the little dumplings are whiter.

GOHAN *(Japanese)*

The staff of Japanese life – plain boiled rice. The varieties used are short and medium grain. *Gohan* actually means 'honourable meal', since the rice is the mainstay of most meals around which the other dishes are eaten. It is also used in *sushi* and in other dishes in which it is incorporated.

GOLDEN BLOSSOMS *(Chinese)*
See *So far gai yuen*.

GOLDEN COIN CHICKEN *(Chinese)*
See *Jin chiang ji*.

GOLDEN NEEDLES *(Chinese)*
See *Gum jum*.

GOLZBKI *(Polish)*

A filling peasant dish, these cabbage rolls can be filled with any combination of ground beef, pork or veal. The whole cabbage is parboiled and the top leaves removed and stuffed with a mixture of rice, onion, spices and the meat. The rolls are then braised in a meat, mushroom or tomato stock and are served with the reduced sauce and, frequently, sour cream.

GOMES DE SA, a ***(Portuguese)***
Meat or fish cooked in the style of Gomes de Sa – meaning with potatoes, eggs and olives.

GOO LO YUK ***(Chinese)***
The Cantonese speciality best-known in the West – sweet-and-sour pork. Small pieces of pork are dipped in batter, deep-fried, and then covered with a sauce of vinegar, sugar, tomato paste and soy sauce, dotted with green pepper and – less authentically – pineapple.

✕ *GOOSEBERRY: CHINESE*
Better known today as Kiwi Fruit and exported in great numbers from New Zealand. The name I'm told was changed for sound marketing reasons since USA citizens at one time patriotically shunned anything which suggested association with 'Red' China.

GORGONZOLA ***(Italian)***
The foremost Italian cheese after Parmesan. It is a blue-veined cow's cheese, with a greenish-blue mould which is particularly spicy. The rind is coarse and reddish-green in colour, often slightly powdery. It is *stracchino* cheese, made from the milk of summer-grazing Alpine cows, who then wintered and were milked at Gorgonzola, where the strange penicillin mould first took hold. Today it is produced in the Po Valley in Lombardy, but no longer at Gorgonzola. It is usually eaten as a dessert cheese – it has a particular affinity for ripe pears – but it is sometimes used in cooking, as in *Tagliatelle con Quattro Formaggio* (also with Parmesan, fontina and mozzarella). It should be sharp and clean in taste and smell, but not overly ripe and ammoniac.

GOSHT ***(Indian/Pakistani)***
The generic Indian term for meat. Various curry dishes have *gosht* in the title, such as *Kuma Gosht* and *Bhuna Gosht*.

GOUDA ***(Dutch)***
Less immediately recognisable than the red-wax Edam, Gouda cheese is nevertheless even more important to the Dutch economy, responsible for over two-thirds of national cheese production. It too is exported all over the world. It may have a few small holes, and the young version, which accounts for most sales, has a buttery, light flavour. Older cheeses are dark yellow-brown inside and much sharper and richer in flavour. It grates well and is used for cooking at both stages, as well as in *kaasdoop*, Dutch fondue.
There are small wheels of baby Gouda made, of about 4lbs in weight, which are sold whole or sliced after one month. The full sized 44lb wheel may take about four months. The aged cheese is kept for about one year or more. There are also versions with cumin seeds, caraway and nettle. Today there are both factory-made and

unpasteurised farm versions available, (the latter only in Holland or at better delicatessens), though the traditional hand-slapping ceremony, with the painted cheese slings, black beribboned hats and clogs outside the 17th century weigh-house at Gouda only remains as an entertainment for tourists.

GRANNY APPLE, POTATO SALAD *(Australian)*
A classic Australian salad with blue cheese and Granny Smith apples.

✗ *GRAPEFRUIT*
One of the youngest fruits in existence being less than two hundred years old. Its first reported sighting was by John Lunan in Jamaica who described this new find as tasting like a grape – which it doesn't of course and leads me to wonder what he'd been drinking the night before. Later explanations for the name were attributed to its habit of growing in bunches which again is not so, although as it's a very heavy cropper it can give that impression.

After the Wall St. crash in 1929 impoverished American housewives could get them free with food stamps although many of the ladies subsequently complained to the Welfare Board that no amount of boiling could make them edible!

GRATIN, au *(French)*
Named for the shallow ovoid dish that the recipe was traditionally baked in, it now means any dish (usually vegetable or fish) topped with breadcrumbs and/or cheese and finished under the grill.

GRAVAD LAX (GRAVLAKE) *(Swedish/ Norwegian/Danish)*
Marinated salmon. The traditional method involves slicing a whole filleted salmon down the length, filling the centre with equal measures of sugar and salt, together with fresh dill and pepper, sandwiching the two sides together, covering with more seasoning and placing the fish under a weight for two days. It is then cut into thin strips or slices and served with a dilled mustard sauce. The Danes often add a dash of cognac or aquavit to their marinade.

GRÉCQUE, à la *(French/International)*
A Frenchification of Greek cuisine which has gradually found its way into an international idiom. It is basically fresh vegetables simmered in a light bouillon or lemon and wine mixture, then strained and cooled in spiced and seasoned oil and a reduction of the cooking liquid. Usual variations include leeks, artichokes, mushrooms and green beans *à la Grécque*.

GROUNDNUT STEW, CHICKEN *(Nigerian/West African)*
An aromatic casserole of chicken pieces, groundnuts (peanuts), onions, tomatoes and broth. The sauce is either liquidised, or the peanuts ground before adding to the sauce, to obtain a smoother consistency.

GRUNER KASE *(Swiss)*
See *Sapsago*.

GRUYÈRE *(Swiss)*

Made in the canton of Frebourg for over 200 years, this cow's milk cheese is today made in Vaud and Neuchatel as well. Its manufacture is similar to that of *Emmental* (qv), but it is half the size. Its flavour is also fuller, fruitier and sharper and there should be few holes. Its fat content is higher than Emmental and it is generally aged longer – six months to one year. It cooks beautifully and is much used in sauces, soufflés, fondues and cheese pastries.

GUACAMOLE *(Mexican)*

A creamy avocado dip which is highly versatile, capable of being used as an *hors d'oeuvre* (with *tortilla chips* (qv)), garnish, filling for *tacos* (qv), or thinned as a salad dressing. The traditional recipe uses onion, lemon or lime juice, dried chilis, chopped tomato and fresh coriander, mashed together with the ripe avocado.

GUAJOLOTE RELLENO *(Mexican)*

See *Pavo al horno*.

GUASACACA *(Venezuelan)*

A spicy sauce made from mashed avocados and pulped tomatoes, lime juice, chopped hard boiled eggs, red chili peppers and other spices. It is served as a condiment for barbecued or grilled beef and pork.

GUCHULPAN *(Korean)*

The 'Nine Varieties', one of Korea's most delicious traditional dishes. Small pancakes are piled in the centre of a large tray and are surrounded by various ingredients for filling them. These include mushrooms, carrots, white radish (daikon), courgettes and fillet of beef, all thinly shredded and briefly stir-fried. The desired ingredients are picked up with chopsticks, placed in the centre of a pancake which is then rolled up and dipped into a sesame seed, vinegar and soy sauce before being eaten. This is usually served as an appetiser, but can be eaten as a main dish.

GUFELHUPF *(Austrian)*

A circular cake, with sculpted sides and a hole in the centre. It is baked in a traditional *bundt* ring. The consistency of the cake is dryish and buttery; it is served as a coffee cake in the many cafes. Gugelhupf will either be left plain, dusted with sugar, or covered with chocolate and almonds.

GULAB JAMUN *(Indian/Pakistani)*

Small balls made from milk powder, flour and *ghee*, flavoured with cardamom and sometimes almonds, are fried, and then drenched in sugared rose water syrup until they swell and are spongy.

GULASHSUPPE *(Austrian)*

A thick beef and vegetable soup which is highly spiced, particularly with paprika. It is served as a hearty or late breakfast or supper dish, or in smaller portions as a winter first course.

GULE AERTER *(Danish)*

Traditional yellow-pea soup, a staple of both Denmark and Sweden, where it is called *Arter med flask*. The soup also contains chunks of bacon, sausage and vegetables (potatoes, carrots, celery, etc.) and in Sweden the solids are usually served separately after the broth. In Sweden it is the traditional Thursday supper, and usually substitutes pork for the bacon.

GUM JUM *(Chinese)*
Also known as 'golden needles', these are tiger lily buds sold in dried form which must be soaked before using. They are often combined with *Wun Yee* in dishes.

GUMBO *(American)*
The classic dish of Louisiana's Creole cuisine, *gumbo* relies on okra for its distinctive texture and appearance. 'Gumbo' means okra in the dialect, and the stew is a combination of poultry (usually chicken) and/or seafood (usually crab and shrimp), okra, rice, peppers and tomatoes. Another distinctive ingredient is *filé* (qv), which gives it a special dark colour and kick. (See also *Okra*.)

HAGGIS *(Scottish)*
The national dish of Scotland, it is also the main feature of Burns' Night, on the 25th January. It is composed of minced sheep's heart, lights and liver mixed with suet, oatmeal, herbs and spices, stuffed into a sheep's stomach, tied and boiled. The usual accompaniments are mashed potatoes and turnips – *Clapshot*. The size of haggis varies from individual to large versions for several people. The entire pudding, including the skin, is edible.

HALVA *(Indian/Pakistani)*
A solid sweetmeat, made by sautéeing, puréeing and then reducing vegetables or cereals in a sugary syrup. It is served cut into squares. A favourite constituent is carrot (*Gajjar halva*). Others are coconut and semolina (*Halva Madras*) and with sultanas and semolina (*Halva Bombay*).

HALVA *(Turkish)*
Made in large blocks or slabs this very sweet confection can be bought by the slice and a little is quite nice especially with some coffee to wash it down. Usually made from a mixture of flour, butter, sugar and honey with various additions e.g. pistachio nuts.

HAR KAU *(Chinese)*
Shrimps or prawns in a transparent wheat and corn-flour pastry, thinly rolled and shaped like small Cornish pasties. These are deep-fried and served with hot dipping sauce as part of *dim sum* (qv) or as an appetiser.

HAR YEE KAI *(Chinese)*
Literally 'Beggar's chicken' – an entire chicken is stuffed with onions and herbs, mushrooms and vegetables and is wrapped in large dark lotus leaves. The whole is then moulded in a clay covering and baked. The chief guest breaks the clay covering with a

specially-presented mallet, releasing a cloud of wonderful aroma.

HARIRA (*Moroccan*)

A spicy chicken-based soup thickened with rice or noodles, and chick peas. It is traditionally eaten to break the fast at sundown during Ramadan.

HARISSA (*Moroccan/Tunisian*)

A hot red chili sauce used as a condiment with many North African dishes. It is made of red pimentoes, soaked, drained and pounded with garlic, coriander, caraway and mint. At the end a little salt and oil is stirred in. It should be kept in a sealed bottle, and once opened, in the refrigerator.

HASENPFEFFER (*German*)

A rich Bavarian stew made from hare, well-flavoured with spices, pepper and red wine. It is often served with dumplings.

HAVARTI (*Danish*)

A mild, bland, cow's cheese, peppered with small holes, and made in flat rounds or loaves. It is slightly acid when young, but becomes sharper with age. The more common is the dry rind version; a washed rind version is less bland.

HEUNG NEW FUN (*Chinese*)

'Five spice powder' – a mixture of aniseed, fennel, cloves, cinnamon and pepper. It is piquant, spicy and should be used sparingly.

HEUNG SO NGAP (*Chinese*)

Whole duck marinated in spices and colouring, steamed, then deep-fried. After cooking, the crispy duck is chopped into small pieces and garnished with coriander or spring onions.

HIGADO (*Spanish*)

Liver (usually lamb, but in the country those of small songbirds are used), sautéed in olive oil and garlic and served garnished with sweet pepper or paprika. If it is cooked *a la astureana* it is sautéed with garlic, onions, tomatoes and ground onions.

HO YAU NGAU YUK (*Chinese*)

A Cantonese speciality. Though this recipe is reproduced in other parts of China, oyster sauce is the mark of Canton. The thinly-sliced beef is marinated in rice wine, oyster sauce, soy sauce and cornstarch, then stir-fried with ginger and green pepper.

HOISIN SAUCE (*Chinese*)

A sauce sold in bottles or cans, much used in stir-fried dishes. It is thick and glutinous, made from fermented red bean curd and salt.

HOLLANDAISE (SAUCE) (*French*)

A classic of French cuisine, a rich yellow sauce of egg yolks, butter, lemon juice and vinegar emulsified in a double boiler over heat. It should not be overheated and is always served lukewarm, usually with fish or vegetables.

HOLSTEIN-SCHNITZEL ***(Austrian/German)***
Named after Bismark's foreign secretary, Count Holstein, this is a more extravagant version of *Wiener Schnitzel* (qv). The breaded and fried veal cutlet is garnished with criss-crossed strips of anchovies, capers and if served '*mit spiegelei*' (with mirror egg), it has a fried egg on top.

HOMINY ***(American)***
A traditional Southern speciality, hominy is hulled white corn, of a particularly mealy consistency. It is simmered until tender, then mixed with butter and fried as cakes or baked. It can also be made into fritters, while fried hominy is ground, boiled and mixed with butter to be served as an accompaniment to a traditional Southern breakfast.

✕ *HONEY*
This product is flower nectar predigested, manufactured and stored by bees after which man steps in, takes it away and sells it.

✕ *HOPS*
This plant is best known as a flavouring for beer although the young sprouting shoots were often eaten as a vegetable and are today making a come-back in that form usually in 'expense account' restaurants. I found them in a local supermarket recently and tried them. A pint of bitter tastes a lot better.

HORCHATA ***(Spanish)***
A milky concoction made from ground tiger nuts. It originated in Valencia, but today is found throughout Spain. Made fresh, it tastes vaguely like coconuts, with a slightly lemon-like sourness. It has now been bottled, but the fresh is much the best. Served cold, it is a delicious refresher on a hot day.

HOTCH-POTCH ***(Scottish)***
A soupy stew made with lamb chops and a medley of vegetables, depending on season and availability. A common combination includes green peas, beans, cabbage, lettuce, carrots and onions; but on remote islands and northern districts nettletops, wild spinach, carrot and garlic, and other foraged food replaces cultivated vegetables.

HOUMOUS (HOMMUS) ***(Middle Eastern, Greek)***
A creamy, pale beige paste made from pounded or ground chick peas, mixed with oil, crushed garlic and lemon. It is used as an appetiser; pitta bread pieces are dipped into it and eaten.

HSIANGSU YA ***(Chinese)***
'Crispy, Fragrant Duck' – a Chongjing dish from the West, now adopted by the Szechuan school. The duck is steamed with ginger root, garlic, rice wine and five-spice powder for a few hours, then marinated in its own juice, then deep fried. It is eaten with steamed

buns or pancakes and shredded vegetables, like Peking duck (*Bei jing kao ya*).

HSIEUH ROU DOU FU (*Chinese*)

Crab and ginger, simmered in stock, with bean curd added at the end. Serve with rice.

HUEVAS (*Spanish/Mexican*)

Eggs are one of the main staples of peasant cuisine in Spain, and also assume a more elegant character for certain first courses. Chief among the latter are *huevas rellenos* – eggs stuffed with a variety of fillings made from the mashed yolk and mayonnaise, together with such things as tuna, shrimp, anchovies, pâté or tomato purée. *Huevas con arroz* are hard-boiled eggs which have been halved and stuffed with a mixture of the yolks, air cured ham and brandy, served with red-pepper flecked rice.

As for peasant dishes, recipes include *Huevas a la gitanilla* – 'gypsy eggs' baked on a purée of garlic, bread, saffron, paprika and almonds; *a la flamenca* eggs baked on a bed of tomato purée, surrounded by ham, sausage, asparagus and peas; *en panecillos*, eggs baked in hollowed out bread or fried croutons; or another version *al nido*; 'eggs in a nest' hollowed rolls filled with tomato sauce and egg yolk, wrapped in beaten egg white, and fried until they puff up. (See also *tortilla española* and *revueltos*.)

Huevas do not feature to such a degree in native Mexican cooking, and *huevas rancheros* – tortillas covered with eggs scrambled with chilis, and covered by a hot sauce – is the main egg dish. It may also be garnished with avocado, sour cream and coriander.

HUI KOU MO YIOU (*Chinese*)

Heart of Chinese cabbage braised with mushrooms and bamboo shoots and a sweet-and-sour sauce. It is especially good served cold.

HUO TUEI DAN CHAO FAN (*Chinese*)

'Ten variety' or 'special fried' rice – a staple at all Chinese–Western restaurants, and originally from Shanghai. Boiled white rice is stir-fried with egg, diced ham or pork, prawns and green peas.

HUSH PUPPIES (*American*)

Two quite different dishes go by this appellation.

Corn meal and water, mixed together and fried in bacon fat on a griddle can probably stake the oldest claim to the name. They were so-called because they were supposedly thrown to the howling hounds after a day of squirrel or rabbit hunting with the admonition 'hush puppy'.

A later claimant is the dish popular with east coast Ivy League students: a plate of 'french fries' or chips, soaked in ladles of chicken gravy.

IDLI (*Indian/Pakistani*)

A round, very flat pancake-like bread made from rice flour. It is pale in colour and may be flavoured with lentils, coconut or other vegetables or spices. It is often served with a fruit chutney or a *sambar* (qv) for breakfast in southern India.

IKAN *(Indonesian)*

Fish. There are several types of fish dishes in Indonesia, ranging from sweet and sour to hot. The usual fish used are tuna, Spanish mackerel, kingfish, or snapper – they are interchangeable with the recipes, depending upon availability. One of the most common dishes is *Ikan Panggang* – grilled fish with spices, including chilis, lemon grass, and coconut milk, ginger powder and shrimp paste. The fish is marinated in the sauce before grilling, then basted with it.

Ikan Bali is Balinese style fish steaks sautéed with garlic, laos powder, lemon juice, soy sauce and chili sauce. *Guli Ikan* and *Ikan Bumbu Santan* are both whole fish cooked in coconut milk and spices, though the latter is boned and butterflied, while *Ikan Asam Manis* is fish marinated in a sweet-and-sour garlic and cumin sauce (see *Sate Manis*) and grilled. *Guli Ikan Padang* is a spicy curry of fish pieces in coconut milk.

ILE FLOTTANTE *(French)*

This dessert, 'floating islands' is a nursery favourite popular with French adults. It is composed of whipped egg-whites, or meringues, poached then floated in a vanilla egg custard. The whole is sprinkled with almonds.

IMAM BAYALDI *(Turkish)*

'The priest fainted' – a good name for this piquant dish, usually served as a first course. Split and hollowed aubergines are stuffed with a mixture of onions, tomatoes, herbs, currants and the aubergine pulp, all previously sautéed in olive oil. The stuffed aubergines are then baked on a low heat and served either hot, cold or even reheated which, some say, improves the taste.

INDIAN PUDDING *(American)*

Coarse of texture, dark brown, spicy, with the unmistakable, smokey flavour of molasses, Indian pudding is an old-fashioned New England dessert still found at inns and tables in the north-east. The main ingredients are cornmeal, brown sugar, milk, molasses, butter, cinnamon and ginger mixed together and baked in a *bain marie* until set. It is usually served with double cream or ice cream.

INLAGD SILL *(Swedish)*

Pickled herrings which are marinated for up to three weeks in a mixture of sugar, salt, herbs, spices and almonds. They have a rather sweet, cinnamony flavour and a reddish hue.

INVOLTINI *(Italian)*

Small roll-ups, usually made of veal escalopes with a filling or stuffing. The filling is often of prosciutto slices and sage leaves; the roll-ups are then skewered and braised. Another variation, *alla cacciatora*, has a stuffing of chicken livers, prosciutto and herbs wrapped up and tied in veal escalopes, then braised in chicken stock and marsala.

ISHIKARI NABE (*Japanese*)
A salmon stew, enlivened with *shiatake* mushrooms, greens, *shungiku* (qv) bean curd (*tofu*) and Chinese cabbage. It is a speciality of the northern island.

JA (ZHA) (*Chinese*)
This word in a Chinese recipe means 'deep fried' over high heat.

JALEBI (*Indian/Pakistani*)
Rice and wheat flour coils, coloured yellow/orange by saffron, are deep-fried, then soaked in a sweet syrup, then drained and served. They should be allowed to cool to room temperature before eating.

JAMBALAYA (*American*)
A Cajun dish of Spanish origin, jambalaya is one of the classics of Louisiana cuisine. A casserole based on tomato-flavoured rice – usually combined with chicken and diced ham, or with shrimps, or all three – it should be well spiced with garlic and cayenne.

JAMBON (*French*)
Jambon is served in various guises throughout France, usually as a first course or as a sandwich filling. *Jambon de pays* or *de campagne* is country ham, smoked – or simply salted – and left hanging from the rafters to age. It is eaten raw, sliced extremely thinly and served with *cornichons* (qv) and butter. *Jambon de Bayonne* is a particularly delicate form of this raw ham, a speciality of the south-western corner of the country. *Jambon de Paris* or *blanc* is a pale cooked ham, usually boiled. It is served cold, usually in salads or sandwiches.

JANSSONS FRESTELSE (*Swedish*)
One of Sweden's better-known contributions to world cooking. 'Janessons' Temptation' is composed of layers of anchovies, potatoes and onions, doused in cream and baked in the oven. Unbelievably it can be served as a first course.

JARLSBERG (*Norwegian*)
With Danablu is probably the best-known cheese outside Denmark. It is an Emmental cow's milk type, though its flavour and texture are more like *Gouda* (qv). It is now entirely factory produced, and much of it is exported to Britain and the US. It is used in cooking as well as a dessert cheese.

JIAN (*Chinese*)
This word in a recipe title means 'shallow-fried' over a medium heat. It also usually implies that a sauce – such as yellow or black bean – is added at the last minute.

JIANG BAO JI DING (*Chinese*)
A Peking speciality, chicken and nuts (cashews or peanuts) stir-fried with a *hoisin* and yellow bean sauce.

JIANG YU JI (*Chinese*)
'Red cooked chicken'. A roasting chicken is simmered in dark soy sauce and Chinese wine, then cooled and brushed with sesame oil, chopped into large strips then reassembled and served at room temperature. The

cooking liquid is reserved and used for other 'red-cooked' dishes, thus gaining in flavour and richness.

JIN CHIANGJI (*Chinese*)

Pieces of chicken, ham, pork and mushroom, cut into rounds, are skewered and roasted. Alternatively, boned chicken legs are stuffed with ham and mushrooms, steamed, and cut into rounds. Either way, the name means 'gold-coin chicken'.

JING NG FAR NAM (*Chinese*)

'Five-flavoured pork'. The belly of pork is cut into small pieces, marinated in garlic, wine and spices, and rolled in cooked and ground rice. It is then steamed until exceptionally tender.

JINGISUKAN NABE (*Japanese*)

A special convex pan, heated from underneath, which occurs in other Oriental cookery (see Vietnamese *Nem Nuong*), is used to produce this dish. Beef or lamb is grilled on it, as are thinly cut vegetables, on the table top, with diners serving themselves. Small sauces containing a selection of spices and another containing chili sauce or *wanabi* are available for the cooked pieces of food to be dipped in before eating.

JOE FROGGERS (*American*)

Spicy molasses cookies, popular in America since Colonial times. They are distinguished by their flatness and large size – like the lily pads of Joe Frog, a half-black local of Marblehead, Massachusetts, after which they were supposedly named. They have a dark, rich flavour of rum and molasses, spiked with ginger, cloves, nutmeg and allspice.

JOLLOF RICE (*Nigerian*)

A hot, spicy risotto, named for a part of Eastern Nigeria. It contains tomatoes, onions and spices, and may also contain pieces of chicken.

JUGGED HARE (*English*)

A west country favourite, often served on Boxing Day. The hare is jointed and marinated in wine, vinegar and juniper berries overnight, then drained, browned and cooked with the marinade, carrots, celery and bayleaves. About half an hour before serving, port wine and redcurrant jelly are stirred into the pot. True 'jugged hare', like *civet* (qv) uses some blood to thicken and colour the sauce.

JUHUA GUO (*Chinese*)

A variation on the Mongolian Hot Pot (*Shau yang rou*), this is the 'chrysanthemum pot', in which chicken breast, tripe, fish, maws, fish balls, spinach, snow peas, cabbage and perhaps pork or oysters are cooked in the moat of the burner all at one time. Edible chrysanthemum (*shungeku*) are scattered over the top. This is a Chengdu speciality from the West, and the burner uses spirits instead of charcoal. Each piece of fish, meat, poultry or vegetable is dipped into a 'four seasoning mix' – ginger, onion, pepper and salt – before being eaten.

KADAYIF *(Turkish)*
'The shredded wheat dessert' – long cylinders of stringy pastry, filled with nuts, or cream and nuts, soaked in a honey and orange-water syrup.

KAFTA (KEFTA) *(Arabian)*
See *Kofta*.

KAI *(Thai)*
Chicken. This is the most frequently encountered poultry in Thai cooking. It can be fried with ginger shreds (*Kai phat khing*), or deep-fried in yellow bean sauce (*Kai tod taucheo*). An especially succulent dish is *Kai Yang* – a garlic-smothered chicken grilled or roasted over hot coals.

KAISERSCHMARRN *(Austrian)*
Reputedly invented for Emperor Franz Joseph, this is a sweet souffléd omelette which is cooked flat on the hob, then torn apart and browned in butter. Served sprinkled with icing sugar and accompanied by stewed plums or cranberry sauce.

KALAMARAKIA *(Greek)*
Baby squids. These are either served deep-fried with lemon, or sautéed in oil, then simmered in a wine sauce and served cold.

KALIBRAKA *(Russian)*
One of the triumphs of Russian cookery, a large loaf-shaped pasty filled with a mixture of flaked salmon, rice, onions, mushrooms and hard-boiled egg, flavoured with dill. It is served cut into slices.

KALLAJE *(Lebanese)*
A cheese similar to Greek *Halumi*, which is served grilled on *aish* (bread).

KANG KEOW WAN *(Thai)*
Green curry paste made from fresh green chilis, blended with pepper, garlic, coriander, cumin, lemon rind, shrimp paste, and *serai* (lemon grass powder) and *laos* (galangal powder – related to ginger). It can be hot or mild depending on whether the seeds of the chilis are included.

KAO *(Chinese)*
This word in a Chinese recipe means 'roasted'. Roasting is usually done as barbecuing, or in a restaurant oven, since traditional Chinese homes do not have an oven.

KAPI *(Thai)*
Shrimp paste – made from dried and soaked shrimps. It is a principal constituent in Thai cooking.

KARELA *(Indian/West Indian/Malaysian/Thai)*
The bitter gourd, this vegetable is often sold under its Indian name, *Karela*. It is a long, green, knobbly gourd, filled with bright bitter seeds. These must be scraped away and the interior salted then dried. They can be lightly boiled, and are much used in curries in both India and the West Indies. They are also stuffed with meat or chicken or other vegetables, then fried.

KASHA *(Russian/Polish)*
Buckwheat groats, soaked overnight then baked. The stock is sometimes flavoured with mushrooms and/or onions.

KASSLER *(Austrian/Swedish)*
The boned 'butt' of pork, smoked. It is either baked or sliced and fried.

KTAPOTHI *(Greek)*
A favourite of quayside Greek tavernas – octopus. These are often hung out to soften, then pounded against the quayside stones before being cut into small pieces and grilled, to be served with small glasses of *ouzo* or *retsina* as an appetiser. Octopus is also served *me saltsa* – sautéed in oil and garlic and then simmered with wine, tomatoes and onions.

KATSUDON *(Japanese)*
Pork, egg-and-breadcrumbed and fried, simmered in *dashi* and served on a bed of *gohan* or boiled rice. Like *Tonkatsu*, it is derived from German influence.

KATSUOBUSHI *(Japanese)*
Small, pale flakes of dried *bonito* or tuna, which look like wood shavings. It is a favourite ingredient for Japanese dishes, imparting a sweet-salty taste to many soups and stewed dishes such as *Oden*.

KAY JEE GHUY *(Chinese)*
Literally 'Chicken Draughtsmen'. See *Dong Gwoo Lap Cheong Jing Gu Yook*.

KEEMA *(Indian/Pakistani)*
Minced meat. In India it is usually lamb, but in Muslim areas and Pakistan it can also be beef. The *keema* is usually shaped into *Kofta* (meatballs) or shaped around hard-boiled eggs to make *Nargisi Kofta*.

KEFTEDHES *(Greek)*
Long meatballs made of minced beef or veal, kneaded together with chopped parsley, onions, oregano and mint, eggs and breadcrumbs. Sometimes they are further seasoned with a little vinegar and olive oil before being fried.

✗ *KELP*
One of the edible seaweeds widely available from 'Health-food' shops. A good source of potassium and iodine plus vitamins A and D. Quite a profitable little commodity too!

KESHI YENA *(Dutch Caribbean)*
A whole baby Edam is stripped of its red skin, hollowed, and stuffed with a spicy mixture of meat, onions, tomatoes and any other ingredients to hand. It is then baked and brought steaming to the table to be carved.

KESKEC *(Turkish)*
A porridge of shredded chicken and bulghur (cracked wheat) simmered for a long time until it is thickened and mushy. It is served sprinkled with paprika and melted butter poured over.

KETCHUP *(British/American)*
Although today we think first of tomato ketchup (catsup in the US) when the term is used, ketchup was originally a fermented or pickled fish extract, a condiment brought to Europe from the East Indies. Today it

can also mean any extract or boiled and strained pulp of fruit, nut, vegetable or fish. The most widely seen, in addition to tomato ketchup, are mushroom, walnut and fish ketchup.

KEY LIME PIE (*American*)

A speciality of Florida, a cool but rich mixture of lime juice, eggs, sugar and condensed milk inside a pastry pie case. It is usually tinted lime green with a little food colouring and topped with meringue. Served cold.

KHAO (*Thai*)

Thai rice. The word is synonymous with food. Rice is cooked by the absorption method or by steaming, and is then served plain – usually moulded – with a spicy curried stew, or fried (*Khao Phat*) with meat, poultry or seafood.

KHAROUF MESHWIEH (*Arabian*)

A whole lamb stuffed with a mixture of rice, minced lamb, pine nuts, spices and almonds, placed on a spit and roasted over coals on an open fire. It is the grand course for banquets and for the fabled Arabian picnics.

KIBBEH (*Lebanese*)

Kibbeh is a Lebanese classic which has filtered through to other Levantine countries. Cracked wheat (burghul) and minced meat are kneaded together until they form a paste, and are then formed into hollow-cases around the index finger, filled with a mixture of cooked mince, spices and pine nuts, or rice and onions, and either deep fried, or served raw as *kibbeh orayeh*, dressed with mint, pepper and olive oil.

KIEVSKIYE (*Russian*)

Better known as Chicken Kiev, this dish was instigated by a French chef in the Russian court. It consists of boned chicken filled with butter, then dipped in egg, then breadcrumbs and fried. When cut into. the butter spurts out of the chicken. Garlic was a later addition.

KIM (*Korean*)

Seaweed which is dried and salted, then oiled and toasted over a flame until crisp.

KIMCHEE (*Korean*)

Pickled Chinese cabbage, one of the country's national dishes, usually served as an accompaniment or condiment at every meal in a restaurant. It is made from Chinese cabbage, onions, chili, garlic, ginger and various stocks and pastes, and can be very hot. Most Westerners find it an acquired taste.

KITSUNE DONBURI (*Japanese*)

See *Donburi*.

KIWI FRUIT (*Chinese/New Zealand*)

These are small plump, oblong fruits with a light fuzzy skin. The interior is brilliant green, with two margins of small black seeds. It is mild tasting, with a gentle hint of gooseberry (its appearance and taste also lead it to be known as the *Chinese Gooseberry*). It is rarely cooked, except for ice-creams and conserves. It is most usually used for flans, fruit salads, and as a dessert fruit.

KNAIDLACH (Jewish)

Dumplings, traditionally served in Passover soups. Always based on egg and matzo meal, they come in a variety of flavours and consistencies, including cheese, potato, plain and chicken (fat).

KOFTA (Indian/Pakistani)

Kofta are simply meatballs, made of *Keema*, minced meat. They are a speciality of Northern India and the Frontier. A particularly rich version from Kashmir uses minced lamb with coriander, chilis, ginger and yogurt, but no onions or garlic, as these are not used in Kashmiri-Brahmin cooking.

KOFTA KEBAB (Turkish)

A relative of *Kafta* (Arabian) and *Kefta* (North Africa), *Kofta* are balls or sausage-shaped mixtures of minced lamb or beef with onions, eggs and spices. They are skewered and grilled over charcoal.

KOKORETSI (Greek)

A 'shish kebab' of lamb's liver, kidney, sweetbreads and heart, wrapped in intestines or caul and skewered. The kebab is then grilled.

KOLDUNY (Polish)

Relatives of *pelmeni* (qv), these filled, ravioli-like dumplings are usually served in light broths, and are a warming winter dish. The filling is usually seasoned minced pork or beef.

KOMBU (Japanese)

Dark, broad leaves of seaweed which is sold dried to be used in *dashi* (qv) and as a 'packaging' for small rice *sushi* (qv). It is also favoured pickled as a condiment.

KON LOH (Chinese)

See *Crosne*.

KORMA (Indian/Pakistani)

A milk curry flavoured with yogurt and/or cream and subtle spices. Can be used for lamb, chicken or prawns. It is the mildest of the common curries.

KOTLETKI (Russian/Polish)

Kotletki are usually of two sorts: those made of pounded poultry breasts or veal – and those made of minced meat – usually beef or pork. Both are dipped in breadcrumbs and fried in batter.

KRAPFEN

See *Faschingekrapfen*.

KRUPUK UDANG (Indonesian)

Shrimp wafers. The best are largish and light pink. They are deep-fried to swell into large, crispy puffs. They can be stored in an airtight container. Buy in Oriental shops or specialist delicatessens.

KULCHA (Indian/Pakistani)

See *Nan*.

KULFI (Indian/Pakistani)

A kind of ice cream, with thickened bits of cream and pistachio hidden within the usual frozen milk mixture. *Kulfi* is thickened with arrowroot and flavoured with the pistachios and rose water, so it has a more solid, sweeter character than ordinary ice cream.

KULICH *(Russian)*
A tall cylindrical loaf of egg and yeast bread, decorated with dribbled white icing. The interior is studded with preserved fruit, almonds and currants, and is coloured by saffron. It is a traditional Easter loaf.

KUNG TOM YAM *(Thai)*
A Thai soup of prawns, lemon grass, lemon leaves, chilis, fish sauce, spring onions and coriander, with a liberal infusion of fresh lemon juice. The lemon juice, grass and leaves should result in a soup with a markedly acid-sour flavour.

KVASS *(Russian/Polish)*
A low alcohol kind of sour beer, made from rye bread and yeast. It is used as a basis for soup and stews.

LA JIAO JIANG *(Chinese)*
Hot chili sauce, used both for dipping and also for some cooked dishes.

LADIES' FINGERS   *(American/African/West Indian/Indian/Far Eastern)*
West Indian name for *Okra*.

LAHM BIL AJEEN *(Arabian/Syrian/Lebanese)*
A type of pizza, made from a yeast dough topped with minced lamb or beef, onions or tomatoes, and baked.

LAHMA MISHWIEH *(Lebanese)*
Skewered kebabs of lamb pieces which are interspersed with tomatoes and onions and baked over coals.

✖ *LAMB*
Louis XVI of France who loved his food is credited with describing lambs as "walking cutlets".

LANCASHIRE *(English)*
Though Caerphilly was probably the original cheese for *Welsh Rarebit*, Lancashire has long been declared the *best* for making it. It crumbles and melts with ease, and its mellow flavour is better suited to the mixture of beer and cheese on toast than any other. It has an unusual method of making, being a combination of curds made from different days milking, thus increasing the acidity of the cheese. Up to three different days' milk may be used. Cartwheels up to 40lb are made, as well as 12lb truckles. It is aged about two months, developing a full, custardy flavour.

LAPIN *(French)*
Rabbit. A favourite meat of the French table, rabbits are raised by farmers and also shot in the wild. Both saddles *(rable)* and whole animals are cooked, the former roasted or braised in wine with onions or prunes, the latter stewed or braised with a variety of sauces. A famous dish is *Lapin avec Deux Moutardes* – although the two mustards can even be increased up to

four. The sauce is enriched with cream and parsley.
Another popular treatment is a *Civet* (qv).

LASAGNA (*Italian*)

A kind of pie, made with layers composed of sheets of
pasta alternated with other ingredients, usually of
meat or vegetables, and cheese. The sheets are usually
either of plain egg pasta or coloured green by spinach.
The principal version is *alla Bolognese* – with meat
sauce, béchamel and parmesan cheese, but other well-
known variations include *pasticcata alla Napoletana*
(Naples style) with meat ragú, sausage, cheese and
hard-boiled eggs, vegetarian-style with spinach, ricotta
and Parmesan, and *alla maniera di Ragusa* – with
minced veal, mushrooms, *mozzarella* (qv) and tomato
sauce.

LASAGNETTE (*Italian*)

Type of pasta, of durum wheat, forming long, broad
ribbon-like noodles, with one or both side edges
ruffled. Usually served with a tomato and anchovy
sauce.

LASSI (*Indian/Pakistani*)

Iced yogurt drink, particularly recommended with
curries and spiced foods.

LAVERBREAD (*Welsh*)

A Welsh speciality made from laver, *Porphyra umbili-
calis*, a seaweed with thin purplish fronds found on the
Gower peninsula and south Pembrokeshire. Its name is
misleading, since it has nothing to do with bread. It is
simply the seaweed which has been washed, boiled and
puréed, then made into cakes rolled in oatmeal. These
are traditionally fried in fat and served with bacon for
breakfast.

✘ LEEK

*The National Emblem of Wales ever since the Welsh fought
the victorious battle against the Saxons in A.D. 640 and
wore leeks in their caps for identification in combat.*

LEICESTER (*English*)

A russet-orange colour cow's cheese with a clean,
medium flavour. Although it is quite moist, it combines
this with a crumbly texture and is a good cooking and
melting cheese. It is matured for eight to twelve weeks;
the farmhouse version for a little longer.

LEIDEN (*Dutch*)

Named after the university town, this cow's milk
cheese is uncooked and pressed, which gives it a rather
crumbly texture. It is made in unpasteurised farmhouse
versions and in factory versions; both are flavoured
with cumin. Some farmhouse exampes qualify as Old
Leiden, having exceeded the usual three month ageing,
and the cumin flavour is strong.

LEITAO ASSADO (*Portuguese*)

Roast suckling pig, cooked on a spit over an open fire or
charcoal. It can be superb in Portugal, where simply
dressed meat and fish are best.

LIÈVRE *(French)*
Hare. Most of the recipes followed for the domestic or
wild rabbit also apply to hare, although the meat is
stronger and is capable of more assertive sauces. The
animal must first be very carefully skinned to remove
the glands which carry unpleasant biles – the animal is
officially classed as a vermin. Red wine sauces and those
with brandy and *marc* (a course brandy, very like
Grappa) go particularly well with the rich meat. (See
lapin and *civet*.)

LEMPER *(Indonesian)*
Rolls of glutinous rice with a minced and spiced pork or
chicken filling. The rice roll itself is wrapped in a
banana leaf or a bamboo leaf, then steamed or barbecued. They should be allowed to cool and be served at
room temperature.

LIMBURGER *(German/Belgian)*
Although Limburger was originally made in the province of Luttich, Belgium, and was named for the town
where it was originally marketed, today it is made
primarily in the Alsace, Germany, though it is also
made in Austria and in the US. It is a semi-soft cheese,
containing some irregular holes. It varies in weight
from about 1lb to 2½lb and is usually square or
rectangular in shape. Limburger is made from cow's
milk which has been heated to a high degree, then
formed, pressed lightly, salted and then cured in open
shelves for two to three weeks, then wrapped and aged
for a further two to three months. The result is an
extremely pungent surface-ripened cheese with a
reddish-yellow rind and yellow paste. It is the 'old-
socks' cheese *par excellence*, but its flavour, while
distinctively ripe, is nothing compared to its notorious
aroma.

LING MUNG GAI *(Chinese)*
Chicken fried with shredded ginger, and simmered in
lemon sauce. It is served with boiled rice.

LINGUIÇA *(Portuguese)*
A short sausage, heavily garlic flavoured, which is often
served on its own with good peasant bread, or sliced
and used in quiches, omelettes and stews.

LINZERTORTE *(Austrian)*
A speciality from Linz in central Austria. A shortcrust
pastry shell is covered with finely chopped almonds or,
alternatively, almonds can be worked into the pastry.
Then a thick layer of raspberry jam, and finally a lattice
crust. It is baked, cooled and the whole dusted with
icing sugar.

LION'S HEAD MEATBALLS *(Chinese)*
See *Su jee tao*.

LIPTAUER *(Austrian/German)*
Also known as *Liptovsky sir* in Czechoslovakia, this is a
spread of cream cheese, mixed with paprika, sour
cream, onions, capers and mashed anchovies. It is

served as an appetiser – often with new white wine – or sometimes as an after-dinner savoury.

LIVAROT (*French*)

A cow's cheese made in and around the Normandy village of the same name. It is a wheel-shaped small cheese of approximately ¾–1lb in weight. A few farm-house unpasteurised cheeses are still made, but now most are made in factories, of skimmed morning and whole-cream evening milk. A washed rind cheese with a moistish brownish-red rind and springy cream centre, it has a very strong smell and flavour, almost ammoniacal even when not over-ripe. It is governed by an *appellation d'origine* and should be ripened about three months before eating. It can be found in the traditional grass binding or in modern raffia. Both are then put in a wooden box.

LOTUS FLOWERS (*Chinese*)

See *So far Har Yuen*.

LOUIS, CRAB OR SHRIMP (*American*)

A speciality of the Western United States – supposedly invented in San Francisco. It is a combination of flaked crab meat, cayenne pepper, grated onion, chili sauce, mayonnaise and cream, bound together and piled back into the shell. It is served as a luncheon salad or a first course.

LOUKANIKA (*Greek*)

A fat, spicy red sausage, made from minced lamb, breadcrumbs, chili, paprika, onion, cumin, garlic and sometimes red wine.

LOX (*Jewish*)

Smoked salmon, usually of a deeper red colour and thicker texture than found in ordinary Scottish smoked salmon. It can be bought 'fresh' or canned. It forms part of the traditional New York breakfast, served with toasted *bagels* (qv), cream cheese and scrambled eggs.

LULA (*Portuguese*)

Squid. Usually cooked with onion, parsley, potatoes and tomatoes *de caldeirada* (in casserole) or stewed in its own ink (*em sua tinta*).

LUMACHE (*Italian*)

Lumache means 'snails', and refers both to the field snail, almost as popular with Italians as with their French neighbours, and to the pasta shapes which are often filled with a vegetable or meat and cheese stuffing and baked in a tomato sauce.

Dishes using real snails include *Lumache alla Milanese*, with oil, butter, garlic, anchovies and wine, and *alla Romana*, served with stewed tomatoes, anchovies, pepper and mint. There is also a curious 'sweet' snail dish from the north-west in which the snail shells are stuffed with macaroons and nuts and baked – *all 'ossolana*.

LUT TZE MUN NGAP (*Chinese*)

Duck simmered with chestnuts, and served with spring onions.

LUTEFISK (*Norwegian*)
A speciality which is, at best, an acquired taste. It is actually 'rotten fish', made from cod steeped in potash. It is left for some time, then cleaned and canned – the fish is ready when the can is swollen by putrefaction. It is eaten with butter.

LYCHEE (*Chinese/Japanese/West Indian*)
Small, round fruits with a brittle shell covered in small points. The flesh is white and juicy and conceals a large single shiny brown seed. The ripe fruit has a pinky-rose hue and peels easily. It is highly regarded as a dessert fruit, though it also lends its subtle flavour to ice creams and fruit salads. It is also very popular in much 'international' style *nouvelle cuisine*, used in recipes for poultry and in many savoury first courses. The Chinese make use of them for savoury dishes, but the Japanese treasure them more as a finish to a meal or as a simple eating fruit.

LYONNAISE, à la (*French*)
In the style of Lyon. It usually implies the use of onions and butter (as in *pommes Lyonnaise*) or additionally vinegar. *Cervelas* and *saucisson Lyonnaise* are both renowned types of sausage.

MA HO (*Thai*)
'Galloping horses'. A light dish – usually served as an appetiser or part of a large buffet. It is a savoury combination of ground pork, garlic, coriander, peanuts, chili and fish sauce, used as a filling or topping for fresh fruits such as pineapple slices, lychees or other exotic fruits.

MA TIE (*Chinese*)
Water chestnuts. They are not chestnuts at all but roots of a kind of vegetable. The name means 'horse's hooves' – referring to their shape before peeling. They are available fresh or in cans, though the latter are much less flavourful.

MA YUNG BAO (*Chinese*)
Steamed sweet bean buns, prepared with a soft white yeast pastry and stuffed with the bean paste. They are smooth-topped or sesame-strewn and are served as *dim sum* (qv).

MACE (*Spice*)
A wavy, light curl of orangey-brown spice with a delicate flavour of nutmeg. This is hardly surprising since it is the light carapace or covering of the nutmeg seed inside the fruit. It can be bought ground or whole, and then ground or pounded immediately before using. It is most commonly used in cakes and pastries, but is also found in soups or stews where a more subtle version of nutmeg flavour is desired. The two spices, nutmeg and mace, are found in the Spice Islands; now part of Indonesia, as well as in Grenada in the Caribbean. The dried, net-like covering is usually marketed in 'blades' of mace, and is used mostly in meat and

poultry dishes, though it can be substituted for nutmeg. It is, however, more expensive per ounce than the nutmeg.

(For translations see the *Herb and Spice* chart.) (See also *Nutmeg*.)

MACHCHI *(Indian/Pakistani)*

Fish. The fish used in Indian cooking tend to be those that can support the use of spices. Thus they are usually strongly-flavoured fish like tuna, pomfret, kingfish, jewfish or sardines. The fish can appear in a curry (*Machchi kari*) or be marinated in a paste of spices, then fried (*Tali machchi*). Other treatments include *Machchi hazur pasanda* (whole spiced baked fish with yogurt – cream sauce) and *Machchi jhal frazi* (sautéed in a black iron pan with several spices).

MANCHA MANTELES *(Mexican)*

This means, literally, 'tablecloth stainer' – and refers to the permanent stains resulting from the dark *mulato* chilis used in its preparation. It is usually made with pork or chicken, which has been marinated in vinegar, then cooked with the chilis, sesame seeds, almonds, tomatoes, cinnamon, garlic and onion which have been reduced to a thick purée. Towards the end of the cooking plantains (green bananas), pear and pineapple pieces are added.

MANCHEGO *(Spanish)*

The best-known cheese of the country, from the central plains of La Mancha. Made from sheep's milk, it varies in style from semi-soft and mild to crumbly and sharp, depending on how long it has been aged. It is often served as an appetiser and appears in many cooked dishes.

MANGO *(Indian/Caribbean/Malaysian/Thai)*

A wonderfully juicy fruit with a light orange flesh, slightly fibrous but, ideally, lusciously pulpy. The skin deepens from green to red-orange-purple when ripe; the fruit is only easy to peel when ready for eating. The large flat seed must be carefully cut out, usually by slicing the two main sides away with their flesh, leaving a thin central slice encasing the seed. The sweet, rich pulp is delicious and probably best on its own, but it is also made into ice cream (India – Caribbean), as well as used in pastries (Caribbean) or in curries and stir-fry recipes (India and Malaysia). They are becoming more popular in Western cuisine, and are found in many sweet and savoury recipes.

MANDOO KUK *(Korean)*

A steamed meat dumpling of minced beef and vegetables, served in a clear beef broth flavoured with sesame.

MANZO *(Italian)*

Young beef, between the stages of veal and ordinary beef – i.e. less than four years old. It is often boiled to make *brodo* or broth, then served in a sweet-sour salad with onions, garlic, vinegar, sugar and herbs. This is *manzo carpionato*. Other treatments include cooking long and slowly in red wine (*alla Lombarda*) or stewed with vinegar and cream (*alla Trentina*) or with bacon, herbs and anchovies (*alla certosina*).

MARBLED EGGS (*Chinese*)

See *Chau Yip Dahn*.

MARILLENKNODEL (*Austrian*)

These little bundles hide a fruit surprise. The potato dough dumplings each contain a stoned apricot. After they are boiled and simmered, they are dredged with fried breadcrumbs and sprinkled with sugar.

MARINARA, alla (*Italian*)

A sauce, usually served over pasta – spaghetti, fettucine or linguine – composed of pulped tomatoes and basil simmered until thick. A Neopolitan favourite. Also on pizza made with tomatoes and garlic.

MAROILLES (*French*)

A pungent cow's cheese from Flanders and the Northeast, it is one of the finest of the washed-rind cheeses. Protected by an *appellation d'origine* most are still made from unpasteurised milk in farmhouses though in its earliest days it was made by monks. It is smooth, pale and homogenous, with a just moist reddish rind. Its flavour is rich, strong, but with a mellow and not acrid or ammoniacal aftertaste. There are both larger squares (just over 2lb) and smaller squares of about ½lb.

MASCARPONE (*Italian*)

An unsalted cow's cheese from Lombardy, unbelievably rich since it is about 90 per cent pure butter fat, and resembles cream. It is mildly sourer than cream, and of a thicker consistency. But like cream it is used almost solely as a dessert, whipped with fruit, or decorated with slivered chocolate, candied fruit or nuts. It is sold in muslin bags or small pots and must be eaten almost immediately.

MASSAMAN (*Thai*)

A mild curry made with beef or chicken. It is quite watery, the 'gravy' including coconut milk, and containing sliced bamboo and sweet potato. It is influenced by the Moslem settlers who came from the west into Thailand.

MAYIRITSA (*Greek*)

A tripe soup – which may also include lamb's liver, heart and intestines – made with spring onions, chopped dill and rice. Beaten egg and lemon juice are stirred in at the end. It is a speciality traditionally served at Easter.

MAYONNAISE (*French/International*)

A cold dressing condiment which is a mainstay of classic French cuisine, but has also spread worldwide. It is an emulsion of eggs, mustard and oil, beaten until a smooth, ivory-coloured sauce is obtained. It is served with all manner of meats, fish, poultry and vegetables and forms the basis of many other classic sauces, including *Tartare* (qv), *Remoulade* (qv) and *Aïoli* (qv).

MAZUREK (*Polish*)

A thin pastry base of nuts (usually walnuts or hazelnuts) or diced fruits (dates, sultanas or figs) mixed with sugar, eggs and rye breadcrumbs, baked till crisp and covered with chocolate icing or powdered sugar.

MELANZANE (Italian)

Aubergines, a staple vegetable in the Italian repertoire, served in pasta dishes, hot or cold as antipasto; or in stews.

Melanzane ripene is the general term for stuffed aubergines – *alla Parmigiana* are halved, stuffed with parmesan and mozzarella and baked in tomato sauce. In *alla catanese* the aubergine is cut into a fan shape and fried. In Calabria two classic treatments include stewing with eggs, herbs and garlic or deep-frying with a stuffing of basil, peppers and cheese.

MECHOUI (North African/Arabian)

Traditionally a mechoui is a whole sheep roasted on a spit on an open fire. It is the universal dish for festivals, weddings and desert picnics. The term is also sometimes used in a wider sense to cover any meats – usually lamb or kid – grilled over a fire.

MELITZANES PAPUTSAKIA (Greek)

Means 'little shoes'. Stuffed aubergines which are close cousins to the Turkish *Imam Bayaldi* (qv). But in addition to the stuffing of tomatoes, onions and chopped aubergine, minced lamb and cheese are also included. It is usually served hot as a main dish.

MERLUZA (Spanish)

The most common fish at the Spanish table, *merluza* is a form of hake. It is found all over the country and appears in numerous dishes, including *Merluza a la Vasca* (with a green parsley sauce with clams and mussels), *a la Sidra* (in a cider and garlic sauce with potatoes), *a la Madrilena* (with ham and cheese), *a la Gallega* (Galician-style with potatoes, garlic and onion), and *con alcaparras* (fried in batter with capers).

MEZE (MEZETHAKI) (Middle Eastern in particular Greek and Turkish)

A general term for a spread of *hors d'oeuvres* which can be hot or cold or both. They can form the appetisers for a meal or the meal itself. They can include such titbits as olives, nuts, sliced cucumbers and tomatoes, small 'miniature meals', such as fried chicken liver or brains, stuffed vegetables – aubergines, vine leaves, etc. – dips of *taramasalata*, *tahina* and chick peas (*humus*) (qv), and various small fish and kebabs. It consists from as few as eight dishes to as many as thirty, and in it the richness of Middle Eastern invention is encompassed.

MIE GORENG (Indonesian)

Egg noodles, boiled then fried with pork, prawns, garlic, chili, shrimp paste and soy sauce, decorated with chopped spring onion and sliced cucumber. A staple of Indonesian cooking.

MILANESE, ESCALOPPE (Italian)

See *Wiener Schnitzel*.

MINESTRONE (Italian)

The most well-known of the Italian soups, it should be the king of vegetable soups, if made well. The classic version must contain white beans, some form of pasta, ham, onion, garlic, herbs and tomato purée; after that any of a number of vegetables – peas, kale, celery, tomatoes, etc. – can be added. Just before eating, each serving is sprinkled with parmesan. (Note, some regions omit any kind of pasta.)

MINHO, A MODA DE *(Portuguese)*

In the style of Minho, the wine-producing, *vinho verde* region. It can mean basted with a spicy chili and olive oil marinade, as in *Frango no espeto a moda de Minho* (spit-roasted chicken), wrapped in cabbage leaves and baked, then unwrapped and served with onions and potatoes (*bacalhau a moda di Minho*), or simply stewed in the wine of the region, whether red or white.

✕ MINT

According to the mythological story, Pluto was entertaining a young lady called Minthe when his wife discovered them and trampled the unfortunate girl into the ground. From that spot a plant grew and her memory lives in its name, Mint.

The custom of serving mint sauce with lamb in Britain hails from the Elizabethan Age when, in order to encourage the consumption of fish and protect the wool industry, Her Majesty decreed that lamb could only be eaten with bitter herbs. The least bitter herb available then was mint and today we're still forcing the stuff down although the jellied variety can be quite palatable and at least doesn't run all over the plate.

MIRIN *(Japanese)*

A golden, sweet rice wine, used sparingly in glazes for ribs and other grilled foods, and as flavouring in vegetable salads and other cold dishes. It is rather like a sweet sherry, which may be substituted if necessary.

MISO *(Japanese)*

Miso – or more correctly *aso-miso* – is the fermented red bean paste which is an ingredient common to a large number of Japanese soups. *Miso shiro* is a simple broth made only from this paste, which is a usual breakfast dish.

MITSUBA *(Japanese)*

Japanese trefoil, whose leaves resemble parsley, though they are always in clusters of three. They are served raw or just wilted in salads, savoury custards, soups, sushi, tempura and one-pot dishes. The flavour is between parsley and celery.

MOHR IM HEMD *(Austrian)*

Translated as 'Moor in his nightshirt', this dessert is a pudding of butter eggs, sugar, almonds and chocolate, steamed, and covered in whipped cream.

MOLE *(Mexican)*

Literally 'sauce', from the Aztec. There are three great national sauces, the *mole rojo* or *Pepian rojo* (see *Pipian de Camarones*), made with tomatoes, pumpkin seeds and chilis; *Mole verde*, a thick green sauce of pumpkin seeds, onion, green tomatoes, green chilis, coriander, almonds and tomatillos – a quite mild sauce used for pork or chicken – and *Mole Poblano* – the great national dish, usually made with turkey, whose name is synonymous with both the dish and the sauce. It is so called because it was originated in the state of Pueblo. Its immediate association with chocolate is correct though misleading, since only one ounce of chocolate is really used. The sauce is a dark red colour, from the dried chilis and the chocolate. It improves if made ahead, and utilizes four types of chilis, pepper, almonds, raisins, cloves, aniseed, cinnamon, tomato purée and chocolate, in which the browned turkey is simmered. Traditionally it should take up to three days to prepare.

MONGOLIAN HOT POT *(Chinese)*
See *Shau yang rou.*

MONTEREY JACK *(American)*
At one time simply called Jack Cheese, now usually distinguished by its place of origin – on the coast of California below San Francisco, where it was first made in the 1840s. It is a 'cheddared' cheese, the curds cut like the classic cheddar, but it is very pale and a much milder cheese. There are two sorts; the more common is the ordinary Jack, a moist cheese ripened up to six weeks; the other is Dry Jack or Old Monterey Jack, used for grating and aged up to six months. The former is much used for Tex-Mex Californian style cooking such as *enchiladas, chilis rellenos* and other favourites.

MOOLI *(Japanese/Chinese/Indonesian/Malaysian/ Indian)*
See *Daikon.*

MORCILLA (MORCELA) *(Spanish/Portuguese)*
A particularly Spanish and Portuguese form of blood sausage, rich and heavily flavoured. It is used in stews, sliced and fried and eaten with eggs or as an appetiser, or even eaten raw. 'Columbian-style' is a version which also contains rice.

MORNAY SAUCE *(French)*
A thick coating sauce made of cream, *Béchamel sauce* (qv), cheese and egg yolks. It is usually used with vegetables (cauliflower, broccoli and spinach particularly) and with white fish.

MOROS Y CRISTIANOS *(Spanish)*
Meaning 'Moors and Christians', this dish has its origins in Spanish history, from the days when the Moors (or Moroccan Arabs) ruled southern Spain. The name refers to the contrast of black beans and white rice – the beans are cooked with garlic, bacon and paprika and placed on a platter; the rice, which has been cooked and moulded in a ring mould, is then placed on top of the beans like a crown. It can serve as either a main dish or an accompaniment to grilled meat.

MORTADELLA *(Italian)*
A large, ovoid pork sausage, speckled with pieces of fat, and flavoured with coriander, peppercorns and, some-

times, pistachios. It is sliced and served cold as an *hors d'oeuvre*. A speciality of Bologna.

MOSTARDA DI CREMONA *(Italian)*
A speciality of Lombardy, usually served with roast meats and game. It is composed of whole baby fruits – or slices – pears, cherries, apricots, pineapples, etc. suspended in a sweet/sour syrup with a heavy flavouring of mustard.

MOUCLADE *(French)*
A speciality of the Charentes, on the west coast above Bordeaux, this mussel dish combines fresh cooked and shelled mussels with butter, white wine, cream, saffron and turmeric (or curry powder). The whole is then warmed under a grill until bubbling and brownish, and served with crusty bread, or more simply, unbrowned in soup plates.

MOULOKHIYA *(Egyptian/Lebanese/Jordanian)*
The deep green leaves of the moulokhiya bush have a mellow flavour and impart a glutinous consistency to dishes in which they are used. *Moulokhiya* is used as a term for a soup or stew – almost the national dish of Egypt – made with the fresh or dried leaves of *moulokhiya* together with chicken or meat stock, garlic, and coriander. It is served as a soup, or with pieces of the meat used to make the stock, over or with rice.

MOUSSAKA *(Greek)*
A meat and vegetable pie made with sliced aubergines layered with a mixture of minced lamb, grated onion and spices; grated or sliced cheese, and sliced tomatoes. The whole is then covered with *Béchamel sauce* (qv) and baked until bubbling and browned.

MOUSSE *(French)*
Literally 'froth' or 'foam'. It is applied to savoury dishes or desserts which have a light, frothy texture, characteristically containing cream, whipped egg whites or both. Examples include: fish mousse, vegetable mousses (served as first courses), chocolate and lemon mousses (desserts).

MOUTABEL *(Lebanese/Syrian/Jordanian)*
As *Mutabbel* (See *Baba Ghannog*).

MOZZARELLA IN CAROZZA *(Italian)*
'Mozzarella in Carriages', a speciality of the Roman area. These are little sandwiches of mozzarella in bread, dipped in milk and egg and deep-fried, usually served with a side dollop of tomato sauce.

MU HSU ROU *(Chinese)*
A Peking speciality in which pork tenderloin is marinated in wine, ginger, anise, ground tangerine peel and soy sauce, then braised or roasted until tender. It is then shredded and wrapped in Mandarin pancakes, like Peking Duck (*Bei jing Ngap*).

MUC DON THAT *(Vietnamese)*
Cleaned squid bodies with minced pork, noodles and spices, fried and then served with sliced or shredded lettuce.

MUGICHA (*Japanese*)

A beverage once idiosyncratic of Japan, made from roasted unhusked barley which is brewed in boiling water like tea. It is a popular summertime beverage, and has made its way to Korea.

MULLIGATAWNY (*Indian*)

An Anglo-Indian invention, a relic of the Raj. It is a curry-flavoured soup, made with beef or chicken stock and many usual curry spices and sometimes coconut milk. The name comes from the Hindi word '*mulegoothani!*' or pepper water.

MUNSTER (*French*)

An *appellation d'origine* cow's cheese, Munster comes in two forms, the *Munster fermier* (farmhouse-made) made from unpasteurised summer milk from the high Vosges, and later from winter milk of the valleys, and as *Munster laitier*, made in factory dairies from pasteurised milk all year round. Both are round, flat, with an orange-red washed rind and yellow, springy body. It has a permeating smell, and the farmhouse version, particularly, should be eaten quite young – after a ripening period of about three months. There is a German version whose title is also spelled *Münster* although in flavour it is less intense.

MURGH (*Indian/Pakistani*)

Chicken. Chicken in curry-style dishes is characteristic of the north, west and central parts of India. They are found particularly in Moghul and Muslim curries, which range from light-flavoured *korma* (qv) curries to the more heavily-spiced *Madras* type. Two particularly fine specialities of the Muslim area are *Murgh Massalam* and *Murgh Moghlai*. The former is a whole chicken, marinated in cumin, saffron, chili, cardamom, cloves, cinnamon, garlic and yogurt, then braised in the marinade. The latter is 'Moghul-style' chicken sautéed in spices, then cooked in milk and finished with almonds and cream.

MUTABBEL (*Lebanese/Syrian/Jordanian*)

As *Moutabal*. (See *Baba Ghannog*.)

MYCELLA (*Danish*)

Cow's milk cheese, known as the Danish gorgonzola, though its green veins and yellowish body could not be confused with the Italian cheese. It is milder than gorgonzola too, though it has the same fat content.

NACHOS (*Mexican*)

Also popular north of the border, these are quartered corn tortillas deep-fried and spread with a topping of grated cheeses and chilis, then baked until heated and the cheese melted. They are served as an *hors d'oeuvre*.

NAGE, à la (*French*)

Literally 'swimming'. Used to describe dishes – usually based on shellfish such as lobster, crayfish or shrimp – in which the main ingredient is poached and then served in a thin court bouillon of fish broth, white wine and herbs. It is occasionally thickened with cream.

NAI NUONG *(Vietnamese)*
See *Nem Nuongo.*

NALESNIKI *(Polish)*
Savoury or dessert pancakes, either filled with meat, cheese, chicken or mushroom mixtures, or sprinkled with sugar or spread with jam and eaten with sour cream.

NAM PRIK *(Thai)*
The ubiquitous sauce of Thailand, used to season almost everything in the country. It occurs as a dip for salad vegetables, for cooked shrimps or prawns, and for anything you wish. It is a medium thick sauce of dried shrimp paste *(kapi)*, pounded garlic, chilis and lemon juice, palm sugar and water, and is usually *very* spicy and hot.

NAMUL *(Korean)*
The generic term for vegetables, which are often served as salads, as in *oyi Namul* (cucumber salad) and *Kong Namul* (bean sprout salad).

NAN *(Indian/Pakistani)*
A flat leavened bread, usually made from white flour, which is cooked on the side of a *tandoor* oven. The result is a puffy, elongated single-serving, which is often served with *tandoori* meats or poultry. It can also be baked stuffed with ground almonds and spices *(peswari nan)* or with ground meat and spices *(keema nan)*. Also sometimes known as a *Kulcha*, it is a speciality of the Punjab.

NANTUA, à la *(French)*
To serve fish, shellfish or chicken in the style of Nantua, a town in the Savoie which is famous for its crayfish. *Sauce Nantua* is a cream sauce enriched with a strained liquor made from pounded crayfish shells, minced lobster or crayfish, and butter. It is served with many fish and shellfish, and boned with forcemeat – stuffed *Poularde* (chicken) *Nantua*.

NARAYANA BAN TOM SINDHU *(Thai)*
A cooling summer drink of rose water and coconut milk thickened with mung bean flour and poured over crushed ice. The name means '*Vishnu in a Sea of Milk*'.

NARGISI *(Indian)*
Any dish using hard-boiled eggs. Probably the most familiar is *nargisi kofta*, hard-boiled eggs encased in minced meat, making large lamb (or beef) meatballs. They are then simmered in a tomato and spiced yogurt sauce. They are named for their supposed resemblance to the yellow and white flowers of the narcissi.

NASI *(Indonesian)*
Nasi is rice. The best-known Indonesian rice dish is *Nasi Goreng*, or mixed fried rice. Traditionally, it is served in a flat dish, the top of the rice – which is spicy and contains beef or pork, prawns and onions – criss-crossed with strips of thinly sliced spicy omelette which sometimes include pieces of red chili and cucumber.

Nasi Uduk is another familiar national version of rice, cooked in coconut milk, flavoured with coriander, cumin, lemon, shrimp paste and kencur powder, and coloured with turmeric.

Nasi Kuning Lengkap is another yellow rice, cooked in turmeric and coconut milk, with curry (*chalcus koenigii*) leaves and garlic, but it is festively decorated with red and green chilis, marbled eggs (achieved with food colouring) and is served on banana leaves.

NEGRESSE EN CHEMISE (*French*)

A sweet or dessert made in the shape and mode of a bombe. It is chocolate mousse or ice cream covered with a coating of cream or vanilla ice cream. Its name means literally 'Moor (or negress) in a shirt'. See also the German/Austrian variation, *Mohr im Hemd*.

NEIGE, OEUFS, à la (*French*)

Oval mounds of egg whites, poached in milk and served in vanilla custard made with the milk. These 'eggs in the snow' are a French nursery favourite equally popular with adults.

NEM NUONG (*Vietnamese*)

Pounded pork marinated with lemon grass, chilis, rice wine, onion and spices and then barbecued on bamboo skewers. Served with rice noodles, coriander, mint and *nuoc leo* sauce (qv), wrapped in lettuce leaves. Also made with venison (*Nai Nuong*).

NEWBURG, à la (*French*)

A rich sauce usually served with lobster or large shrimp (prawns). The lobster meat is removed from the shell and chopped, or the shrimp shelled and deveined, and both are cooked and then finished in madeira wine enriched with cream, brandy and egg yolks.

NEW ENGLAND BOILED DINNER (*American*)

A traditional recipe of the north-eastern United States, which is usually served with mustard and horseradish sauce, and a side plate of corn muffins. The meat is corned beef brisket, which should be boiled together with all the vegetables – onions, potatoes, beets, carrots and turnips – in one large pot. Cabbage is served alongside.

NIÇOISE, à la (*French*)

Served in the style of Nice, on the Côte d'Azur. Usually includes a sauce or garnish of tomatoes, garlic, capers, anchovies and olives, with the optional inclusion of courgettes and artichoke hearts. The usual flavourings are thyme, rosemary and sometimes tarragon and/or oregano. Chicken (poulet) and some fish are often prepared in this fashion. Salade Niçoise is a well known and popular dish often served as a first course and may include pieces of tuna and fine french beans in its composition. Black olives are regarded by many as essential.

NORIMAKI (*Japanese*)

A variation of *sushi* (qv) but instead of rectangles or circles the *norimaki* are formed into cylinders, while the filling inside the seaweed is raw fish, vegetable or egg.

Before serving, the long cylinders are cut into smaller ones.

NORMANDE, à la (French)
In Norman style, from the province of Normandy. It usually implies the presence of fish – commonly white fish and/or shellfish – in a sauce of fish broth and mushrooms enriched with white wine, cream and egg yolks. When not used to denote fish, it refers to a sauce of apples, cider and cream, sometimes with the addition of Calvados. This sauce is especially popular with chicken and veal, and is also used as a filling for omelettes.

NOUGAT (French)
A dessert candy, made all over the south and south-west of France but particularly associated with Montélimar in Provence. It is a sort of almond toffee, with the nuts combined with egg whites, sugar, lemon juice and honey, and sometimes glacé fruits and/or other nuts.

NUOC CHAM (Vietnamese)
A clear dipping sauce with chopped chilis and garlic floating in a mixture of vinegar, fish sauce (Nuoc mam) water and sugar. Used as a condiment for many dishes.

NUOC LEO (Vietnamese)
A spicy dipping sauce of cooked glutinous rice, garlic, bean sauce, stock, sugar, fish sauce (Nuoc mam), chili sauce, peanuts and minced pork (optional). It is often served with Nem Nuong and other meat dishes.

NUOC MAM (Vietnamese)
A very potent fish sauce whose base is tiny 'rice' fish, pounded and mixed with oils and spices. It forms the basis of Nuoc Cham (qv) and many other Vietnamese dishes and sauces.

NUTMEG (Spice)
First discovered by the Portuguese and Spaniards in the Moluccas, the 'Spice Islands' in what is now Indonesia. The nutmeg is the kernel of the nutmeg fruit, found on the Myristica fragrans tree. It is a double wonder, the fruit containing the mace coating the nutmeg seed coat, which contains the nutmeg kernel. The kernel must be grated by hand to obtain the fragrant spice, or can be bought already ground. In European cookery it is used mainly in cakes and sweet dishes, but historically it was used to a large degree in meat and poultry dishes. It is also used with carrots and spinach (notably in ravioli) and in cheese and custard quiches and tarts. In the Caribbean, where it also grows, it is a prime ingredient in the islands' legendary rum punches.
(See also mace. For translations see the Herb and Spice chart.)

ODEN (Japanese)
A mixed stew combining vegetables such as cabbage and white radish (daikon), with fish and squid, meat and eggs, and flavoured with konnyaku, dashi, mirin, katsou-bushi and other esoteric ingredients.

OEUF (French)
Eggs figure largely in French cuisine, often as light luncheon dishes (such as soufflés) or more often as hors

d'oeuvres. Presentations and cooking methods include *oeuf brouillé* – scrambled or lightly creamed eggs (sometimes with *truffes* or other ingredients added), *en cocotte* (baked in a ramekin or individual little container, on its own or with cream, wine or other additives), *oeuf mollet* (soft boiled, usually with a light sauce poured over) or *oeuf poché* (lightly poached egg, often on a crouton). (See also *omelette.*)

OISEAU SANS TETE *(French)*
Small paupiettes of flank steak beef, stuffed with a ground meat filling or with chopped onions, cornichons and carrots, tied and braised in a wine sauce or gravy. Also called *paupiettes* (which can be made of meats other than beef).

OKRA *(American/African/West Indian/Indian/Far Eastern)*
A ridged green vegetable, shaped rather like fingers or chili peppers, though with a frizzy skin and a mild flavour. When cooked it can have a glutinous character, depending upon the cooking method and whether the pod has been punctured during preparation. It can be served stuffed, cut into sections or presented whole; it is much used in Indian curries and African stews, where its rather stringy, glutinous quality is exploited. In European and American cooking it is more usually teamed with tomatoes, either with or without meat. It is a usual ingredient in Louisiana *Gumbos* (qv) and other recipes.

OLIEBOLLES *(Dutch)*
Deep-fried apple filled doughnuts studded with currants. A traditional treat at Christmas and Easter.

OMBLE CHEVALIER *(French)*
A chad, found mainly in the crystal waters of the Haute Savoie, particularly Lake Annecy. It is renowned for its delicate flavour and is a speciality of some of the most expensive restaurants in France.

OMELETTE *(French)*
Whole eggs, lightly beaten, poured into a pan with melted butter, and cooked until a creamy flat surface has been achieved. Omelettes are either savoury or sweet, the savoury treatments include *fines herbs* (with fresh chopped herbs) or various combinations of cheese, poultry, fish or vegetables, lightly rolled and served warm. A selection of types include omelette *Arnold Bennett* (with smoked haddock), *Parisienne* (with braised lettuce or artichoke hearts), *perigordine* (with truffles), *nivernaise* (with ham, chives and sorrel), *Normande* (with apples, cream and Calvados) – sweet; or with shellfish and cream – savoury, *Niçoise* (with tomato, olives and anchovies) and *Savoyarde* (with cheese and potatoes).

ONIGIRI *(Japanese)*
Rice balls, a near relative to *sushi*; stuffed with raw fish, omelette or vegetables and rolled in sesame seeds. Served as a canapé.

✕ *ORANGE*

Reputed to be at least 20 million years old and described by botanists as a berry, it was Louis XIV at Versailles who began the royal fashion of the orangerie where 1200 trees were displayed in silver tubs. Interestingly these were just for show and never eaten. Instead oranges from Portugal were imported for royal comsumption. Oranges grown in or near the tropics remain green even when fully ripe, and it is with the assistance of ethylene gas that they develop the colour we are accustomed to. Oranges are also treated with a mild fungicide solution to prevent contamination and a further light solution of shellac which adds shine to the skin and also blocks the tiny pores to prevent the fruit drying out. These last two practices have caused some concern to some people although I am assured by the trade that the amounts used are well within the World Health Organisation recommendations. If you need to use orange peel or zest for a recipe then the recommendation is for a light scrub or wash with a soft brush. Organically grown and untreated fruit is difficult to find and often cosmetically less appealing, especially as we have become accustomed to our commercially produced fruit and vegetables being of uniform size and polished appearance. However, as we all know there's a lot of truth in the old saying 'Beauty is only skin deep'.

OSSO-BUCCO *(Italian)*
A homely dish from Lombardy, now popular all over Italy and abroad. Rounds of veal knuckle are braised in a white wine and tomato sauce containing garlic and onion. The osso-bucco are served in the reduced sauce, with a fine mixture of chopped parsley, garlic and lemon zest sprinkled on top just before serving. (This is called gremolata.)

OURSIN *(French)*
Sea Urchin. The innards only of this spiny sea creature are eaten, either raw or stirred into scrambled eggs.

✕ *OYSTER*

In bygone days the oyster was a very common food and a popular ingredient in steak and kidney pie. Inevitably this wholesale consumption led to a shortage and of course today they have become a luxury item.

The word ostracise comes from the custom of voting a person 'in' or 'out' by making a mark on an oyster shell as a kind of forerunner to the clubland system of 'blackballing'.

PAAN *(Indian/Pakistani)*
Spices, candied nuts, lime paste and other small sweetmeats, often wrapped in a betel leaf, are offered to guests at the end of a meal. They are designed to clean the breath and bid a sweet farewell.

PABELLON CARAQUENO *(Latin American)*
Goose steak with rice, blade beans and plantains.

PACZKI *(Polish)*
These are the Polish version of *Faschingkrapfer* (qv); the jam filling is traditionally made from plums or rose jelly.

PAELLA (*Spanish*)

A delicately balanced combination of rice, vegetables and either poultry or fish or both. It is flavoured with saffron and should, traditionally, be cooked over an open fire, though today most paella are cooked on the hob. The name derives from *paele* or *Paila*, the shallow pan in which the mixture is cooked. The original recipe specified a combination of eels, snails, rice and green beans only, with chicken or rabbit added for special occasions. But gradually mussels, shrimp, peas, squid, duck and other ingredients found their way into the mixture. Lemon wedges, parsley and strips of sweet red pepper are traditional decorations, and true aficionados eat only bread and spring onions with the paella. After all that, however, it has to be said that there are no hard and fast laws concerning this dish as it often was/is made with whatever ingredients are available and affordable.

PAGLIA E FIENO (*Italian*)

'Straw and hay', a mixture of thin noodles, green and pale yellow. It is usually served with a cream, ham and mushroom sauce, to which peas are sometimes added.

PAKORAS (*Indian*)

Savoury, deep-fried fritters, the Northern Indian version of *Bhajuas*. Unlike the latter, they are flat, and are made of a combination of chick pea flour, spices, garlic and a vegetable or mixture of vegetables.

PALAK (*Indian/Pakistani*)

See *Sag*.

PALATSCHINKEN (*Austrian/Hungarian*)

Pancakes are a popular – if filling – Austrian/Hungarian dessert. The thin pancakes are made as crêpes, then filled with one of several options and rolled up. Served as plainly as possible, they are sprinkled with sugar and moistened with a squeeze of lemon. Popular fillings are curd chese (topfer) or jams.

PAN BAGNA(T) (*French*)

A loaf of French bread, either round or long, which has been split in half and brushed with olive oil liberally. It is then layered with anchovies, tomatoes, black olives, onions and artichoke hearts, reassembled and pressed under a weight for some time in order to blend the oil and the juices of the ingredients. It is then sliced into serving pieces. It is a popular workman's snack or picnic piece in the South of France.

PAN JIM (*Korean*)

Whole spring onions, dipped into a batter of eggs, flour and oyster sauce, then deep-fried.

PANACHE (*French*)

The word means mixed and usually applies to Shandy-lager beer with lemonade, a favourite summer cooler. Also used for mixed salads, either of lettuce and raw vegetables or of fruits.

PANEER (*Indian/Pakistani*)

See *Panir*.

PANIPURI *(Indian)*
Savoury snack from the central part of India, but well-known under other names throughout the subcontinent – *gol gappa* in Punjab, *puska* in Calcutta and Bengal, *pustholes* further south. It consists of thin, delicate crisp wheat flour wafers, filled with a small dollop of spiced potato, chick peas or meat – or sweeter versions with fresh coconut or chutney.

PANIR *(Indian/Pakistani)*
Home-made curd cheese, usually cut into cubes and stirred into vegetable dishes such as *mattar panir* (peas and cheese) or *sag panir* (spinach and cheese). These dishes are from the East of India and Bangladesh.

PANSOTTI *(Italian)*
The Ligurian version of *ravioli*, triangular envelopes of pasta containing a mixture of spinach or chard and *ricotta* cheese, or brains, sweetbreads and herbs. It is traditionally served with walnut sauce.

✖ *PAPAYA*
Sometimes called the 'tree melon' and regarded by experts as an excellent breakfast 'starter', the papaya has the curious ability through one of its enzymes of tenderising meat and is widely used commercially to achieve this.

Properly hung good quality meat, exspecially beef, shouldn't need this treatment; but of course from the producer's point of view it's an expensive business to keep their product hanging around to the point of perfection and so, alas, the money-saving shortcut is often taken, to the detriment of taste.

PAPILLOTE, EN *(French)*
Small joints or cuts of meat, fish or poultry are wrapped in a greaseproof paper or tinfoil pouch or envelope which has been generously oiled. The packet swells up during the cooking and is presented at the table to be cut by the waiter or the diner, releasing the steam. (See also *Chemise, en*.)

PAPPADOM *(Indian/Pakistani)*
Crisp, spicy or plain wafers, which can be bought dried in packets. They must be deep-fried quickly in hot oil before serving; some versions can be grilled. While Westerners tend to eat them as a prelude to an Indian meal, the Indians themselves tend to crush them over their food before eating.

PAPRIKASH *(Hungarian)*
A dish usually made with whole pieces of chicken or veal, cooked in a sauce dominated by paprika and finished with sour cream.

PARATHA *(Indian/Pakistani)*
A flaky, rich, wholemeal round and flat bread, which is griddle-fried in *ghee*. The *paratha* is strongly flavoured with the taste of the *ghee*. Also served stuffed with a vegetable purée.

PARIS-BREST (*French*)
A *patisserie* – and a Paris speciality – made of choux paste piped into a circle, sprinkled with almonds and baked. The baked pastry is split in half, filled with a butter cream, and sandwiched back together.

PARMA HAM (*Italian*)
See *Prosciutto*.

PARMENTIER, à la (*French*)
Antoine-August Parmentier (1737–1817) was an agronomist who wrote numerous treatises on food generally and on the potato in particular, popularising a vegetable that was disdained earlier. Because of this, his name is linked indelibly to potatoes; any dish including *parmentier* in the title being served with a garnish of potatoes.

PARMESAN (*Italian*)
Hailed by many as the world's only true seasoning cheese, Parmesan (or more correctly *Parmigiano Reggiano*) has been made in Italy since before the time of the Romans. It is a cow's milk cheese, aged for grating and cooking from two to four years and as a dessert cheese for about one. It is made in a strictly defined and controlled area of Emilia-Romana and Lombardy, and can be made only between April 15 and November 11 each year from unpasteurised milk of the morning and evening milking. When truly mature it has a dark yellow-grainy texture with small beads of sweat apparent; its rind is dark brown. The flavour is inimitable – fruity, sharp and full – and it is indispensable to most pasta dishes and many other meat, poultry and vegetable recipes. It should never be grated until just before using; Italian or cookery shops sell special small graters with trays to catch the crumbs for sprinkling.

PASHKA (*Russian*)
The traditional unsalted Easter cake, tall and cylinder-shaped, with a puffed top. It is made with flour and cream cheese, and is studded with fruit and almonds. The top and sides are dribbled with a thin sugar glaze.

PASTEL (*Chilean/Mexican*)
Layered meat or poultry, baked. In Chile, *Pastel de choclo* is beef and chicken, shredded and cooked with raisins, eggs and onions; the whole is then covered with a cornmeal batter and a little sugar and baked.
In Mexico, *Pastel de Montezuma* is a variation, using turkey in a *mole verde* (qv) with shredded tortilla and grated white cheese forming alternate layers.

PASTERIOD CANNIR (*Welsh*)
Pasteriod – pasties – are a speciality of Wales, but the most traditional is that containing leeks. The pastry is a cold-water one, using lard and flour. Occasionally bacon is added to make a more substantial version, but that is not strictly traditional.

PASTICCIO (*Italian*)
A pastry pie with a filling of pasta, meat, vegetables and cheese. The pasta used may be macaroni (*di maccheroni*), lasagna (*di lasagna*) or of *anolini*. In the case of *Pasticcio di lasagna alla napolitana* the interior of the pie

is layered with pasta, ricotta, sausage or pork, mozzarella and parmesan, and then baked in the oven. *Pasticcio di maccheroni alla fiorentina* (in the Florentine manner) mixes the macaroni with beef, mushrooms, chicken livers, tomatoes and herbs.

PASTITSIO (*Greek*)

A 'pie' made from pasta – usually macaroni or a long tubular pasta – baked with minced lamb (or less often, beef) tomato sauce and cheese. The macaroni absorbs the sauce and meat juices, so that the dish is somewhat dry and the pasta holds it together.

PATATAS BRAVAS (*Spanish*)

'Bold potatoes'. The tuber version of Spanish chips: potatoes are peeled and salted, then sautéed in olive oil and garlic and dusted with sweet pepper before serving.

PAUPIETTE (*French*)

See *Oiseau sans tête*.

PAVO AL HORNO (*Mexican*)

Turkeys were already domesticated birds in Montezuma's day. This recipe is a Christmas favourite; the turkey (*Pavo*) is stuffed with a white bread, called *bolillo*, together with raisins, almonds, dried fruit and hard-boiled eggs, the whole bound with cornflour and tomato paste. The turkey is marinated in vinegar, onions and garlic before roasting. It is also known as *Guajolote relleno de gala*.

PEAS AND RICE (*Caribbean*)

Mainly Jamaican, this is a combination that constitutes the main meal of many a Jamaican household. There are two kinds of peas (actually beans) used: the small brown 'pigeon' peas, which are combined with rice to make 'Gungo peas and rice' and red beans for 'Red beans and rice'. Both versions usually cook the beans or peas and rice with coconut milk and salt pork, but unlike the Gungo peas, the red peas colour the rice a dull red.

PECENA HUSA (*Czeck*)

A seasonal celebratory dish, produced when the fatted goose is slaughtered. It is rubbed with caraway and other seasonings, stuffed with sauerkraut, and roasted on a trivet.

PECORINO (*Italian*)

A cheese traditionally made from ewe's milk – and thus a generic name for all such cheeses, made from central Italy through to the South and the islands. Generally speaking they are drum (or wheel) shaped with a rough, sometimes combed, rind. They are invariably sharp, pale and close-textured.

Probably the most well-known is *Pecorino Romano*, said to date back to the days of Romulus and Remus. It is particularly sharp and tasty, and has a very hard paste with a dark, wood-ash rubbed rind. Its pervasive flavour is particularly good with pasta and strong country dishes. Another version is *Pecorino Sardo* which some knowledgeable cheese pundits prefer for its particularly dry texture and assertive flavour. A version of the latter is also made with peppercorns.

PEKING DUCK (*Chinese*)
See *Bei jing ngap*.

PELMENI (*Russian*)
Small dumplings of a thin pastry filled with minced beef and onion. If served on their own they are accompanied by butter and mustard; but more usually they are simmered in a thin soup.

PEPERONATA (*Italian*)
A first course of sweet red, green and yellow peppers, grilled and skinned, then arranged with sliced onions and tomatoes, cooked gently in oil and garlic, and served cold. A speciality of Tuscany.

PEPITOS (*Mexican*)
A snack – or torto – eaten in a hurry or as a lunch break. It consists of warmed bread split into two, one side spread with mustard, roast beef and avocado, with a jalapeno pepper or two. Then it is covered by the other half.

PEPPERPOT SOUP (*Jamaican*)
A dark brown soup of salt beef (or pork), made with okra, yams and *callaloo* (or spinach), cooked in stock and coconut milk and seasoned liberally with chilis, cayenne and pepper.

PERGEDEL (PERKEDEL) GORENG JAVA (*Indonesian*)
Javanese-style meatballs, adapted from the *frikkadels* (see *Frikadeller*) of the early Dutch settlers. These meatballs or patties are highly spiced, made with minced beef, garlic, potatoes, shrimp paste, soy and numerous spices. They are deep-fried.

PERGEDEL JAGUNG (*Indonesian*)
Hot and spicy fritters of corn kernels and rice flour, deep-fried and served with chili and mild *sambals* (qv).

PERIGORDINE, à la (*French*)
In the style of Perigord, containing *truffes* and/or *foie gras*. It can, less frequently, apply to garnishes or dishes containing *cèpes* – the *Boletus* mushroom, another speciality of the region.

PESTO (*Italian*)
A green sauce made from pulverised basil leaves, pine nuts and garlic, combined with olive oil and cheese – traditionally *pecorino Romano* (qv) – though *Parmesan* (qv) may be substituted. Classically it is served with *fettucine*.

PETS DE NONNE (*French*)
One of the jokes of French cuisine, the name of this delicate sweet actually means 'nun's farts'. A treat from the Savoie, they are light, puffy fritters of choux pastry dusted with sugar.

PHAT WUN SEN (*Thai*)
'Phat' means 'fried' and prefaces the title of many Thai dishes. *Wun Sen* are vermicelli noodles, made from rice flour. They are stir-fried, after soaking in hot water,

together with meat and/or seafood, chilis, bamboo shoots, garlic, vinegar and fish sauce.

PHO (*Vietnamese*)

A delicate beef broth, simmered for a long time, then served together with cooked noodles and raw vegetables, and a side order of raw or just simmered beef ladled into the soup at the last minute.

PICADILLO (*Mexican*)

A combination of minced meats (usually beef and pork), sautéed with chilis, garlic, olives and raisins in a tomato sauce. It is served separately, or as filling for *empanadas* (qv) or stuffed vegetables such as squash or mild chili peppers. (See also *Chiles Rellenos*.)

PICO DE BALLO (*Mexican*)

A piquant condiment made from grilled mild and hot peppers and tomatoes, mixed with scallions and coriander, and tossed with an oil and vinegar dressing. It should be kept for at least a couple of days before serving with meat or poultry.

PIERNIK (*Polish*)

A rich spice (cinnamon, nutmeg and allspice), raisin, nut and honey cake, enriched with brandy and orange peel. It is served dusted with icing sugar.

PIEROGI (*Polish/Russian*)

Small, envelope-shaped pies of minced meat, spring onion and egg, in a sour-cream pastry. They are often served as accompaniments to *Bakszcz* or *Borscht* (qv).

PILAF, PILAU (*Middle Eastern/International*)

This method of cooking rice is native to Turkey, the Levant, Northern Africa and as far east as India, taken there by the Moghuls. The rice, traditionally a patna or other long-grained variety, is first sautéed in butter, ghee or oil before adding water or stock, covering and allowing to cool. This invariably results in fluffy rice, with every grain separate. The rice can then be mixed with meat, poultry, fish, shellfish or vegetables or a combination of any of these, before serving.

PILAU (*Indian/Pakistani*)

Rice is the staff of life for eastern, southern and central Indians and forms the main part of a meal. *Pilau* rices are those which have been lightly fried in oil or *ghee*, then spiced, sometimes with vegetables and/or meat or chicken added. The most common spices for *pilau* rice are cloves, cinnamon, cardamom, cumin and often turmeric, while the *parsis* and the great moghul dishes often add saffron, as well as sliced pistachios, almonds and sultanas. A *Biriani* (qv) is a particularly rich *pilau*. Indians always use long-grain, Basmati-type rice.

PILUS (*Indonesian*)

Sweet potato and ground rice balls deep-fried until golden brown. They are served plain or with sugar syrup as a dessert.

PINCHOS MORUNOS (*Spanish*)

Small lamb kebabs on wooden skewers marinated in olive oil, garlic and herbs and grilled over charcoal. They are often sold on the streets in large towns.

PINTADE *(French)*
Guinea fowl. A much prized bird in France, combining the fuller flavour of game birds with the plumpness and white meat of chicken. It can be used in almost any dish which suits chicken or turkey.

PIPERADE *(French/Spanish)*
Piperade (in French) or *piparrada* (in Spanish) is a Basque speciality which is either served by itself or as an accompaniment to grilled meats. It consists of onion, garlic, green and red peppers, ham and chopped tomatoes sautéed in oil, then gently scrambled with eggs to produce a moist mixture. It should be served with sautéed bread.

PIPIAN DE CAMARONES *(Mexican)*
Shrimps quickly cooked in a mixture of sauted ground pumpkin seeds, chilis, garlic, onions, tomatoes, honey and allspice. It is a pre-Columbian dish, from before the time of the Conquistadors.

PIRAO *(Brazilian)*
Cornmeal and coconut porridge or *polenta* (qv), moulded in custard cups and chilled. It is often served with coffee as a snack.

PIRI-PIRI *(Portuguese)*
A very hot and spicy chili sauce which comes in bottles and is thin and oily, without seeds. It is also popular in South Africa as a condiment for fish dishes, a round-about taste developed by way of the Dutch/Portuguese West Indies through the Boers.

PITTA *(Middle Eastern)*
Found throughout Turkey, Israel, Syria and Lebanon, pitta is a flat unleavened bread, which when baked develops an air pocket or hollow in its centre. It is thus a 'pocket bread', which is often split and filled with meats and/or salads to serve as a light snack.

PLA *(Thai)*
Fish. In Thai cooking the fish are usually fairly large ones – snapper, bream or jewfish – served whole or filleted. It can be fried whole (*cian*) or in fillets, or steamed (*merung*). The usual garnishes include coriander, ginger, spring onion and chili.

PLANTAIN *(Caribbean)*
A member of the banana family, the plantain is larger, harder and blander. It must be cooked – usually fried – before eating. It is served as an accompaniment to many Caribbean meals, as a first course with hot tomato sauce, or as a dessert, sautéed in butter and brown sugar, and flamed in rum.

PLUM PUDDING *(English)*
A misnomer if ever there was one, this classic Christmas pudding does *not* contain plums. Instead it should be rich with sultanas, raisins, currants and chopped mixed peel in a suet, flour, sugar and egg base, well spiced with cinnamon, nutmeg and cloves. It is steamed in a cloth or mould for several hours, then flamed with

brandy and brought burning to the table. It is customarily served with *Brandy Butter* custard or cream.

PO PEA TORD (*Thai*)
Fresh vegetable spring rolls. They are filled with bean sprouts, Chinese cabbage (*bok choy*) and other shredded greens, wrapped in a stiff pastry shell.

POFFERTJES (*Dutch*)
Available at street stalls and cafes in Holland, these are small, deep-fried batter fritters, served with melted butter and a dusting of confectioner's sugar.

POLENTA (*Italian*)
A thick porridge made only with water, salt and cornmeal, which is a speciality of Northern Italy. If served warm, it may be topped by gravy, tomato sauce or simply butter and cheese. If preferred otherwise, it is spread out on a sheet to cool and congeal. It can then be cut into slices and fried in oil or baked with layers of meat and cheese.

POLLO (POLLITO) (*Mexican/Spanish*)
Pollo in both classical Spanish and Mexican Spanish is chicken. But the two methods of preparation are generally quite different. Well-known chicken recipes in Spain marinate the bird in vinegar, wine and herbs and spices (*Pollo Escabechado*), an influence of the Moorish domination; you can cook it in sherry (*Pollito al Horno* or *de Jerez*) or (another offshoot of the Moors) in orange and mint sauce (*Pollo con Salsa de Naranja y Menta*). Other peasant recipes include garlic chicken (*Pollo al ajillo*), chicken with figs (*Pollo con Higos*) and *Pollo al Vino Tinto* (in red wine with *Chorizo* (qv)). One recipe which is popular in Mexico and Spain is the Aragonese *Pollo Chilindron* (chicken with red peppers). It was the Aragonese who supported the exploitation of the New World, and the East, from both of which came the hot, spicy peppers. Today, Mexican chicken dishes include *Pollo Bravo* – with very hot chilis, red and green tomatoes; *Pollo Verde* – in a thick green purée of peas, *Pollo en salsa de chilpotle* – in a smoked jalapeno sauce, with mushrooms and vinegar, and *Mancha Manteles* (qv).

POLO (*Iranian*)
A generic term for several rice dishes served throughout the country. It is a layered dish, with the rice alternated with lamb or chicken enhanced with vegetables or fruit and nuts. Apricots, pomegranate juice, sugar, strips of orange or tangerine, pistachios and/or almonds can all appear in a *polo*. The rice is often saffron-flavoured.

POLPETTE (*Italian*)
Meat balls, Italian style, usually containing beef and spiced pork sausage, as well as soaked and squeeze-dry bread and herbs. They are a favourite of Sicily and the south, and are usually served in a tomato and garlic sauce.

PORCINI (*Italian*)
The *Boletus* mushroom. See *Cèpe*.

✕ *PORK*
Of all the creatures on Earth none has a more fascinating history of usefulness than the pig, and even despite certain religious laws banning its consumption it remains the world's most widely eaten meat. Second only to the dog as a man's earliest domesticated animal, nothing else can rival its ability as a meat provider, almost every part of it being edible, which fact did not prevent the 19th century writer Charles Monselet from observing unkindly that 'The pig is nothing but an immense dish which talks while waiting to be served'.

PORT-SALUT *(French)*
This full-flavoured cow's milk cheese, originated by the monks in the department of Mayenne in the 13th century, was further improved and adapted to modern cheese-making methods by Trappist monks who came to the abbey in the 19th century. It was called *Port du Salut*, but after the Second World War the name was sold to a factory which now makes the commercial version most familiar to the customer – a semi-soft, springy cheese with a smooth, homogeneous mellow-flavoured paste and an orangy washed rind. The monastery cheese, which is made in smaller wheels than the commercially produced version and has a slightly tangier taste, is now sold as *Entrammer* (qv).

✕ *POTATO*
It took the dreadful Irish famine of 1845 for botanists to declare, after a desperate search for an alternative, that there is no substitute for the potato. Today it is the British nation's principle source of Vitamin C but sadly, yet again for economic reasons, only a few varieties are widely available commercially and the horrors of convenience preparation are well illustrated in this magazine extract from John and Karen Hess: 'The potato is one of nature's best designed products, it is born in a sturdy package, with wonderful shelf life. Yet we haul it from field to factory, peel and slice it by machine, cook it in hot grease, dose it with additives, wrap it in petroleum or natural gas dervative, freeze it, store it in a frozen warehouse, take it across the country in a diesel refrigerated truck, store it in another frozen warehouse, deliver it to a supermarket freezer move it to a kitchen freezer, and eventually we reheat it. Then, we eat it.'

PROVOLONE *(Italian)*
Once made from buffalo milk, this smooth uncooked cheese is now made from cow's milk and is a native of Compania and Lombardy. Its flavour depends on ageing. The young cheese is treated with calves' rennet and aged up to three months, the *picante* variety is coagulated with kid's rennet and aged up to two years. The milder variety is now more prevalent and is often smoked. It occurs in many shapes, from simple rounds

or ovals – small to enormous – to handmoulded melons, pigs, sausages and people.

POULE AU POT (*French*)

The famous 'chicken in a pot' of Henry IV, who declared that every family should have one. A boiling chicken is simmered in a court-bouillon of carrots, leeks and celery in water, accompanied by an onion stuck with cloves and a roasted onion. The chicken is served with some of the strained reduced broth and sea-salt is passed round.

POULET (*French*)

A chicken – technically a young cock chicken in contrast to the English pullet, a young laying hen. It is in practice used interchangeably with *coq*, *poularde* and *volaille*. The most well-known area for its poultry is Bresse, whose chickens have their own *appellation controlée*, but many other regions of France have fine, tender chickens with their own sauces to go with them. Other sauces are named after events (*Poulet Marengo* (qv)) or people (Henry IV, Agnes, Sorel, etc.). See also *Niçoise, Marengo, Nantu, Normand*, etc.

POUNTI (*French*)

A local dish of the Auvergne. Pork and bacon are finely diced and mixed with eggs, cream, grapes and/or prunes and shredded Swiss chard. The whole is baked in the oven until it puffs up, forming a substantial soufflé-like loaf, which is then sliced and served warm or cold.

PROSCIUTTO (*Italian*)

Air-dried ham, sometimes smoked but usually raw. It is sliced very thinly and served as an *hors d'oeuvres*. Similar to *jambon de pays* (qv), only even more finely cut, the finest variety is *prosciutto de Parma*, often known simply as *Parma ham*.

PURI (*Indian/Pakistani*)

Made from wholemeal flour like *chapatis* and *parathas*, and at first flat and round like them, *puris* differ in that they are deep-fried in *ghee*, producing a puffy, golden crisp circle of bread. They are most often eaten with vegetable and dry curries.

PUSS PRAYERS, STUFFED (*Jamaican*)

Avocado halves filled with a mixture of *ackee* (qv) and salt fish (qv), in a dressing of coconut milk and lime juice. Served cold.

QUESADILLA (*Mexican*)

A street snack sold by vendors all over Mexico, but also popular as an appetiser. It is made with either raw or cooked corn or wheat tortillas, which are stuffed with cheese or chicken, rolled into a cigar-shape, and deep-fried. The wheat-flour tortilla version is more common to Sonora, the corn-flour version to the coast and Mexico City.

RAAN (*Indian*)

Kashmiri-style roast leg of lamb. The meat is rubbed with spices, then marinated in a purée of honey and spices for some time. Those flavourings include cumin, turmeric, cinnamon, cardamom, cloves, saffron, yogurt and almonds. The lamb is then roasted as usual.

RABLE *(French)*

A saddle of hare or rabbit *(lièvre* or *lapin)*.

RABRI (RABARHI) *(Indian/Pakistani)*

A thick, condensed milk dessert, flavoured with rose water and studded with almonds and pistachios.

RACLETTE *(Swiss)*

A generic name for types of mountain cheeses, mostly made in the Valais. These are cheeses which toast easily in front of a fire or a special 'raclette grill', and can then be scraped with a special implement onto a plate. The melted cow's cheese is then traditionally eaten with boiled potatoes and pickle.

RAITA *(Indian/Pakistani)*

See *Dahi*.

RAS *(Indian/Pakistani)*

Cream cheese balls. These are usually served in syrup *(ras gula)* or in cream *(ras malai)* as a dessert.

RAS EL HANOUT *(North African)*

A mixture of spices characteristic to the cooking of Morocco, Tunisia and Algeria. Spice merchants in bazaars sell 'secret formulae' and housewives have their own recipes. Often reputed to contain as many as 100 herbs and spices, it more usually is composed of about 15 or 20. Cinnamon bark, dried roses, ginger, cloves, peppers and several other aromatics are pounded together in a mortar to produce the 'grocer's head'.

RASAM *(Indian/Pakistani)*

Rasam is 'pepper water', a digestive aid commonly served with or after an Indian meal, to reduce flatulence (hence the *asafoetida* in the broth) and settle the stomach. Usual ingredients also include pepper, cumin, mustard seeds and fresh coriander leaves. It can also be thickened with *dahl* (lentils).

RASPBERRY VINEGAR (VINAIGRE DE FRAMBOISE) *(English/French)*

Actually popular in England long before *nouvelle cuisine* as an accompaniment to such traditional dishes as Yorkshire Pudding and toad-in-the-hole, it has enjoyed a renaissance through the offices of the new French cooking. It is made from fine white wine vinegar, infused with raspberries and sugar, then strained and bottled. Today it is much used in *salade composée* – particularly those containing poultry, pâté or game – and in delicately sauced hot dishes.

RAZNJECI *(Yugoslavian)*

Boneless pork and veal cut into cubes and marinated in oil and onions before being skewered with bay leaves and grilled. They should be basted with the marinade while cooking.

REBLOCHON *(French)*

A semi-soft cow's milk cheese made in unpasteurised farmhouse versions and in *latiers* with pasteurised milk. Both are governed by *appellation d'origine*. The cheese originated from the particularly rich milk left at the end of the day's milking, which the cowherds would appropriate for their own use, milking the cow after the day's milk quota had been checked by the owner. Some *goût verité* versions are made the old way, with milk still warm from the cow. The cheese, whether *fermier* or not, uses the milk of Tarentaise cattle and is made in the Haute Savoie around Thones. It is characterised by a washed pinkish-grey rind and smooth, creamy paste; the flavour is sweet and fruity and not as strong as the mouldish smell might suggest. Sold in a flattened disc just over 1lb in weight, it is pressed between two thin chipboard sheets after being ripened four to six weeks.

RED COOKED CHICKEN *(Chinese)*
See *Jiang yu ji.*

RED EYE GRAVY, HAM WITH *(American)*
A traditional southern dish in which slices of ham are fried, and then coffee stirred into the pan juices to be poured over the ham on serving.

RED FLANNEL HASH *(American)*
This staple of the 90s gold-rush mining towns has become a classic businessman's lunch and sure-fire late supper dish. It is a combination of corned (salt) beef, boiled potatoes, onions, cream and diced beetroot. The latter ingredient is responsible for the name and the characteristic colour.

REFOGADO *(Portuguese)*
A thick onion, olive oil and bread purée that forms the basis of a number of national dishes.

REFORM CLUB, LAMB CUTLETS *(English)*
A recipe originated in the London club of that name, it comprises well-trimmed cutlets or end chops, coated with a mixture of minced ham and breadcrumbs, and then fried. They are served with a rich Espagnole sauce, containing julienne of carrot, truffle, ham, gherkin and redcurrant jelly.

REMOULADE *(French)*
A mayonnaise sauce or dressing with the added ingredients of mustard, and chopped capers, gherkins and hard-boiled eggs, served with vegetables (as in *céleri remoulade* – see *celeriac*) or with cold meats or poultry.

REMPEYEK *(Indonesia)*
Lacy dry pancakes or wafers which are made of peanuts *(kacang)*, prawn *(udang)* or coconut *(kelapa)*, spices, rice flour and eggs. They are fried, then drained and crisped. They can be eaten with meals or as nibbles before dinner or with drinks.

RENDANG *(Indonesian)*
The Indonesian version of curry, usually made with beef (though lamb is sometimes substituted), and distinguished from the Indian version by the meat and the use of coconut milk and tamarind liquid. It appears in two versions, a milder *Rendang*, with desiccated coconut, chili, fennel, cumin, coriander, ginger, cinnamon and cloves joining the beef, coconut milk and tamarind, and a hotter version *Rendang Daging*, which is also

drier, and contains lemon grass, curry leaves, more chilis and sugar.

REUBEN SANDWICH *(American)*
A favourite delicatessen and lunch counter order, made with rye bread piled high with hot corned (salt) beef, Swiss (Emmental) cheese, and sauerkraut. It is topped with another slice of rye and usually served with a dollop of *Russian Dressing* (qv) and a Polish gherkin.

REVUELTOS *(Spanish)*
Scrambled or soft-set eggs. These eggs are produced in an exceptionally gentle way. The egg is beaten then stirred until just set in the top of a double boiler. This results in very creamy eggs. Variations include *de langostino y espinacas* (with shrimp and spinach), *de ajetas* (with spring onion), *'El Coll'* (the yolks stirred with chopped tomatoes, then the whites beaten and stirred in at the end to produce a fluffy whipped pudding), and the classic *Duelos y Quebrantos*, mentioned in *Don Quixote*. The name means 'sorrow and suffering', and is a simple scramble of bacon, *chorizo* and eggs.

✕ *RICE*
"A meal without rice is like a beautiful girl with only one eye". (Old Chinese saying.)

RICOTTA *(Italian)*
A fresh, very moist and unsalted 'cottage type' cheese, which was originally always made from the whey of any milk – cow's or ewe's – which has been reheated and evaporated to a white 'cake' with striated sides. The ricotta from Rome, Tuscany, Sardinia and Sicily were traditionally made from ewe's milk; that from the Piedmont from cow's. This is the version most usually encountered in Britain. In its most common form it is soft, unsalted and very bland; it can also be salted and dried and even matured to a hard, grating consistency. It is much used in Italian cookery for pasta fillings, mixed with herbs and vegetables. It is also mixed with coffee, liqueurs, candied and fresh fruits to make desserts and makes a fine cheese cake. (See *Crostata di Ricotta*.)

RIGATONI *(Italian)*
Short, plump tubes of pasta, ribbed along the length. They are dryish, commercially made, and hold sauce well. They are usually served with a tomato sauce, or baked *gratinati* in the oven.

RIJSTTAFEL *(Indonesian)*
Actually a Dutch invention, using the rich variety of Indonesian cooking to create a vast buffet or 'rice table'. The *rijsttafel* is really a procession of dishes, sometimes reaching as many as 18 or 20, and is usually only found at large Indonesian restaurants or at banquets. The dinner may start with soup and various sates and continue through *Nasi goreng*, plain rice, *gado-gado*, several chicken and beef curries and grills, and

many different *sambals* and other accompaniments. A smaller version of *rijsttafel* known as *Nasi Rames* is available for more ordinary occasions.

RILLETTES *(French)*

Rillettes are made all over south-western France, from the Loire down. One of the most famous versions is from Tours, where jars and crocks are filled with long-cooked and shredded pork meat, spiced and pounded with its own fat, and then sealed under a final layer of fat. An equally renowned variation is from the Dordogne, which traditionally replaces the meat and fat of the pig with that of the goose. The rillettes – like *boudin noir* (qv) or *black pudding* (qv) – were made from the leftovers of the fatted pig, killed with great ceremony in the autumn and made into hams and rolled loins.

RISI E BISI *(Italian)*

A thick, creamy soup-like concoction of rice, bacon, onion, fresh peas, butter and Parmesan cheese. It is a speciality of the region around Venice.

RISOTTO *(Italian)*

The staple starch dish of Northern Italy, the equivalent to the southern and central preoccupation with spaghetti and other plain pastas. Genuine *Risotto* is rice briefly cooked in butter or oil, which then has broth added a little at a time whilst the rice is constantly stirred. As the broth is absorbed more is added and eventually the rice achieves a creamy consistency. Additional butter and cheese are then usually added. The whole operation takes about thirty minutes and demands your constant attention but the result is well worth the effort.

The rice used is *arborio* rice – a large, rounded white grain which cooks to a softened consistency on the outside while remaining slightly chewy within. It gives the *risotto* its inimitable texture. There are almost as many styles of *risotto* as there are ingredients, but some of the more noteworthy include *bianco* (plain risotto with butter); *di fruitti di mare* (with seafood and cooked in fishstock); *alla Milanese* (cooked in wine and chicken stock with saffron, beef marrow and Parmesan); *al funghi* (with mushrooms); *con la zucca* (with pumpkin); *alla Parmigiana* (in beef broth, with chicken livers, butter and Parmesan); *alla Siciliana* (with artichokes, beans and peas), and *nero* (with cuttlefish and its black ink).

ROCKEFELLER, OYSTERS *(American)*

Named after the turn-of-the-century New York millionaire philanthropist, the classic recipe combines a purée of butter, spinach, celery, green onions and parsley, placed on the half shell and topped by an oyster, then baked or broiled and served on a bed of rock salt.

RODGROD *(Danish)*

'Red pudding' – a dessert composed of red berries – redcurrants, strawberries and raspberries – cooked until pulpy then thickened with cornflour. It is eaten with great dollops of whipped cream (*flode*).

ROGHAN JOSH (*Indian*)

This lamb curry dish receives its name from its rich red sauce, derived from the liberal use of chilis, although it is not excessively hot. It also contains onions, garlic, bay leaves, cloves, coriander and several other spices.

ROQUEFORT (*French*)

The 'Queen of Cheese' the green-blue veined ewe's cheese is world famous. Although originally only available for a few months of the year because of the availability of the Larzac sheep milk from which it was made, today Corsican sheep's milk is imported to extend the production to almost year-round though it is still difficult to come by good cheese in winter. Though the blue mould once grew naturally, today powder containing the mould *penicillium* is sprinkled over the cheeses and steel wires pushed through them to encourage its penetration. True Roquefort can only still be made in the Causse and ripened in the caves of Combalou. Its clean sharp smell and taste, followed by a slightly salty aftertaste is inimitable, and the real thing can be identified by the silver foil wrapping with a red sheep imprinted on it. The cheese is delicious for dessert, as well as being used by the French in certain savoury dishes such as mousses, soufflés, salads and sauces.

✕ ROSEMARY

Originally named Rosmarinus, (Dew of the Sea) devotion to the virgin Mary brought about its present name and its flowers, which once were white, took on their present-day familiar blue when the virgin spread her mantle to dry upon a nearby bush. A nice little story and quite a nice herb too if used carefully.

ROSTI (*Swiss*)

Potatoes parboiled in their skins, then peeled, grated, and packed into a frying pan and fried in butter until golden brown one side, then turned over and cooked until brown on the other side.

ROTI (*Dutch Surinam*)

A dough pancake stuffed with spiced chicken and potatoes. It has echoes of the curried dishes found in the Dutch East Indies.

ROUPA VELHA (*Brazilian/Portuguese*)

Literally meaning 'old clothes', casserole of goose skirt, cooked shredded.

ROUX (*French*)

The basis of many French sauces. Butter is first melted, then mixed with flour. If the butter and flour are allowed to brown, a brown sauce will result. Other ingredients such as stock, wine and cream are then added to make the appropriate sauce.

RUJAK (*Indonesian*)

A mixed fruit *sambal* (qv), served as an accompaniment to curries and rice dishes.

RUSSIAN DRESSING (*American*)

Not Russian at all, but an American invention, now a staple of every fast food diner and restaurant in the country. It is really a variation of *remoulade* (qv), replacing the mustard with tomato purée and eliminating the capers. It is thus a combination of mayonnaise, tomato purée, chopped gherkins, parsley and perhaps a little sweet pepper. It is used as a dressing for green salads and on sandwiches and hamburgers.

RYGEOST (*Danish*)

Not found outside Denmark, this cow's milk cheese is the traditional snack for Midsummer's Eve, meant to be eaten round the traditional bonfire. It is a naturally smoked cheese, and is today made only by a few small dairymen.

SABA NO SUTATAKI (*Japanese*)

Mackerel salted and chilled for several hours, then sliced thinly and marinated in vinegar, salt and sugar. It is served with a garnish of thinly sliced carrot, *daikon* and watercress, and a ginger and soy dipping sauce.

SABLE, GATEAU DE (*French*)

'Sand cake'. A light shortbread cake, usually baked in a ring shape. It is a speciality of the *Maire* and is often credited as the origin of Scottish shortbread (brought over with Mary, Queen of Scots).

SACHERTORTE (*Austrian*)

A Viennese delight, made to the recipe of Franz Sacher, once Prince Metternich's chef and later founder of the Hotel Sacher. It is a rich chocolate cake, with a layer of apricot jam under the mirror-like chocolate icing. It has become one of Vienna's most famous products and is traditionally eaten with *schlag* (whipped cream). Today it is imitated all over the world and is also exported in various sizes by the hotel itself.

SAFFRON (*Spice*)

A pungent, golden spice from the autumn crocus, a member of the family *Iridaceae*. The spice is the stamens of the flowers, and because of the work involved for the scarce return – 80,000 flowers are needed for 1lb of dried stamens – it is the world's most expensive spice. Only about 1g (or 5 threads) are needed to flavour 1pt (600ml) of liquid. It imparts a distinctive colour and flavour (somewhat tea-like) to numerous Spanish and Indian dishes. The finest saffron is Spanish, that from India is less pungent. Always buy the threads and not the powder, which may be adulterated.

SAG (SAAG) (*Indian/Pakistani*)

Sag actually means greens, though in most cases it will be spinach. It is used in *sag bhaji* (the dry vegetable curry, (qv)) and in *sag panir* (see *Panir*). It also appears in the North Indian speciality of lamb and spinach, *sag gosht*. The North Indian word for spinach is *Palak*, also used to denote the same dishes. *Sarson ki sag* is a salad made from mustard and cress.

SAKE *(Japanese)*

The legendary rice wine of Japan, sake is served hot, poured into small handleless cups from a carafe called a *tokbuse*. It is pleasant and somewhat sweet, and quite easy to drink. In polite society, one is never allowed to pour one's own sake, but must wait to be served by one's neighbour at table. Thus keeping an eye on your neighbour's needs is one assurance that yours will be looked after.

SALT FISH *(Caribbean)*

Can be found in other parts of the Caribbean, but a speciality of Jamaica, where it is usually served with *ackee* (qv). Salt fish – salted, preserved cod – is also shredded to make fritters. They are traditionally accompanied by *rundown sauce*, made from the juice which 'runs down' a freshly split coconut.

SALTIMBOCCA alla ROMANA *(Italian)*

Thin slices of veal are covered with ham and sage, then either rolled up or left flat and sautéed in butter and Marsala. Other variations include *alla partenopea* – veal spread with ham and cheese on tomato sauce, and *alla marchigiana* – beef covered with bacon and ham and sautéed in wine.

SALMAGUNDI *(English)*

An old English dish of Elizabethan origin, consisting of layers of sliced meats or poultry alternating with various colourful fresh and pickled vegetables, decorated with sliced hard-boiled eggs and capers, and built upon a bed of lettuce and salad. It is dressed with oil and vinegar, and is a feast as much for the eye as the palate.

SALLY LUNN CAKES *(English)*

These sweet, spongy cakes, about four inches in diameter and six inches high, have been made since the late 18th century, when they were hawked about the streets of Bath by a street vendor, supposedly called Sally Lunn. Another explanation is that her cry was in a bastardized French spoken locally – 'Solet lune' – referring to the golden yellow texture of the cake. Whatever the explanation, these cakes are still linked with Bath, and are made at the Red House shop in the city. The cakes are allowed to rise for several hours before being brushed with egg yolk and baked. They should be split open while hot and eaten with whipped cream.

SALZBURGER NOCKERL *(Austrian)*

A kind of soufflé, made in three mounds, which is simply a combination of eggs, lemon peel, sugar, flour and vanilla extract. It is a speciality of the Austrian city after which it is named.

SAMBAL *(Indonesian)*

Sambals are sauces, usually very spicy ones. They are placed in small dishes on the table to be used with the main courses – with discretion. Some common ones are:

Sambal ulek: a simple *very* hot chili paste.

Sambal kacang: a simple, hot peanut sauce.

Sambal kelapa: chilis, prawn paste, garlic, tamarind and coconut.

Sambal bunces: green beans, garlic and chilis.

Sambal bajak: red chilis, garlic, *kemiri* nuts, tamarind liquid, shrimp paste, onions, all fried together. Not as hot as many sambals.

Other sambals, though still meant as an accompaniment, are more substantial and are meant to be served with rice. These are generically known as *sambal sambalan*, and include *sambal goreng udang asam* (piquant fried prawn sambal with ginger, garlic and chilis), *sambal cumi-cumi pedis* (with squid and chilis) or *sambal goreng hati* (liver and garlic-chili sauce).

SAMBAR *(Indian/Pakistani)*

A curry of mixed vegetables and *arhar dahl*, or small brown pigeon peas. It is a favourite South Indian dish, usually served with the pancake-like *Idli* (qv).

SAMOSA *(Indian/Pakistani)*

Small, savoury, deep-fried pastries, usually in the shape of little triangular packets, stuffed with spiced vegetables or lamb mince. They can be bought on the street as a *chat, and are also served as a tea savoury in India. In England and elsewhere they are more likely to be served before the main course of a meal or with drinks.*

SAMPHIRE *(English)*

A succulent shore plant which grows wild, notably on the East Anglian coast. It should be lightly boiled, then served smothered in butter. It is a fine accompaniment to fish. To eat, pull the fleshy leaves through the teeth, leaving the strings behind. Samphire can also be pickled although this treatment overpowers its delicate flavour.

SAMSO *(Danish)*

Named for the Island of Samso, it is a cow's milk cheese which has become Denmark's most original contribution to cheese. It is a firm, yellow cheese, with a character strongly combining bits of Cheddar and some of Emmental. It has the rich flavour of a Cheddar, with the nuttiness of the Emmental. Its optimum ageing period is six months. Made in large wheels but often sold pre-packaged when factory made, it has few holes. It is much used in cooking as well as for eating.

SAN BU JAN *(Chinese)*

A well-known Peking sweet, a strange mixture of sugar, egg yolks and corn starch fried in lard and scrambled. Very sweet, its name means 'won't stick three ways' – it won't stick to your spoon, chopsticks or teeth.

SAPSAGO *(Swiss)*

Also known as *Grüner käse*, this is a small, cone-shaped greenish, hard cheese, coloured by the addition of powdered clover leaves. It is made from slightly sour skimmed cow's milk cheese, which has had buttermilk added. The curd is cooked, strained, pressed and ripened for about five weeks. It is then dried and ground together with salt and the ground clover to make the mixture, which is then packed into cone-shaped moulds. It is grated over bread for breakfast or on other regional dishes.

SARDINHAS (*Portuguese*)

The most familiar fish in Portugal, the sardines are either brushed with oil and grilled (*grelhadas*) or seasoned with oil, garlic and herbs and baked.

SASHIMI (*Japanese*)

Fillets of the freshest raw fish are thinly sliced and artistically arranged with garnishes. Common types used include tuna, salmon, bream and small octopus and squid. It is served with soy sauce and a hot green horseradish called *Wasabi* (qv).

SATAY SAUCE (*Indonesian*)

A piquant dipping sauce, usually accompanying sates – skewered cubes of pork, chicken or beef. The sauce is based on a groundnut (peanut) paste, thinned with oil, tamarind liquid or lemon juice, and spiced with chilis, garlic and soy sauce.

SATE (*Indonesian*)

Pork, chicken or sometimes fillet of beef pieces which are marinated in a sauce for several hours, then barbecued or grilled. They are often served with a *Satay sauce* (qv).

The marinade for the saté can be sweetish (additional sugar, less spice), spicy (several additional sambals, spices and garlic added) or mildly flavourful. The basic ingredients are garlic, onion, palm sugar, peanut oil, tamarind liquid, soy sauce and spices. *Sate manis* indicates a sweet version, *sate bumbu* a very spicy one. *Sate ayam* is chicken sate. *Sate udang* is grilled skewered prawns. Traditionally, the skewers used are bamboo, soaked before using to inhibit burning.

SAUERBRATEN (*German*)

A richly-flavoured country dish, which requires an inexpensive cut of roasting beef to be marinated two days in wine, onion and pickling spices, then cooked slowly. The beef is served sliced thinly, and the piquant cooking juices are thickened with cornflour and sour cream. Boiled potatoes or noodles are the usual accompaniment.

SAVOYARDE, á la (*French*)

In the manner of the Savoy, in the Alpine region of France. It traditionally means a dish cooked with potatoes and cheese – as in *Omelette Savoyarde*, a flat omelette, and *Gratin Savoyarde*, potatoes baked in cheese and stock.

SAVOYARDE, POMMES à la (*French*)

Thinly cut round of potato baked in stock and cheese, producing a bubbly, browned *gratin* (qv). Little squares of bacon may also be found in some interpretations.

SAYUR *(Indonesian)*
Spiced vegetable dishes. The most common include *Sayur kol* – cabbage in spicy and peanuty coconut milk; *Sayur Lodeh* – mixed vegetables in the same sauce; *Sayur Buncis* – green beans and chicken fried with many spices and moistened with coconut milk, and *Sayur Tumis* – stir-fried vegetables.

✕ SCALLOPS
A host of legends surround this, one of the loveliest of seafoods, except when overcooked. My favourite true story concerns the young lady scallop preparation worker, interviewed by the 'New Yorker' Magazine. When asked for her honest opinion of the shellfish she said "They don't have much personality".

SCHWARTZWALDER ART, REHRUCKEN *(German)*
Venison cooked in the manner of the Black Forest; marinated in wine and spices, roasted and then served with its sauce heightened with brandy and sour cream. It is accompanied by broad noodles and cranberry sauce.

SCOTCH BROTH *(Scottish)*
A broth of lamb (mutton) or beef, with a wealth of finely diced vegetables floating in it, including peas, turnips, carrots, onions, leeks and cabbage. The distinguishing feature is the inclusion of barley.

SCOTCH EGGS *(Scottish)*
Now popular as a picnic and pub snack all over the British Isles, made from shelled hard-boiled eggs rolled in sausage meat or savoury mince. The balls are then breadcrumbed and deep-fried.

SCRAPPLE *(American)*
A traditional Pennsylvania Dutch breakfast dish. Pork trimmings – including meat and offal – or alternatively, pork sausage, is fried with onions, then mixed with cornmeal, milk, herbs and spices and allowed to set. Afterwards it is cut into squares and fried in butter.

SEE JEE TAO *(Chinese)*
'Lion's Head' meatballs – the pork, water chestnut, dried shrimp and ginger root meatballs are supposed to resemble a lion's head. The meatballs are simmered in stock with stir-fried cabbage. A dish from Jiangxi in the east.

SELLOU *(Morroccan)*
Traditional dessert eaten during Ramadan (after daylight) made from flour, oil, butter, honey and almonds.

SEMUR DAGING *(Indonesian)*
Cubed beef cooked in a spicy, sweet and sour soy sauce. Served with rice and *sambals* (qv).

SERBIAN BOHNENSUPPE *(Austrian)*
A legacy of the Austro-Hungarian Empire, this spicy bean soup is a favourite in every Austrian *Gasthaus* and *Ratskeller*.

SERUNDENG *(Indonesian)*
Dry spiced coconut and peanuts, served as an accompaniment to rice meals, or served crushed over the top of Indonesian curries.

SEV *(Indian/Pakistani)*
Wiggly nibbles of chick-pea flour spiced and deep-fried, which are served as snacks or *chat*. They are combined with *channo* and *channa Ri dhal* (chick peas and split peas) to make Bombay mix, a popular drinks snack.

SEVICHE *(Mexican)*
See *Ceviche*.

SHABU-SHABU *(Japanese)*
Paper-thin beef, Japanese rice noodles, a selection of vegetables and bean curd are simmered in broth piece-by-piece, swished backwards and forwards (Shabu-shabued) until the food is cooked. There are two classic sauces – one made with sesame seeds, sesame chili, oil and soy; another with lemon juice and another kind of soy.

SHAO *(Chinese)*
This word in a Chinese recipe title means braised (or literally 'burned'). The ingredient is first fried, then simmered in stock until almost dry.

SHARK'S FIN SOUP *(Chinese)*
See *Yu Ar Tang*.

SHASHLYK *(Russian)*
Marinated lamb, beef or pork, similar to the Turkish *Shish Kebab* (qv), alternated with mushrooms and onions, skewered and often served flaming. The meat can either be grilled over coals or a fire, and is usually served with pomegranate or sour plum, garlic and coriander sauce.

SHAU YANG ROU *(Chinese)*
The Mongolian Hot Pot – which has been adopted by the Peking and Northern school of cooking. The hot pot is a strange-looking utensil, a funnel in which charcoal is burned, surrounded by a dished circle in which stock or water is kept boiling. The name actually means 'rinsed lamb in fire pot', and refers to the rinsing motion used to cook the thinly-sliced lamb in the boiling liquid. The other ingredients, also cooked the same way, include chinese cabbage, spinach, bean curd and cellophane noodles. The sauce into which the meat and vegetables are dipped is mixed according to personal preference in little, individual saucers placed by each diner's chopsticks. It is a combination of chopped spring onions, garlic, ginger, soy sauce, Chinese wine, *Hoisin* sauce, chili sauce and sesame seed oil. Each diner helps him or herself to a slice of meat or vegetable, cooks it in the hot pot stock, and then dips it into the sauce before eating.

SHAWARMA *(Egyptian/Arabian)*
A close relative of Turkish *Doner Kebab* (qv), shawarma rotates packed sliced marinated lamb on a vertical skewer in front of a charcoal fire.

SHIITAKE (*Japanese*)
Delicate umbrella-capped mushrooms with a long stem and small top. They are dark and strong flavoured and are available dried and fresh for use in stews and in lightly-sautéed dishes. Though originally used only in Oriental dishes, today they are much favoured by *nouvelle cuisine* chefs of American and French cuisines for many of their new dishes.

SHINGARA (*Indian/Pakistani*)
Bengali savoury stuffed pastries resembling *samosas* (qv), but which use plain flour and are always filled with spiced vegetables and nuts, never meat.

SHISO (*Japanese*)
A herb, served raw or put into soup or other hot dishes at the last minute. It comes in green and purple versions; the purple most often used for pickling. Both leaves are broad, flat, jagged and slightly fuzzy. The green version is used in *sushi*, salad and as a garnish to *sashimi* or *tempura*. The flavour is complex: somewhere between citrus, mint and licorice.

SHORTBREAD (*Scottish*)
Indelibly linked in the popular mind with Scotland, shortbread probably developed from the *petit galettes*, little sand cakes, brought from France by Mary Queen of Scots. Today they are a popular tourist souvenir, and are usually sold cut into bars or 'petticoat tails', in tins and packets. It is usually made from a simple mixture of wheat and rice flour, butter and sugar. Worked with the hands, it is rolled out and baked until crisp and crumbly. See also *Sable, gateau de*.

SHOYU (*Japanese*)
Soya sauce, Japanese style. It is actually quite different from the Chinese, since it has no additives and no caramel, so it is lighter in colour and thinner in consistency. It also has a greater wheat content, making it sweeter and less salty.

SHUNGIKU (*Japanese*)
Edible chrysanthemum leaves which resemble the ornamental version which is *not* edible. The leaves are more deeply lobed and fuller, and are used raw or barely melted in salads, soups or in one-pot dishes.

SHUI MAI (*Chinese*)
Tiny steamed pork-stuffed pastries, served as *dim sum* (qv). They are supposed to resemble little money bags.

SHUSO LO (SHINSONRO) (*Korean*)
The 'soup of kings' or 'royal casserole' is made in a large casserole at the table and contains meat broth with seaweed, fish, sliced meat, vegetables and sliced boiled eggs and nuts. It is really a version of the ubiquitous oriental steamboat, and is served on special occasions. It is sometimes served in traditional individuals pots with coals in the central chimney to keep the soup simmering while eating.

SKIRLIE (*Scottish*)
An accompaniment to meats and game, skirlie is a mush of chopped onions and oatmeal, cooked in grated

suet or dripping. When cool, it can also be rolled into dumplings and cooked in Scotch Broth (qv).

SMÖRGÅSBORD *(Swedish)*
Sweden's most famous culinary delight. It is often thought to be merely a cold table, but that is incorrect. A true smörgåsbord contains hot, filling dishes, as well as cold ones. They should be eaten in a traditional order – first herring (available in ten or more different salads and marinations), served with boiled potatoes. Then comes the other fish – salmon, cod, sprats, eels, together with scrambled eggs, etc. Then the hot meats, then vegetable salads, then cheese. The usual accompaniment is beer (lager) with perhaps some aquavit.

SMORRESBRØD *(Danish)*
Open sandwiches – literally 'buttered bread' – a distinctive offering of Danish cuisine. These sandwiches are available all day long in pubs and restaurants, with sometimes as many as 200 types offered at once. They are made with several different kinds of bread, and the toppings can number almost any combination or variation of fish, meat or cheese, whole slices or pastes, as well as vegetables like asparagus, peppers, pickled gherkins, onions etc. The garnishes are mayonnaise, remoulades and sour cream, with decorative swirls and colourful additions like parsley, radish, gherkin, etc. The usual accompaniment is strong lager or aquavit. Called *Smorgas* in Sweden.

SNAILS *(French)*
See *Escargots*.

SNERT *(Dutch)*
See *Erwentensoep*.

SO FAR GAI YUEN *(Chinese)*
Chicken pieces, dipped into spiced batter and then deep-fried. The name means 'golden blossoms'. They are served as appetisers, together with *So Far Har Yuen* (qv).

SO FAR HAR YUEN *(Chinese)*
'Lotus flowers' – prawn, water chestnuts and spring onion balls, dipped into egg-white batter and deep-fried. They are served as appetisers.

SOFT SHELLED CRABS *(American)*
An east coast seasonal delicacy, soft-shelled crabs are available in late spring and summer as small, ordinary sea crabs shed their shells. They are dipped in flour, sautéed in butter and traditionally served on toast with liberal squeezings of lemon.

✘ *SOLE*
'Le Répertoire de la Cuisine' that great classic chef's handbook lists over 330 recipes for sole of which Dover Sole in the British Isles is king. The connection with Dover dates from the 19th century, when a certain fish dealer arranged

an express delivery service to London thereby earning fame for his town and no doubt a fortune for himself.

SOPAIPILLAS *(Mexican/American)*
These are a Tex-Mex speciality, a derivative of the *mueganos* of interior Mexico, which are a street snack of small fritters bound together with muscovado sugar syrup. *Sopaipillas* are much larger, flour-and-lard deep-fried puffs which are bathed in a honey, rum, butter and cinnamon sauce. They are scrumptious.

SOTO AYAM *(Indonesian)*
Classic Indonesian chicken soup, highly spiced, with egg or cellophane noodles and garnished with sliced spring onions and chopped hard-boiled eggs, dried chilis and onion flakes.

SOUSE *(Caribbean)*
Pig's trotters stewed with lime juice and spices then left to cool for a day, served cold, usually as a snack or first course.

SPAGHETTI *(Italian)*
The Italian pasta, known and internationally beloved, although most often served in hackneyed versions of *alla bolognese* (with minced beef, pork, mushrooms, tomatoes, garlic and herbs) or *alla napoletana* (with garlic, tomatoes, onions and olive oil). The best spaghetti is made only from hard durum wheat and water. It is formed into long, thin strands either by machine or hand, and is most usually purchased dried.

Other, more interesting sauces include *alla carbonara* (with strips of fried bacon, and raw eggs stirred into the cooked pasta at the last minute, and finished off with a large dose of Parmesan cheese), *alla amatriciana* (with bacon, tomatoes, onions, chili and cheese), and *alla puttanesca* – 'whore's style'! – with an easy going use of garlic, capers, tomatoes, peppers, olives, anchovies and herbs. *Alla vongole* (with clams), and *alla siciliana* (with tomatoes, aubergines and *ricotta* (qv), also known as *alla Bellini*) are two more fine alternatives.

SPANAKOPITTA *(Greek)*
A spinach and cheese pie, layered with fillo (qv), pastry. It is usually baked as a large pie, then marked into diamond-shaped squares. It can also be made as small separate envelopes or triangles. The cheese may be *feta* or a sharpish cheese like Gruyère (which substitutes for home-made Greek cheese of the same type).

SPECIAL FRIED RICE *(Chinese)*
See *Huo Tuei Dan Chas Fan.*

SPEKKOEK *(Indonesian)*
Spice cake. One of the great treats of Indonesian cooking, a series of many thin buttery layers, alternately plain and spicy, flavoured with cloves, cinnamon, nutmeg and vanilla.

SPOONBREAD *(American)*
A moist cornmeal dish, halfway between a bread and a pudding, spooned out of its baking dish and served

with butter as a side accompaniment to the main course.

STAR FRUIT (CARAMBOLA) *(Chinese/Malaysian/West Indian)*

A waxy yellow fruit with five long vertical ribs which, when cut across, approximates a five-sided star, exposing its small oval black seeds. It is best eaten raw, in salads or as a dessert fruit. In the Far East it is preserved in honey or is served with main courses, such as chicken or pork, as a garnish. Also called the *pomme canelle*, the star apple, and the *blimbing* (in Malaysia).

STARGAZEY PIE *(English)*

A Cornish speciality in which pilchards are stuffed with chopped onions and breadcrumbs, and arranged over the bottom crust of a lard pastry pie. The fish are then surrounded by layers of bacon, hard-boiled eggs and onions, and the top crust laid over. The fishes' heads are allowed to poke out the outer rim of the pie – 'star-gazing' – and when the whole is baked the oil from the heads moistens the pie.

STECCHINI *(Italian)*

Literally 'on little skewers'. *Stecchini alla Bolognese* is composed of veal, gruyère, mortadella and bread, dipped in egg and breadcrumbs, then skewered and deep-fried. *Stecchini alla genovese* combined offal (sweetbread, brains, chicken livers, etc.) and veal with cheese, artichokes and mushrooms.

STEFANKA *(Polish)*

A multi-tiered white cake, whose layers are bound together with chocolate cream filling, and covered with a mirror-like chocolate glaze. It is named for Stephen, one of the great saints of the Middle European Catholic church.

STIFATHO *(Greek)*

A rich, pungent stew made from beef, baby onions, chopped tomatoes, rosemary, bay leaves and coriander seeds, simmered in red wine and lemon juice or vinegar. It is served with rice.

STILTON *(English)*

Comes in two versions: the famous blue-veined cheese with the creamy paste and the lesser known white Stilton, made in the same way as the blue except that the *penicillium* mould is not allowed to develop and so the cheese is not aged as long. The flavour is naturally milder than its famous relative. Known as 'The King of English Cheeses' (as Brie is of the French!), the blue cow's cheese has a distinct tang – milder when young but rich and pungent when mature. It is made in small farmhouse creameries in the Midlands, most of which use pasteurised milk. The best is made from unpasteurised summer milk and is characterised by a yellower paste and a more powerful flavour. It should be aged about six months. A traditional accompaniment is port – but it should *never* be poured into the cheese. Mind you the last time I saw that actually being done was at the Restaurant Jammet, Dublin in 1962 so that particular malpractice has probably died out.

STOVIES (*Scottish*)

The Scottish way with potatoes. Small peeled potatoes are cooked in butter or bacon fat and the minimum of water in a covered pot over a low flame. When the potatoes are ready they are sprinkled with fine oatmeal, mixed, and left for ten minutes. These potatoes were traditionally served as the main course in poor crofting families.

STRACCIATELLA (*Italian*)

A light broth, of chicken or beef, with beaten egg, semolina and parmesan stirred in, producing the 'rags' in the name of the recipe.

STROGANOFF, BEEF (*Russian*)

Although it is now a standby of Russian-inspired international cuisine, beef Stroganoff is not a truly intrinsic Russian dish. It was invented by the French chef of the eponymous Russian Count, and consists of thin strips of top-quality sirloin or fillet, sautéed with onions and mushrooms and enhanced with sour cream and mustard. The result is served over boiled rice.

SUAN-LA TANG (*Chinese*)

Hot and sour soup, a speciality of Szechwan. The hotness is supplied by chili powder and ginger and the sourness by vinegar. The meat is chicken and/or pork, with mushrooms.

SUCCOTASH (*American*)

An Indian dish bequeathed to the pilgrims, *succotash* is a mixture of corn kernels and lima (broad) beans, cooked in butter and cream. It is available canned and frozen in the US.

SUKIYAKI (*Japanese*)

Paper-thin sliced pieces of meat (usually beef), together with sliced vegetables, bean curd and noodles are fried on a special plate over a spirit stove in front of the diner. In a private home, this quick frying is done by the host; at a restaurant by a special chef. As the beef, onions, bamboo shoots, mushrooms and noodles cook, the cook tosses them with a mixture of soy, sake and sugar. The diner dips each morsel in raw egg before eating.

SUNG SHU YU (*Chinese*)

Fried sea bass in a sweet-and-sour sauce, garnished with spring onions, ginger root, red pepper and coriander. A Cantonese speciality.

SUNG-Z JI TSU (*Chinese*)

A Mandarin dish, of chicken breast shredded then fried with chili and vegetables. Served with lettuce leaves which are rolled round the chicken filling, then dipped in a chili sauce and eaten.

SUNOMONO (*Japanese*)

A variety of cold salads come under this heading, usually mixing fish or shellfish with vegetables and seaweed. Dressings may also vary, but consistent ingredients include rice vinegar, sugar, soy sauce and *mirin* (qv).

SUPPLI AL TELEFONO *(Italian)*

'Telephone wires' – an amusing name for a delicious Roman *hors d'oeuvres*. It is composed of freshly made or left-over risotto rolled around cubes of mozzarella or other soft stringy cheese. The balls are then dipped in egg and breadcrumbs and deep-fried. When pulled apart to eat, the cheese forms long strings between the pieces – the telephone wires!

SUSHI *(Japanese)*

Elaborate little pop-in-the-mouth creations, often consumed at special *sushi* bars as lunch or a light snack. They look like canapes, and are made from cold, vinegared rice and a little sugar, either arranged in rectangles topped with raw fish, or rolled and bound with a circlet of raw fish and seaweed. Cucumber and other tiny slivers of vegetable may also be used. *Wasabi* (qv), a hot mustard of aquatic vegetables, is often included in the combination.

SUVLAKI *(Greek)*

Meat cubes, usually pork or lamb, marinated in a mixture of olive oil, lemon juice and bay leaves, then skewered and cooked over charcoal.

SWEET-AND-SOUR *(Chinese)*

For shrimp, see *Chao haah look*, for pork, see *Goo lo yuk*.

SWEETSOP *(Caribbean/South American/Southeast Asian)*

See *Custard Apple*.

SYLLABUB *(English)*

An Elizabethan dessert, 'syllabub' refers to a type of sparkling drink or champagne used in its earlier incarnation. Today sherry has replaced it. That, together with brandy, forms the alcoholic base. This is mixed with spices, lemon juice and peel, and sugar, then strained. Cream is either whipped into the liquor, or poured over it, but either way it should be served in tall champagne flutes.

SYRNIKI *(Russian)*

The Russian version of Jewish cheese *Blinzes* (qv), made of curd cheese and mashed potatoes patted into patties and fried in butter. They are served with cold sour cream, and some fresh whortleberries.

SZE CHUEN JAR GAI *(Chinese)*

Quick-fried chicken pieces. The pieces are dipped in a mixture of cornflour and five spices, then fried in batches, and finally after all are cooked, returned to the wok with chilis, garlic, ginger and spring onions. This is a hot-flavoured Szechwan style dish.

SZE CHUEN TONG *(Chinese)*

A thick soup full of good things, including, mushrooms, prawns, pork, bean curd and cellophane noodles, flavoured with chili oil, soy sauce, vinegar and

Chinese wine. It is, as the name implies, a favourite 'hot and sour' Szechwanese soup.

SZE CHUEN TSUI NGAP *(Chinese)*
Szechwanese-style roast duck. The duck is rubbed with a red-coloured paste of spices, then left to marinate overnight. After roasting, it is served in Mandarin pancakes with plum sauce and shredded spring onions, in the manner of Peking Duck *(Bei jing ngap)*.

TABBOULEK *(Lebanese/Israeli)*
Cracked wheat is soaked in lemon juice and water until puffed, then mixed with chopped tomatoes, onions, parsley and mint, and moistened with olive oil. Traditionally it is eaten with vine leaves or lettuce used as spoons, often from a communal dish.

TACOS *(Mexican)*
In Mexico, *taco* simply means snack – always wrapped up in a hot folded corn tortilla. Usual fillings include mashed avocado *(guacamole)*, turkey in chili and spices *(mole poblano* (qv)), refried beans *(frijoles refritos* (qv)), lamb or pork with chili sauce, *(chorizo* (qv)) or minced beef and hot tomato sauce. The latter has become a staple in the south-western US, though the *taco* is also usually 'improved' with the addition of shredded lettuce, grated cheese and hot sauce.

TAFELSPITZ *(Austrian)*
A cut of tender boiled beef from close to the tail. It is usually served with a caper sauce.

TAHINA *(Greek/Turkish/Israeli)*
A paste or dip made of sesame seeds ground and emulsified with lemon juice, oil and garlic. It is used as the basis for other dressings and dips, and is also served on its own with warmed pitta.

TAHU *(Indonesia)*
Bean curd. Fried Tahu is sometimes used on *gado-gado* and other mixed vegetable dishes, as well as being deep-fried and served with a spicy sauce. *(Tahu goreng kecap)*.

TAJINE (TAGINE) *(Middle Eastern/North African)*
A generic term for a stew made in a specially shaped dish of the same name. The *tajine* pot is made of earthenware, with a tall, cone-shaped lid which concentrates the moisture and flavour of the food inside and directs it back into the stew. It is traditionally placed on a brazier and cooked over coals, but can also be used in an oven. The more common tajines include either lamb – in chunks or meatballs – or chicken. Additions may include preserved lemons, olives, hard-boiled eggs, onion, tomato, chili peppers, spinach and/or olives. The home of the *tajine* is Morocco, Tunisia and Algeria, but it can also be found in other Arab countries and in Israel.

TALEGGIO *(Italian)*
Named after a small town near the Austrian border, this cheese is of the *stracchino* type – made from mountain grazing cow's milk – and has a dry mellow curd with a pinkish-grey rind. It is a strong aromatic

cheese, which becomes stronger and more pungent as it ages. It is one of the few Italian cheeses which can be deliberately aged when bought to accentuate texture, colour and taste. It can be made with either pasteurised or unpasteurised milk, though the latter is, of course, preferable.

TAMALE PIE (*American*)

A homely dish from the south-western United States in which a mixture of browned beef mince, chilis, tomato paste, onions and black olives are baked under a crust of corn bread.

TAMALES (*Mexican*)

Among the oldest of Mexican dishes, it is claimed that tamales were served at Aztec banquets. They are made from a simple corn dough spread on corn husks, filled with a sweet or savoury stuffing, and then rolled upon the corn husk and steamed. The savoury filling for the *tamal* dough can be minced beef or chicken, with red sauce (tomato and chili) or green tomatillo sauce. For sweet tamales, the filling is usually a mixture of nuts, fruit, sugar and sultanas. Tamales can also be deep-fried or baked with a tomato sauce or a meat and chili sauce.

TANDOORI (*Indian/Pakistani*)

Food – usually chicken or lamb, whole or in pieces – cooked in a *tandoor*, or clay oven. The poultry or meat is first marinated in spices before being baked in the oven. The result is a moist, flavourful meat, often with a reddish tinge from the paste. It is usually served on a bed of lettuce with a choice of chutneys or *sambals*.

TANG TSU HWANG YU (*Chinese*)

A Shandong speciality from the North-west of China, this recipe uses yellow fish or carp from the Yellow River, deep-fried in oil then bathed in a sweet-and-sour sauce of ginger, oil, onions, garlic, vinegar, sugar and soy sauce.

TAPAS (*Spanish*)

A term which covers all the little dishes served in bars as accompaniments to an aperitif. One or two may stimulate the appetite, while an entire meal can be made from several. Tapas can include *Albondigas* (qv) mussels, sausage slices, deep-fried prawns, olives, stuffed mushrooms, anchovies, and many more intricate recipes designed to be eaten in small quantities. The name is supposed to mean 'lid' from the old Spanish drinking custom of placing a piece of bread on top of one's glass to keep the flies out.

TARAMASALATA (*Greek*)

A dip, lightly pink in colour, served with *pitta* bread (qv). The basic ingredient is lightly-smoked cod's roe, pounded or processed to a paste with garlic, breadcrumbs and lemon juice, and emulsified with oil (olive or vegetable or both) until it attains a smooth consistency.

TARTARE SAUCE (*French/English*)

A cold sauce based on mayonnaise, thickened with sieved egg yolks, chopped onions, gherkins, capers, parsley and mustard. It is usually served as a condiment with grilled and fried fish, or to accompany cold vegetables and salads. Also employed as a dressing in France for cooked mussels.

TARTUFI (*Italian*)
Italian truffles – or *tartufi* – unlike those of France, are white. And unlike the French variety they are most often served uncooked, simply grated over rice or pasta, mixed with anchovy and served on croûtons or in a *bagna cauda* (qv); or in a light salad. Their smell is strong but their taste is ambrosial.

TEMPE (*Indonesian*)
A slab or cake of soya bean paste, which looks like a cheese with white skin. It is made from soya bean soaked with yeast and pressed. It varies from soft to crunchy in texture, and tastes slightly nutty. Eaten as a snack or used like bean curd or *tahee* in cooked dishes.

TEMPURA (*Japanese*)
Vegetables, fish and/or shellfish (prawns are usual) are dipped in a thin batter which puffs up beautifully, and are deep-fried. *Tempura* bars can be found all over Japan; at restaurants it may be made at a special bar and served to the client, or diners may be served from the kitchen. The dipping sauce accompanying the tempura includes soy sauce, *dashi* and *mirin* (qv).

TEPPAN-YAKI (*Japanese*)
Literally, this means 'cooking on an iron plate'. The diners sit around a large hotplate, at which a specially trained chef tosses and grills a wide variety of meat, fish, shellfish and vegetables. This version of Japanese 'theatre of cuisine' has become immensely popular in America and is now spreading to Europe.

TERIYAKI (*Japanese*)
Meat – usually beef – poultry or fish, marinated in a mixture of soy sauce, *sake*, *mirin* and ginger for a short period of time before being sautéed or grilled, and served with a reduction of the marinade. The sauce can also – as in *Gyniku* (beef) *Teriyaki* – be used for basting the meat while cooking.

THALI (*Indian*)
The South Indian manner of serving a meal – on a 'tray' or *thali* made from a banana leaf or an actual silver platter. The term is also used to describe the meal itself, in which various different spiced vegetables are arranged in little mounds or in small bowls called *katori*, around the leaf or tray. Chapatis or other breads are used to mop up or combine the various ingredients and act as a spoon.

THERMIDOR (*French*)
Lobster thermidor was created during the French Third Republic as a tribute to the Revolution. The lobster is halved and the meat removed and grilled. The meat is sliced and replaced in the shell, together with a thick sauce of *béchamel*, white wine, cheese and

mustard. The dish is then browned under the grill before serving.

THOSAI *(Indian/Pakistani)*
See *Dosai*.

TIAN *(French)*
A provençal baking dish, made of earthenware and fairly shallow. The term is used to cover the kind of food cooked in such a dish – typically the layered vegetable entrées which sometimes include eggs, rice and cheese.

TIKKA *(Indian/Pakistani)*
A kebab cooked in a tandoor oven. The tikka is usually of chicken or lamb cubes which are first rubbed with a wet *masala* paste, then left to marinate, and finally cooked.

TILSIT (TILSITER) *(German)*
A cow's milk cheese first made by Dutch settlers in Germany. The cheeses are usually flat and cylindrical, about 10in in diameter and about 10lb in weight, although today smaller loaves are being made. Today, since Tilsit itself is in the USSR, production has moved to northern Germany, where it is made in both whole-milk and skim-milk versions. The cheese usually requires five to six months to mature, but may be aged less. The result is a medium-firm, light yellow, mildly pungent cheese, with occasional small holes. Sometimes caraway seeds are added.

TIM SUEN JEUNG *(Chinese)*
The famous Cantonese sweet-and-sour sauce, so loved on pork balls or with fried *won ton*.

TIMBALE *(French)*
A mould, rather thimble-shaped, which was designed to imitate pastry crust. Usually timbales are small portions of pasta, rice or vegetable purées, served with a complementary sauce. They can accompany the main course, or stand on their own as a first course.

TOAD-IN-THE-HOLE *(English)*
A favourite since Victorian times, this homely dish is composed of meat baked in a batter of eggs, milk and flour. In its early form, it was often a combination of chops and other meats which were buried in the pudding; today it is fried sausages.

TOD MAN PLA *(Thai)*
Minced fresh fish and green beans, mixed with curry paste, formed into small patties and deep-fried. They are served with a dipping sauce of *nam prik*.

TOFU *(Japanese)*
A staple of Japanese cookery a white, cheesy-custard-like paste made from fermented soy beans. It has a delicate flavour and a soft smooth texture, and is much valued as a source of protein. It is served drained raw, or deep-fried and served with other vegetables, such as

bean sprouts. The Chinese version is *dow foo* and is less sweet than the Japanese version.

✘ *TOMATO*
Once known as the 'Apple of Love' and also the 'Golden Apple' – early European varieties were coloured yellow – the familiar tomato of today was once regarded with fear, distaste and suspicion due in part to its close relationship to the poisonous deadly nightshade. In the USA just over a century ago the recommended 'safe' cooking time was no less than three hours! In England their acceptance generally as a worthwhile food did not really begin until after World War 1 although they had been cultivated as an ornamental plant for centuries. Today's commercial tomato, in the interests of big business, has been scientifically 'improved' to such a degree that it is virtually useless in terms of taste, texture and nutrition and I can only recommend if possible that you follow Jane Grigson's excellent advice and grow your own using the seeds of the Marmande variety.

TOM BAM *(Vietnamese)*
Shrimp paste. A thick mash of raw pounded shrimp, oil, pork fat, sugar and fish sauce, used as a flavouring in soup, or fried shrimp toasts *Bank mi cheen tom* (qv) and moulded on sugar cane and grilled, *Chao Tom*.

TONKATSU *(Japanese)*
Pork escalope marinated in *mirin*, soy sauce and spices, then fried in egg and breadcrumbs. It was introduced to Japan by the Germans and has a definite resemblance to *Wiener Schnitzel* (qv).

TOPFENSTRUDEL *(Austrian)*
Made with the same transparent dough as apfelstrudel, this version is instead filled with sugared curd cheese, sour cream and sultanas. It is dusted with icing sugar before serving and is often accompanied by vanilla sauce.

TORIMAKI *(Japanese)*
An omelette rolled and stuffed with *mirin* flavoured chicken. It is served sliced on a bamboo mat.

TORTELLI *(Italian)*
A term used interchangeably with ravioli to mean square-shaped envelopes of pasta stuffed with minced vegetables. If stuffed with spinach or chard, eggs and cheese it is called *di erbette*, but pumpkin is another usual filling along the northeastern coast and Bologna area. One version, called simply *di zucca* (with pumpkin) also combines mostardo (pickled fruit), cheese and crushed macaroon.

TORTELLINI *(Italian)*
Rings of stuffed pastas – like 'little navels' – a speciality of the Emilia-Romagna. The stuffing is usually meat – pork, sausage and ham – served in a tomato sauce (*alla bolognese*) or cream sauce (*alla crema*), but it can be

filled with chicken and truffles, or even spinach and ricotta.

TORTILLA ESPANOLA (*Spanish*)
The *tortilla* is a Spanish classic and has nothing in common with the Mexican version except for the root *torta*, meaning round cake. It is a flat potato omelette, cooked in olive oil, and served hot or cold, cut into wedges. Other variations include chorizo sausage and pimento or cured ham, and peas, green beans and asparagus (*Tortilla Paisana*), or tuna, chick peas or even dates. (See also *Tortilla Mexicana*.)

TORTILLA MEXICANA (*Mexican*)
Flat pancakes made with a special cornmeal flour – *masa harisa* – water and salt. They are used for several traditional dishes, including *tacos* (qv) and *sopes* (qv) and are also made into chips for dips like *guacamole* (qv) and for appetisers. A less frequently encountered tortilla is made from wheat, and is larger and softer than the corn version. It is used for *burritos* (qv) and is served, folded with butter, as bread during a meal.

TOSTADA (*Mexican*)
The tostada is made with deep-fried corn *tortillas* which are spread with refried beans, then topped with shredded lettuce, chicken, sliced tomatoes, onion rings, sour cream, *guacamole* and grated cheese. They are eaten as a 'light' meal, or sometimes, in a smaller version, as an appetiser.

TOURTIERE (*Canadian*)
A popular French Canadian dish, which was once a traditional Christmas dish. It is a shortcrust pie, whose filling of ground pork and onion is liberally flavoured with cloves.

TRIGLIE (*Italian*)
Red mullet, a favourite dish of the Italian coast. Usual dishes include *all' anconetana*, a speciality of the Italian marche. The fish are cleaned and marinated in lemon juice and rosemary, then coated in breadcrumbs and wrapped in slices of Parma ham. The marinade is poured over, with some olive oil, and the fish are then baked.

✄ TRUFFLES (*Nicknamed Black Diamond*)
The truffle is an underground member of the funghi family, which thus far has refused to be cultivated, and they are 'hunted' for with the assistance of dogs and pigs, who can detect their scent from beneath the soil. The black truffle of France is the most famous with tiny, thumbnail sized slivers used as a dramatic garnish for certain classic dishes – thinly sliced black olives can achieve the same visual effect. They are available in small tins at big prices and even the peelings are sold for use in pâtés and sauces. However, unless in the months between November and March you can afford to sample the unique flavour and

scent of the fresh article I wouldn't even bother thinking about them.

TSAO GU (*Chinese*)
Dried straw mushrooms. These are their true name, as opposed to the generic term for dried mushrooms *Dung Gu* (qv).

TSUI GHUY (*Chinese*)
Literally 'drunken chicken'. The whole chicken is simmered in a stock or court buillon. It is then cut up, salted, and then marinated for forty-eight hours or more in rice wine and the cooking stock. It is served cold.

✖ TUNA
Most familiar as a canned product this is the fish which, remarkably, never rests due to the fact that its gills are incapable of independent action and therefore must maintain constant movement to ensure the flow of life preserving oxygen. Gastronomically speaking its flesh has been compared to veal and in appearance at any rate there is some similarity. In Italy the best cut is the stomach, (ventresca) which enjoys the notable recommendation of Elizabeth David. Prime quality tuna in Japan is often served raw, which may well taste a lot better than the hefty garlic smothered sample I encountered on a working visit to Maderia. Though luckily my palate was handsomely compensated by some wonderful Cossart Malmsey!

✖ TURKEY
Benjamin Franklin writing in 1784 expressed the wish that the Eagle had not been chosen to represent his country describing the bird as being of "bad moral character" and "often very lousy". "The turkey", he continued "is a much more respectable bird and a true original native of America". His wish thus far has not been realised although in Great Britain millionaire turkey producer Bernard Matthews has succeeded through the medium of television advertising in popularising the Norfolk dialect pronounciation "Bootiful" in describing his various related products.

✖ TURNIP
Nature has seen fit to endow the turnip and its cousin the cabbage with the violently poisonous element, arsenic! However, it's only a trace which, I'm told, may actually be good for one. The lesser-known name for this modest root is Rutabaga and if you examine the label of your dark pickle jar you will see that it plays quite a prominent part in its composition.

TURRON (*Spanish*)
A rich almond and honey candy, a kind of nougat, which is originally of Arab origin. It appears in two versions, a hard bar – Alicante-style – and a soft

marzipan-type, native of Jijona. It is eaten on its own and is also used in many desserts, ice creams and cakes.

TZE BO GAI (*Chinese*)
Chicken slices, together with ham pieces, dipped in a mixture of soy sauce, sugar, cornstarch and oil, wrapped in parchment paper and deep-fried.

TZE GHEUNG MUN GAI (*Chinese*)
Chicken in small pieces braised with lily buds, ginger and garlic, and lightly tossed with honey and soy sauce.

✕ UDDERS
On a flying visit to the famous Lancashire seaside resort of Blackpool in search of regional food specialities, I managed to locate the last UCP shop (United Cow Products) in town and there, among the various cuts of tripe, sheeps trotters, puddings and pies was displayed a tray of elder, which is cooked cows udder. A rare and delicious find I have since been told and I'm sorry to report here that I lacked the courage to try it.

UGALI (*East African*)
A thin stew from Tanzania, authentically made with goat. In Britain and in more Europeanised centres in East Africa, it may be made with lamb. It is customarily served with maize porridge or *coo-coo*, a cake of corn-meal and okra.

UITSMIJTER (*Dutch*)
Literally 'bouncer'. It is buttered bread (usually brown bread) topped with ham, cheese or roast beef and one to three fried eggs. This is the traditional budget hunger-breaker, at lunch or any time of day.

VADA (*Indian/Pakistani*)
Gram-flour pastries, deep-fried and then served with spiced *dahl* (qv). They are a popular snack in southern Tamil India.

✕ VANILLA
This plant, a member of the orchid family, has become one of the most popular flavours known to man. Expert opinion varies but it seems most likely to be a native of Central America, and the Aztec Emperor Montezuma is said to have used it to flavour his sole beverage, chocolate. Picking the vanilla pod at just the right moment is time-consuming, painstaking and consequently expensive, which means inevitably that synthetic substitutes abound, which used haphazardly can spoil, rather than enhance a good recipe. As is often the case, there is nothing like the real thing – if you can be sure you've found it.

VINDALOO (*Indian/Pakistani*)
A Goan curry with a slightly soured flavour from the addition of vinegar and tamarind juice. It is one of the

hotter curries, and should contain potatoes and peppers. Usually made with lamb, pork or chicken.

VITELLO TONNATO (Italian)
A Piedmontese speciality. Slices of cold roast veal (usually left from a roast) are covered with a smooth tuna, anchovy, caper and mayonnaise sauce, which is left overnight for flavours to absorb before serving.

WAAKYE (West African)
A variation of the *peas and rice* so common in the Caribbean, this made with rice and black-eyed peas (beans), cooked in a stock and sometimes extended by the addition of meat or chicken pieces.

✖ *WALNUT*
In ancient Rome the walnut was taken to be a model of the human brain and consequently they decided that it was useful as a headache cure. Of course, 'nut' is a slang word for head and is this, I wonder, its origin?

WASABI (Japanese)
A very strong horseradish, which is rendered a sage green through the addition of seaweed. It is usually bought powdered and made up when needed.

WATER CHESTNUTS (Chinese)
See *Ma tie.*

WATERZOOTJE (Belgian/Dutch)
A fish stew, not unlike *Bouillabaisse* in consistency, if not in flavouring. It is made with freshwater fish (eel, carp, pike etc.), cut into chunks and slow-cooked in a celery and herb-flavoured stock enriched with butter. The fish and reduced stock are served with toasted or fried bread. The dish can also be made with chicken and white wine. (In French-speaking Belgium, the dish is called *Waterzooi.*)

WEISSWURST (German)
A pale, whitish veal sausage, flavoured with herbs and wine, served sautéed or grilled. It is very mild and stays fresh for only a brief time. It is popular in Bavaria and Austria.

WELSH RAREBIT (English/Welsh)
Also called Welsh Rabbit, this is an old peasant recipe for a meatless larder. It is traditionally made with crumbly Caerphilly cheese, ale, butter, Worcester sauce and mustard, melted together, poured over slices of toast and browned. Nowadays it may be made with any dry cheese, which is necessary to absorb the maximum amount of ale. See also Buck Rarebit.

✖ *WHEAT*
Together with rice, wheat as a cereal is the world's most important food, at least for people. Remarkable as it may seem to those who luckily live in the well-fed West, cereals account for 80 per cent of all the calories consumed by the entire human race. According to one food writer, in the Middle East, wheat bread is so holy that a piece of it

dropped on the floor must be picked up and kissed in atonement.

✘ WHEY
This is the thin watery companion of curdled milk, immortalised by 'Little Miss Muffet'. The facts behind the popular nursery rhyme are these; Dr Thomas Muffet, a 16th century entomologist, had a daughter called Patience who one day whilst dutifully eating her curds and whey was surprised by an escapee spider from her father's collection.

WIENER ROSTBRATEN *(Austrian)*
A speciality of Austria's capital. It is composed of beef sirloin steaks, sautéed in butter and topped with crisp sautéed onions.

WIENER SCHNITZEL *(Austrian)*
'Vienna schnitzel', named for the capital city of Austria, was an idea brought over the Alps from northern Italy, where it was already an established dish. (See *Milanese Escalopes.*) It is a thinly pounded escalope of veal coated in flour, egg and breadcrumbs, and then fried in lard and butter. The classic 'Veal Viennoise' features the garnish of lemon slices, anchovy fillet plus a side decoration of chopped hard boiled white and yolk of egg with chopped parsley.

WENSLEYDALE *(English)*
This cow's milk cheese comes in two versions – white and blue. The former is more often seen. It is a semi-hard cheese, only lightly pressed, with a mellow, clean flavour. It makes a great accompaniment to apple pie. While the white is aged only a month or two to preserve its flavour and texture, the blue version is aged about six months and develops a full, rounded flavour. A prime specimen could rival Stilton though it lacks its bite.

WON TON *(Chinese)*
Small squares of noodle dough enclosing a savoury mixture of minced pork and prawns. They are usually served simmered in soup of the same name, or deep-fried and served as *dim sum*.

WOO DIP HAR *(Chinese)*
A favourite appetiser at Chinese restaurants – 'butterfly prawns'. Large king prawns are marinated in a garlic and soy sauce, then dipped in flour, egg and breadcrumbs and deep-fried. Served with hot chili sauce.

WUN YEE *(Chinese)*
Cloud Ears or Wooden Ears – dried tree fungus (*Auricularia auricula*). It must be soaked before using and when cooked has a mild flavour and crunchy texture.

YAKKAE JANG KUK *(Korean)*
A thick soup or stew made with shredded beef, spring onions, rice vermicelli, bean sprouts, sesame oil and

chili. Beaten whole eggs are drizzled and stirred into the soup just before serving.

YAKITORI (*Japanese*)

Yakitori is, literally, grilled chicken; and many small bars dedicated to this are found in Japan. Here the bar may be contained within a restaurant. The cooking is done behind a counter, the chef in full view of the diners. In addition, the bar may also produce grilled pork and beef. The chicken and meats are threaded onto small wooden skewers, then dipped into a soy, *mirin*, sugar and cayenne sauce before being grilled. This process is repeated several times; the result is a delicious titbit with a fine glaze.

✗ YAM

Not to be confused with the sweet potato which it resembles, the yam has been described by Laurens van der Post as being a food of vast importance in West Africa where the Ashanti Tribe serve it up with great ceremony at times of birth, death, marriage and recovery from accident or disease. Whether his friend Prince Charles includes it in his careful diet is not known.

YAM (*Thai*)

Used as a prefix to any Thai salad, it means, literally, 'tossed with the hands'. Types include *Yam Krachup* (water chestnut) and *Yam Tang Kwa* (cucumber salad).

YANG CHOW HAAH KOW (*Chinese*)

Chopped cleaned shrimp formed into balls with egg white and cornstarch (or pork fat). These are deep-fried and usually then stir-fried with baby corn cobs, mushrooms, onions and ginger root.

YA YEUNG FU GWA (*Chinese*)

Bitter melon stuffed with chopped fish and prawns, ginger and egg white, cooked in a black bean and garlic sauce.

YOGURTLU (*Turkish*)

Slices of doner kebab or shish kebab served on a bed of toasted pitta bread and covered with a sauce of puréed tomatoes, onions and yogurt. Sometimes also called '*Special Bursa*'.

YORKSHIRE PUDDING (*English*)

A savoury batter pudding originally from the north of England, which has now become synonymous with English cuisine. In the old days the pudding – a simple mixture of eggs, flour and milk – was cooked on a pan under the beef roast, so that it absorbed the drippings. It was then served as a first course, to take the edge off the appetite before the beef – a dear commodity in a low income family. In some northern homes this is still the custom, though it is now more usually served with the beef, often as individual puddings.

YOSENABE (*Japanese*)

A dish of simmered seafood, chicken or pork, cooked with cellophane noodles, vegetables, *kombo* and soy

sauce in stock. It is served in bowls, accompanied by a
dipping sauce of soy, *dashi* and *mirin*.

YU AR TANG *(Chinese)*

The famed shark's fin soup. This is practically impossible to prepare in the west, since ingredients are
unavailable. The shark's fin is cooked for several days,
cleaned, simmered for hours to become transparent,
and then steamed with flavourings. It is then cooked
with crab's roe, rice wine, ginger and lard. The soup
finally becomes a smooth golden colour, with the
delicate fin now floating glutinously in it. This is a
'Palace dish', and was traditionally served at the
Emperor's banquet.

ZABAGLIONE *(Italian)*

Egg yolk and marsala wine warmly beaten into a
delicious froth seved with a sponge biscuit. It is a light
and lovely alternative to stodgy 'pud'.

✕ ZAHIDI

*This is the name of a variety of date grown in California.
Fresh dates, Tom Stobart informs us in 'The Cook's
Encyclopaedia' contain 54 per cent sugar and 7 per cent
protein which makes them a good, high energy food and
thus, an ideal companion for climbers and long walkers.
Jane Grigson's chapter on dates in her terrific fruit book
contains some excellent recipes for dates and also this advice
from France: 'If you love elegance, replace the date stone
with a small bit of unsalted butter.'*

ZAKUSKI (ZAKUSKY) *(Polish/Russian)*

A selection of hot and cold appetisers, accompanied by
vodka. The groaning table might include caviar (real
sturgeon or lumpfish), herring, pickled mushrooms,
sausages, cheese, salads and other titbits.

ZAMPONE *(Italian)*

A speciality of Modena and the Emilia-Romagna, this
consists of highly-spiced ground pork, encased in the
skin of a pig's foot. It is usually boiled and served hot
with lentils, potatoes and, perhaps, other boiled meats
(See *Bollito Misto*).

ZARZUELA *(Spanish)*

Literally 'musical comedy'. One of the great Spanish
dishes, a stew of various fish in any combination – often
comprising, monkfish, mussels, mullet, turbot, large
prawns and/or squid – cooked in a spicy, piquant sauce
containing tomatoes, wine and brandy.

ZITE *(Italian)*

The largest of the tube pastas, like a large thick
spaghetti with a sizeable hole. It is usually served with a
thick beef, ham, tomato and wine sauce, which clings
well to the *al dente* macaroni. It is also sometimes served
stuffed (*ripiene*) although this is a painstaking business.

ZRAZY *(Polish)*

Often called 'beef olives' in English, the roulades of
thin beef topside are filled with thin slices of bacon,
dill, carrot and onions, tied and simmered in a sauce of

onions, beef stock and mushrooms, finally enriched
with sour cream before serving.

ZUPPA *(Italian)*

The Italian term for all heavy, thick soups – usually
containing bread or poured over bread. Variations
include *Zuppa di fontina* – with bread and cheese; *di
cozza* – with mussels; *di pesce alla romana* – fish and
shellfish soup, and *alla Bolzanese* – tripe soup with
cream, lemon and cabbage served with *polenta* (qv).
Zuppa di Castagne is a chestnut soup of the north-west,
while *Zuppa scaligera* is a Venetian combination of
turkey, pigeon and cheese, layered between slices of
bread, with broth poured over. It is then baked in the
oven.

Zuppa ingelese ('English soup') is something quite
different: a trifle-like concoction of sponge cake soaked
in Marsala and layered with custard. It is a speciality of
Emilia-Romagna.

ZWIEBACK *(German)*

A twice-baked bread of a dry, rusk-like quality. It is
made from ordinary bread dough to which eggs and
butter are added. The loaves are baked and sliced, then
baked again, which dries the bread so it becomes crusty
and light. Zwieback is available plain or sugar covered.

KEY TRANSLATOR OF MAIN FOODS

BERRIES

(m – masculine)
(f – feminine)

ENGLISH	FRENCH
Blackcurrant	Cassis (m)
Blackberry	Mûre (m)
Blueberry/Bilberry	Myrtille (m)
Cherry: Red	Cerise (f)
Black	Cerise noire (f)
Gooseberry	Groseille à maquereau (f)
Loganberry	Ronce-frambroise (f)
Raspberry	Framboise (f)
Redcurrant	Groseille (f)
Strawberry:	
Ordinary	Fraise (f)
Wild	Fraise de bois (f)

BERRIES

SPANISH	GERMAN	ITALIAN
Grosella negra (f)	Korinth (f)	Ribes nero (m)
Zarzamora (f)	Brombeere (f)	Moro (m)
Azuramore (f)	Blaubeere (f)	Mirtillo (m)
Cereza (f)	Kirsche (f)	Ciliegia (f)
Cereza negra (f)	Schwarze Kirsche (f)	Ciliegia nera (f)
Grosella espinoza (f)	Stachelbeere (f)	Uvaspina (f)
Fruta obtenido del cruce de la zarzamora y la frambuesa (f)	Kreuzung von Himbeere und Brombeere (f)	Frutta che somiglia alquanto al lampone (f)
Frambuesa (f)	Himbeere (f)	Lampona (m)
Grosella (roja) (f)	Johannisbeere (f)	Ribes rosso (m)
Fresa (f)	Erdbeere (f)	Fragola (f)
Fresa silvestra (f)	Wilde Erdbeere (f)	Fragola di campo (f)

FISH

(m – masculine)
(f – feminine)

ENGLISH	FRENCH
Anchovy	Anchois (m)
Brill	Barbue (f)
Caviar	Caviare (m)
Cod, fresh	Cabillaud (m)
Cod, salted	Morue (f)
Crab	Crabe (m)
Crayfish: Freshwater	Ecrevisse (f)
Salt water	Langouste (f)
Haddock	Merlan (m)
Halibut	Flétan (m)
Herring	Hareng (m)
Hake	Colin (m)
Lobster	Homard (m)
Mackerel	Maquereau (m)
Monkfish (Angler fish)	Lotte (f)
Mussel	Moule (f)
John Dory	St-Pierre (m)
Oyster	Huitre (f)
Bass	Bar (m)/loup de mer (m)
Pike	Brochet (m)
Plaice	Flet (m)
Prawn: Small	Ecrivette (f)
Larger	Langoustine (f)
Red mullet	Rouget (m)
Ray/Skate	Raie (f)
Salmon	Saumon (f)
Salmon, smoked	Saumon fumé (m)
Sardine	Sardine (f)
Scallop	Coquille Saint-Jacques
Shad	Alose (f)
Sole, Dover	Sole (f)
Trout	Truite (f)
Turbot	Turbot (m)
Tuna	Thon (m)

FISH

SPANISH	GERMAN	ITALIAN
Anchoa (f)	Sardelle (f)	Accuiga (f)
	Seebutt (m)	
Caviar (m)	Kaviar (m)	Caviale (m) Not common
Merluza (f)	Dorsch (m)	Merluzzo (m)
Bacalao (m)	Stockfisch (m)	Baccala (f)
Buey cangrejo (m)	Krabbe (f)	Granchio (m)
Cigala (f)	Flußbrebr (m)	Astaco (m), gamberi di fiume (m pl)
Cigala (f)/ Langostino (m)	Languste (f)	Scampo (i)
Merlango (m)	Schellfisch (m)	Merluzzo (m)
Halibut (m)	Heilbutt (m)	Sogliola Atlantica (f)
Arengue (m)	Hering (m)	Aringe (f)
Merluza (f)	Hechtdorsch (m)	Merluzzo/ Nasello (m)
Langosta (f) (large) bogavante (m)	Hummer (m)	Aragosta (f)
Caballa (f)	Makrele (f)	Sgombro (m)
Pejesapo (m)	Meerteufel (m)	Coda di rospo (f)
Mejillón (m)	Muschel (f)	Cozze (f pl)
Pez de San Pedro	Not common	Piesce San Pietro (m)
Ostra (f)	Austern (f)	Ostrica (f)
Lubina (f)	Seebarsch (m)	Spigola (f)
Lucio (m)	Hecht (m)	Luccio (m)
Platija (f)	Scholle (f)	Passerino (m)
Camaron (m) Gamba (f)	Krabbe (f) Hummerkrabbe (f)	Gamberetti (m pl) Gamberi/Scampi (m pl)
Salmonete de fango (m)	Rote Meerbarbe (f)	Triglia (f)
Raya (f)	Glattroche (m)	Razza (f)
Salmon (m)	Lachs (m)	Salmone (m)
Salmon fumaro (m)	Raucherlachs (m)	Salmone affumicato (m)
Sardina (f)	Sardine (f)	Sardina (f)
Vierra concha de peregrino (f)	Jackobsmuschel (f)	Ventaglio (m)
Alosa (f)	Alse (f)	Alosa (f)
Lenguado (m)	Seezunge (f)	Sogliola (f)
Trucha (f)	Forelle (f)	Trota (f)
Rodaballo (m)	Steinbutt (m)	Rombo (m)
Atún (m)	Thunfisch (m)	Tonno (m)

FRUIT

(m – masculine)
(f – feminine)

ENGLISH	FRENCH
Apple	Pomme (f)
Apricot	Abricot (m)
Avocado	Poire d'avocat (f)
Banana	Banane (f)
Date	Datte (f)
Fig	Figrie (f)
Grape	Raisin (m)
Grapefruit	Pamplemousse (m)
Lemon	Citron (m)
Mango	Mangue (f)
Melon	Melon (m)
Nectarine	Brugnon (m)
Orange	Orange (f)
Peach	Pêche (f)
Papaya	Papaye (f)
Pear	Poire (f)
Pineapple	Ananas (m)
Plum	Prune (f)
Passion fruit	Fruit de la passiflore (m)
Tangerine	Manderine (f)
Lime	Limon

FRUIT

SPANISH	GERMAN	ITALIAN
Manzana (f)	Apfel (m)	Mela (f)
Albaricoque (m)	Aprikose (f)	Albicocca (f)
Aguacate (m)	Avocatobirne (f)	Avocado (m)
Plántano (m)	Banane (f)	Banana (f)
Datil (m)	Dattel (f)	Dattero (m)
Higo (m)	Feige (f)	Fico (m)
Uva (f)	Weintrabe (f)	Uva (f pl)
Pomelo (m)	Pampelmuse (f)	Pompelmo (m)
Limon (m)	Zitrone (f)	Limone (m)
Mango (m)	Mangopflanze (f)	Mango (m)
Melón (m)	Melone (f)	Melone (m)
Nectarina (f)	Nektarine (f)	Pesco-nettarovie (f)
Naranja (f)	Orange (f)	Arancia (f)
Melocoton (m)	Pfersich (m)	Pesca (f)
Papaya (f)	Melonenbaum (m)	Papaia (f)
Pera (f)	Birne (f)	Pera (f)
Ananas (m)	Ananas (f)	Ananas (m)
Ciruela (f)	Pflaume (f)	Susina (f)
Granadilla (f)	Eßbare Passionsblume (f)	Granadilla (f)
Mandarina (f)	Mandarine (f)	Mandariono (m)
Lima (f)	Limone (f)	Lima (f)

HERBS AND SPICES

(m – masculine)
(f – feminine)

ENGLISH	FRENCH
Allspice	Toute-épice (f)
	Piment Jamaïque
Aniseed	Anis (m)
Basil	Basilic (m)
Bay Leaf	Laurier (m)
Caraway	Carvi (m)
Cardamom	Cardamome (m)
Cayenne	Cayenne (f)
Chervil	Cefeuil (m)
Chili	Piment fort (m)
Cinnamon	Cannelle (f)
Clove	Clou de girofle (m)
Coriander	Coriandre (f)
Cumin	Cumin (m)
Fennel	Fenouil (m)
Garlic	Ail (m)
Ginger	Gingembre (m)
Mace	Fleur de Muscade (f)
Marjoram	Marjolaine (f)
Mint	Menthe (f)
Mustard	Moutarde (f)
Nutmeg	Muscade (f)
Oregano	Oregan (m)
Paprika	Paprika de Hongrie (f)
Parsley	Persil (m)
Pepper	Poivre (m)
Rosemary	Romarin (m)
Saffron	Safran (m)
Sage	Sauge (f)
Tarragon	Estragon (m)
Thyme	Thym (m)
Turmeric	Curcuma (m)

HERBS AND SPICES

SPANISH	GERMAN	ITALIAN
Fruita del pimiento de jamaica (f)	Jamaikapfeffer (m)	Pimento (m)
Anis (m)	Anis (m)	Anice (m)
Alabega (f)	Basilienkraut (m)	Basilico (m)
Laurel (m)	Lorbeer (m)	Lauro (m)
Alcarvea (f)	Kümmel (m)	Comino (m)
Cardamomo (m)	Kardamome (f)	Cardamomo (m)
Cayena inglesa (f)	Cayennepfeffer (m)	Pepe di Caienna (m)
Perifollo (m)	Kerbel (m)	Cerfoglio (m)
Chile (m)	Roter Pfeffer (m)	Diavoletto (m)
Canela (f)	Kaneel (m)	Cannella (f)
Clavo (m)	Givürznelke (f)	Chiodo de garofano (m)
Coriandro/ Cilantro (m)	Koriander (m)	Coriandolo (m)
Comino (m)	Kreuzkümmel (m)	Comino (m)
Hinojo (m)	Fenchel (m)	Finocchio (m)
Ajo (m)	Knoblauch (m)	Aglio (m)
Jengibre (m)	Ingwer (m)	Zenzero (m)
Macia (f)	Muskatblüte (f)	Macis (m)
Mejorana (f)	Majoran (m)	Maggiorana (f)
Hierbabuera (f)	Minze (f)	Menta (f)
Mostaza (f)	Senf (m)	Senape (f)
Moscada (f)	Muskat (m)	Noce moscata (f)
Oregano (m)	Oregano (m)	Origano (m)
Paprika (f)	Paprika (m)	Paprika (f)
Perejil (m)	Petersilie (f)	Prezzemolo (m)
Pimienta negra (f)	Pfeffer (m)	Pepe nero (m)
Romero (m)	Rosmarein (m)	Rosmarino (m)
Azafrán (m)	Safran (m)	Zafferano (m)
Salvia (f)	Salbei (m or f)	Salvia (f)
Estragán (m)	Estragon (m)	Dragoncello (m)
Tomillo (m)	Romischer Quendel (m)	Timo (m)
Curcuma (f)	Gelbwürz (f)	Curcuma (f)

VEGETABLES

(m – masculine)
(f – feminine)

ENGLISH	FRENCH
Artichoke	Artichaut (m)
Asparagus	Asperges (f pl)
Bean, French or Runner	Haricots verts (m pl)
Beetroot	Betterave (f)
Broccoli	Brocoli (m)
Brussels sprout	Chou de Bruxelles (m)
Cabbage	Chou (m)
Carrot	Carotte (f)
Cauliflower	Chou-fleur (m)
Celeriac	Céleri-rave (m)
Courgette/Marrow	Courgette (f)
Cucumber	Concombre (m)
Endive	Chicorée (f)
Leek	Poireau (m)
Lentil	Lentille (f)
Lettuce	Laitue (f)
Fennel	Fenouil (m)
Mushroom	Champignon (m)
Onion	Oignon (m)
Parsnip	Panais (m)
Pea	Petit pois (m)
Green Pepper	Poivron vert (m)
Potato	Pomme de terre (f)
Sweetcorn	Mais (m)
Tomato	Tomate (f)
Turnip	Navet (m)

VEGETABLES

SPANISH	GERMAN	ITALIAN
Alcachofa (f)	Artischocke (m)	Carciofi (m)
Espárragos (m pl)	Spargel (m)	Asparago (m)
Judias (f pl)	Zwergbohne (f)	Fagiolini (m pl)
Remolacha (f)	Crote Rube (f)	Barbabictoia (f)
Brecol (m)	Spargelkohl (f)	Broccoli (m pl)
Col (f) de Bruselas	Rosenkohl (m)	Cavoli di Bruxelles (m pl)
Col (f)	Kohl (m)	Cavolo (m)
Zanahoria (f)	Karotte (m)	Carota (f)
Coliflor (f)	Blumenkohl (m)	Cavolfiore (m)
Apio-nabo (m)	Knollensellerie (m)	Sedano capa (f)
Calabacın (m)	Eierkurbis (m)	Zuchini (m pl)
Pepino (m)	Gurke (f)	Cetriolo (m)
Escarola (f)	Endive (f)	Cicoria (f)
Puerro (m)	Lauch (m)	Porro (m)
Lenteja (f)	Linse (f)	Lente (f)
Lechuga (f)	Lattich (m)	Lattuga (f)
Hinojo	Fenchel (m)	Finocchio
Champiñon (m)	Champignon (m)	Pilz-fungo (m)
Cebolla (f)	Zwiebel (f)	Cipolla (f)
Chirivia (f)	Pastinake (f)	Pastinaca (f)
Guisante (m)	Erbse (f)	Piselli freschi (f pl)
Pimiento verde (m)	Spanischer Pfeffer (m)	Peperone (m)
Patata (f)	Kartoffel (f)	Patata (f)
Maiz (m)	Mais (m)	Granturco (m)
Tomate (m)	Tomate (f)	Pomodoro (m)
Nabo (m)	Weiße Rübe (f)	Rapa (f)

THE HISTORY OF BEVERAGES

Both these beverages are of such importance that with the kind assistance of the London Coffee Information Centre and the Tea Council I have decided to include here the following comprehensive information.

TEA

Tea, an evergreen plant, is a member of the Camellia family. Its oval-shaped leaves are smooth, shiny and pointed in appearance, not unlike a larger edition of the privet hedges which surround many British gardens. It was first discovered more than 5,000 years ago by the Chinese Emperor, Shen Nung. One legend says that whilst travelling around his Empire he sheltered under a tree to boil his drinking water and a leaf from the tree – a *Camellia Sinensis* – fell into his boiling pot of water resulting in the first brew of tea.

Camellia Sinensis is indigenous to China and part of India. Left to grow wild the tea plant develops into a tree many metres high, but under cultivation *Camellia Sinensis* is kept to a height of approximately three feet. Today tea is grown in more than twenty-five countries around the world, but the main producers are India, Sri Lanka, Kenya, Malawi, Indonesia and China. It is cultivated as a plantation crop, likes acidic soil and a warm climate with at least fifty inches of rain per annum.

Little is known about the early beginnings of tea in Britain. The East India Company, under their charter granted by Elizabeth I, recorded ships reaching China in 1637. But it was not until 1644 that any record of tea appeared in their dealings with the Chinese merchants.

However, sailors returning from the Far East did bring packets of the strange leaf back as presents for friends and relatives. It was through these sailors that tea first found its way into London's coffee houses. Thomas Garraway of Garraway's Coffee House, Exchange Alley, Cornhill, London, was one of the first to buy and sell tea and he was quick to see the advantages of the new beverage. His first public sale of tea was held in 1657.

In 1660, Garraway issued a broadsheet offering tea for sale at £6 to £10 per pound and extolling its virtues. Amongst these were "wholesome, preserving perfect health until extreme old age, good for clearing the sight . . .". He also claimed that tea could cure "gripping of the guts, cold, dropsies, scurvys and it could make the body active and lusty". The first tea advertisement appeared on September 30, 1658. The owner of The Sultaness Head Coffee House took space in the newspaper *Mercurius Politicus* announcing the sale of "China Tcha, Tay or Tee". By 1700 there were more than 500 coffee houses in London selling tea.

Tea rapidly gained popularity amongst the beverages sold in these establishments. Tavern keepers were disgusted since their premises were soon deserted as the coffee house vogue swept into being. Neither did the Government relish the decline in revenue brought about by the decreased sales of wine and liquor. Charles II claimed that coffee houses had become centres of sedition and intrigue. In a proclamation of 1675 he forbade the sale of tea, coffee, chocolate and sherbet from people's homes and it was illegal for anyone to keep a public coffee house.

This aroused such ill feeling amongst his subjects that he tactfully forgot to enforce the law. However, tea did appear on the statute books in 1676 with Act XII, under which keepers of coffee houses had to take out a licence at Quarter Sessions. This Act also tried to impose duty on all liquor sold within such establishments but it proved impossible to enforce. A keen advocate of the new beverage was the diarist Samuel Pepys who first tried "a cup of tee (a China drink) of which I never drank before" on Sunday September 25, 1660.

Throughout the 300 years that the British have been drinking tea it has had a remarkable influence on the nation's culture and lifestyle patterns. Queen Catherine, wife of Charles II, first introduced tea drinking as a social and family habit to the English in 1662, when she brought chests of tea to Britain as part of her wedding dowry. It is a habit which has been firmly adhered to by today's royal family. The British tradition of the "tea lady" was first introduced in 1666 by a Mrs Harris, who was the wife of the Housekeeper and Beadle of the East India Company. Little did she think that, when she made tea for the Committee Meetings held by Directors of the Company, she was laying the foundation stone for a tradition that would not only last for more than 300 years but would also cause a national outcry when companies decided, in the 20th century, to replace the traditional tea lady with vending machines.

Tea breaks are another tradition which have been known in Britain for approximately 200 years. Initially, when workers commenced work at around five or six thirty in the morning, employers allowed a break at some point in the morning when tea and food were served to the workforce. Some employers even repeated the operation late in the afternoon. However, between 1741 and 1820 various clerics, industrialists and landowners tried to put a stop to the tea break, maintaining that the imbibing of this beverage made the working people slothful. Although it was before the inception of unions, people stood up for their rights and the tea break remains with us to this day.

When tea was first drunk in the homes of the middle and upper classes, it was normally consumed as the culmination of an evening's entertainment or prior to the ladies of the house retiring to bed for the night. The "tea tray" was brought into the salon and all the assembled company would enjoy a relaxing cup of tea before departing for home or retiring to bed.

As the popularity of tea spread throughout the land it also became an essential part of people's entertainment outside the home; so by 1732 an evening spent dancing or watching fireworks in Vauxhall or Ranelagh Gardens (1742) would be rounded off – certainly by the ladies – with the tea tray being served. This was soon extended to the gardens being opened on Saturday or Sunday for a family day, with tea being served as the high point of the afternoon.

Tea gardens sprung up all around London and in some of the major towns around the country. Dancing was included as part of the day's festivities, so from the tea gardens came the idea of the tea dance. Anna, 7th Duchess of Bedford, is reputed to have originated the idea of afternoon tea in the early 1800s. The reason was that she grew very hungry between lunch and dinner and therefore conceived the idea of having tea served at around four or five in the afternoon to ward off the hunger pangs. More to the point she conceived the idea at approximately the same time as the Earl of Sandwich invented the idea of putting a filling between two slices of bread.

For the working and farming communities, afternoon tea became a high tea. A meal which was a mix of the delicate meal being enjoyed in ladies' drawing rooms of an afternoon and the dinner enjoyed in the house of the gentry after seven or eight in the evening. High tea was the main meal for the working and farming community and the beverage served to go with the meats, bread and cakes was hot tea.

Tea shops were the idea of a manageress of the Aerated Bread Company who persuaded her directors to allow her to open a shop which served tea and refreshments. This was in 1864 and the habit soon spread with the tea shop becoming as much a British tradition as tea itself. Incidentally, the tea shop, when it first opened, was the only place an unchaperoned lady could arrange to meet a friend or friends without damaging her reputation.

As the tea shops and tea rooms fashion spread, the tea dance, which had its early beginnings in the tea gardens, was revived. It remained a fashionable pastime for all the nation until World War II, when circumstances forced it to disappear from the social scene.

However, modern Britons are picking up where their great grandparents left off and tea dances are again gaining in popularity throughout the country.

A GUIDE TO TEAS

There are approximately 1,500 different tea blends. Tea is a natural plant, only differing in taste and character because of the area in which it is grown; the type of soil (tea plants like an acidic soil); the altitude and the climatic conditions of the area. Tea is a year-on-year commodity, and its supply is very dependent on the vagaries of the weather.

In some parts of the world tea is seasonal. In other parts it is picked all year round. The character of the tea from an area changes slightly depending on climatic conditions around the time of that particular 'flush' or picking. Incidentally, because tea is a year-on-year commodity, there can be no such thing as a tea "mountain".

The constant quality and flavour of our well-known brands rely on the tea tasters' and blenders' skills. It is they who ensure that these brands achieve that consistency, regardless of supply, from day to day, year in and year out. Your everyday popular brand-leading blend of tea contains between 15 to 40 different types of tea.

The British are now rediscovering tea and like our grandparents are consuming more of the fine or 'speciality teas'. A speciality tea is a particular blend of tea. It can be made up of teas from an area which gives its name to that blend, or it can be a blend of different teas from various areas which produces a tea with a special and characteristic aroma and flavour.

FROM INDIA

Assam
A blend of teas grown in Assam, North India. Assam tea is a full-bodied tea with a rich, malty flavour. It is an ideal tea to drink for that first cup in the morning. It really wakes you up. Such teas are used in your everyday popular blends because of their full-bodied richness.

Darjeeling
Known as the 'Champagne of Teas', Darjeeling tea is grown many thousands of feet above sea level in the foothills of the Himalayan mountains. Darjeeling is a very light and delicate tea, characterised by a muscatel, or grape aroma and flavour. It is an ideal tea to complete a delicious dinner. It can also be enjoyed with sandwiches in the afternoon, perhaps with a slice of lemon instead of milk.

Nilgiri
From Southern India – the Nilgiri Hills. Light, 'bright' and delicate in taste.

FROM SRI LANKA

Ceylon teas are usually present in everyday blends because of their fine flavour, but they are speciality teas in their own right and are ideal with a slice of lemon as a mid-morning drink. They also make a refreshing cup after a rather heavy lunch. Blend some Ceylon tea with Assam tea and you have your own traditional English Breakfast blend giving you flavour and strength.

Dimbula
Grown 5,000 feet above sea level. Gives a typical 'high grown' flavour – with a golden colour.

Nuwara Eliya
Delicate, light, 'bright' tea with a fragrant flavour, excellent with lemon.

Uva
A fine-flavoured tea from the Eastern slopes of the Central Mountains of Sri Lanka.

FROM EAST AFRICA

Kenya
Kenya grows tea all the year round. The teas are full-bodied and 'bright' giving a warm coppery-coloured tea. Kenya tea has a good rounded tea flavour, making it an ideal tea to be drunk anytime during the day. Although Kenya teas are readily available as speciality teas they are important as an integral part of British popular brand-leaders.

FROM CHINA

Keemun
From Anhui Province – light, delicate and ideal with Chinese food.

Oolong
Oolong teas are semi-fermented teas (in layman's language a semi-green tea). They are light, very delicate teas characterised by a fruity aroma and flavour closely akin to the smell and taste of peaches or roses. Milk

and sugar should not be added to Oolong teas. If you do add them you will kill the light, delicate taste. Oolong makes a marvellous and unusual tea to serve after a Chinese dinner or a white meat or fish meal. They are very carefully picked and mostly hand-rolled, although some tea estates have now installed machinery for this operation. Oolong teas are generally available from around £5 – £28 per pound, but even the most expensive still costs as little as five pence a cup to make – really good value for money.

Lapsang Souchong

Lapsang Souchong is a black China tea blend easily distinguished by its smoky, tarry aroma and smoky taste. It is best taken in the afternoon with a slice of lemon, and makes a very refreshing and cooling cup of tea on a sticky, close summer day.

According to the history books, Lapsang Souchong obtained its characteristics because the Chinese when they first discovered tea decided that they would like to sell it. Being unable to dry enough of it in the sun they then burnt rope underneath the drying tea to quicken the process. Today, Lapsang Souchong tea is still smoked when it is dried – although modern technology has improved the method.

A BLEND BY NAME

Some teas take their names from people or events and probably the most famous of these is:

Earl Grey

Traditionally Earl Grey is a blend of black China and Darjeeling teas which have been treated with the citrus oil of bergamot. It is this oil which gives the blend its characteristic 'scented' aroma and flavour.

Earl Grey is one of the most popular of the speciality teas and makes an ideal afternoon tea. The blend is said to be named after the 2nd Earl Grey, who delighted a Chinese mandarin with his praise of tea, so the honoured Oriental gentleman concocted this special blend for his noble English friend.

Flavoured tea

There are many flavoured teas on the market. The finished tea can easily pick up any smell or flavour. For example, Jasmine tea is a blend of tea which has had the flowers of Jasmine dropped into the blend and the tea assumes the delicate scent and flavour.

Storage

Tea is easily contaminated and this is why you should always store your tea in an airtight caddy, which should be kept in a cool, dry place. In doing this you enable the tea to keep its natural flavour and avoid it picking up other flavours in your larder or kitchen. There is a story of a tea broker who many years ago made a fortune by buying up chests of tea which had been shipped to this country with cartons of sacks of oranges. The tea chests got damaged en route and on arrival in London the tea smelt of oranges. He promptly bought the whole assignment and packeted it selling it as orange flavoured tea.

How to make tea

When brewing 'speciality' teas, make your tea in the usual way – warm the pot, a teaspoon of tea per person, plus one for the pot (use the same rule for tea bags). Boil freshly drawn cold water. As the kettle comes to the boil take the teapot to the kettle and pour boiling water (after turning off the heat) onto your tea. Infuse for at least five to six minutes (or as instructed on the tea packet), stir and then pour.

The art of tea tasting

Samples from all the teas being bought and sold in auctions are tasted and evaluated by the tea brokers and also by the buyers of the tea that goes into your packet. They look at the colour of the dry tea leaf, sniff the wet leaf and the tea liquor. They smell these and then sip or 'slurp' the tea liquor before spitting it out. Tasters and blenders have some 100 special words describing what they taste. Bright, brisk, full-bodied, etc. In all cases they are looking for quality and flavour – they also compare teas from the estates against previous growths from the same places. Company tasters and blenders are also looking for the qualities and flavour that will remain consistent day in day out, year after year. No easy task when you consider that tea is an annual crop, affected by the vagaries of the climatic conditions in the region in which it is grown. It takes at least five years to train as a taster, and most tasters who have spent a lifetime in the tea trade will tell you they are still learning.

THE HISTORY OF COFFEE

No one knows for certain how or when coffee was discovered and there are many legends about its origin.

One tale says that it was discovered by an Arabian Sheikh who had been sent into exile. He would have died of hunger but saved himself by making a broth from the berries of the coffee shrubs he found growing in the wilderness.

Of all the stories about how coffee was discovered, the best known is the tale of Kaldi and the dancing goats. Kaldi was an Arabian goatherd who is said to have lived in that part of Africa now known as Ethiopia in about the third century AD. He noticed that his goats behaved in a very strange way after they had eaten the red berries of a certain bush. They leapt about as if they had suddenly become young again.

When Kaldi told his story to the abbot of a nearby monastery, the abbot decided to test the power of the berries for himself. He poured boiling water on them to make a drink. When he drank it he found that he could stay awake for hours on end. From then on he and the monks drank the berry liquid every night and no longer felt sleepy during the long hours of prayers. The news of the wakeful monastery spread rapidly and soon the coffee tree was in great demand.

Though the story of Kaldi is only a legend, it is true that the coffee tree was found growing wild more than a thousand years ago. The discovery of the drink led to the commercial cultivation of the coffee plant in the Yemen district of Arabia in the fifteenth and sixteenth centuries.

THE FIRST COFFEE HOUSES

The Arabians were jealous of their trade in coffee and tried to prevent other countries joining in it. Coffee beans were not allowed to leave the country unless they had first been dried or cooked in boiling water. This destroyed their power to germinate. But it was impossible to stop coffee being smuggled out.

One reason was the thousands of pilgrims who visited the holy city of Mecca each year. By the middle of the sixteenth century coffee drinking had spread to Aden, Egypt, Syria and Turkey. In those countries, coffee became known as 'the wine of Araby', because Muslims regarded it as a substitute for wine, which they were forbidden. It was not only drunk at home but also in the many public 'coffee houses' which were opened in every city of the Near East.

People went to these coffee houses for all kinds of reasons. They drank coffee, listened to music, watched the dancing, played chess and other games and discussed the news. Many came to listen to the wandering story-tellers reciting the marvellous tales of the Thousand and One Nights or even simply to sit and listen to the conversation. So much could be learned at the coffee houses that in Turkey they were called the 'schools of the wise'. (Later, when coffee houses became popular in England in the seventeenth century, they became known as the 'penny universities', because it cost a penny to get in.)

Europeans first heard about coffee from travellers returning from the East. They had visited coffee houses and had also seen coffee pedlars. These were people who made their living by going about the streets carrying coffee in copper pots heated by spirit lamps and selling it in tiny cups.

The Italians were the first to bring coffee to Europe. The first shipment arrived in Venice from Turkey in 1615, and the first Western coffee house or 'café' was opened there about thirty years later. Coffee drinking quickly became fashionable. By the end of the seventeenth century there were coffee houses in England, Austria, France, Germany and Holland.

Coffee arrived in Vienna at a dramatic time in the history of Western Europe. The Turks had mobilised a huge army to conquer Europe. In 1683 it reached Vienna and the city was cut off from the world. The story goes that a Polish officer called Kolschitzky helped to save the day. He had lived for many years among the Turks and knew their language and customs. Wearing a Turkish uniform, he managed to slip through the enemy's lines and swam the River Danube many times with messages for the Austrian and Polish troops. In the great battle that followed, the Turkish invaders were routed. They fled and left their supply wagons behind. These contained many bags filled with coffee beans. When the booty was divided, Kolschitzky, who was the only person who knew how to prepare coffee, claimed the sacks as part of his reward. Later, he opened Vienna's first coffee houses and became rich and famous.

The first coffee house in England was opened in Oxford in 1650. The first one in London was opened two years later. Soon there were hundreds of coffee houses in London. Each had its own special customers. For instance, Jonathan's Coffee House in Change Alley was where stockbrokers met, and it soon became the birthplace of the Stock Exchange. Ship-owners and marine insurance brokers went to Edward Lloyd's Coffee House in Lombard Street. It grew into Lloyd's of London, the centre of the world's insurance business. Wills' in Covent Garden was a favourite of writers and poets. More famous people came to the Turk's Head. Among them were David Garrick, the actor, Sir Joshua Reynolds, the painter, and Dr Johnson, who compiled the first English dictionary.

After the eighteenth century, coffee became less popular in England, though from about 1945 people began to drink more again. In other European countries and in North America, however, coffee remained a popular drink. In many big cities, cafés were the centre of social life.

Coffee was brought to Virginia from Britain in the seventeenth century. Coffee houses like those in England were soon opened in all the American colonies. Nevertheless, tea was the favourite drink until 1773. Then the Boston colonists revolted against King George's harsh tax on tea. They boarded the English merchant ships lying in the harbour and threw their cargoes of tea into the sea. After the incident, known as the 'Boston Tea Party', the colonists turned to coffee. It is still the favourite American breakfast drink.

THE FIRST COFFEE PLANTATIONS

The Dutch were the first to transport coffee successfully. In the seventeenth century, they began to grow coffee in their colonies, and Amsterdam became a trading centre for coffee from Java and other islands of the Dutch East Indies.

In 1714, the Mayor of Amsterdam sent a young and vigorous coffee tree to King Louis XIV of France, who had been trying to start coffee growing in the French colonies. The tree was planted with great pomp and ceremony in the Royal Botanical Gardens in Paris. A young naval officer called de Clieu took a seedling from this tree to the Caribbean in 1723. His voyage was a dramatic one. First his ship had to escape from pirates. Then there was a terrible storm. Finally it was becalmed and drinking water ran low. De Clieu managed to keep his coffee plant alive by sharing his tiny water ration with it. It was planted on his estate in Martinique and, by 1777, there were over 18 million coffee trees on the island. All the trees on the big estates of the West Indies came from seedlings grown from de Clieu's tiny plant.

Colonists, missionaries and traders took the coffee plant to Central and South America. By the end of the eighteenth century, coffee had become one of the New World's most profitable export crops.

Nowadays, there are coffee plantations in more than fifty countries. The most important are in the tropics, between latitudes 25 degrees North and 30 degrees South. Coffee has become one of the most important commodities in world trade and as many as 20 million people earn their living from it.

COFFEE GROWING

The trees which produce coffee all belong to the genus *Coffea*. There are many *Coffea* species, but only two are commercially significant.

Coffea Arabica produces the finest quality coffee and is sold for the highest prices. The tree grows well on steep slopes at altitudes from 600 to 2,000 metres above sea level.

Coffea Canephora (Robusta) is easier to grow than Arabica and provides much of the coffee used for manufacturing soluble coffee. It grows well in regions from sea level to 600 metres.

One strange feature of the coffee tree is that it may bear its fruit, leaf and blossom at the same time. Sometimes, in fact, delicate white flowers, green berries and ripe red cherries all appear together on the same branch.

The blossoms last about three days. They smell strongly of jasmine. In countries where coffee grows near the coast its lovely perfume can be smelt as many as five kilometres out to sea. The leaves grow in pairs along the branches. They are lance-shaped, waxy, bright and ever-green.

The coffee berries are dark green at first. As they ripen they change to yellow. After six or seven months they become deep red cherries. This is the name for the coffee fruit. The skin of the cherry covers a sweet pulp which has two coffee seeds inside it. They are shaped like two halves of a bean.

The beans are covered with a husk or parchment. Under this is a delicate semi-transparent silver skin. Sometimes there is only one seed; this is called a pea-berry and has a rounded shape.

Coffee can only grow in certain conditions. Coffee trees grow best where there is plenty of rain at certain times of the year and well-drained, rich, volcanic soil. The plant does not like sudden changes in temperature, and frost can kill it. Although it likes a warm climate, it cannot take too much direct sunlight and is therefore often shaded by larger trees.

Coffee trees grow from seeds first planted in nursery beds. When the seedlings are about one year old, they are transplanted to the fields where they are set in well-manured holes. The holes are about 300mm deep and 300mm wide and 2.5m to 3.5m apart, depending on the type of coffee grown.

The young trees have to be carefully looked after. They must be watered often and the ground between the rows has to be weeded regularly and mulched. Fertiliser is often used to improve the soil, and both young and adult trees must be pruned and sprayed to control pests and diseases which can harm them.

The trees begin to bear fruit after three to five years. They continue to produce full crops for up to fifteen years. Trees that are over one hundred years old may still bear fruit. Coffee cherries are picked by hand. Men and women, and sometimes even children, walk between the rows of trees with baskets or bags slung over their shoulders and pick the ripe cherries from the trees. The cherries ripen at different times and should not be picked until they are fully ripe. Harvesting by machine is difficult and still very rare.

Over 4,000 cherries are needed to produce 1kg of roasted coffee. A picker can harvest as much as 90kg of fruit in one day. This gives about 13.5kg of green coffee – the description given to beans when they are ready for roasting. Obviously, these figures vary somewhat from country to country.

In some countries the fruit is allowed to ripen on the trees until it falls naturally or can be shaken onto a cloth spread on the ground. The cherries are then collected and sifted to remove the dust, leaves and twigs.

COFFEE PRODUCTION

There are two methods of preparing or 'curing' the coffee beans. Better quality coffee is prepared by the 'wet' method. The older 'dry' method is simpler and requires less expensive machinery.

The stages for the 'wet' method are as follows. First, a machine called a pulper removes the pulp of the ripe cherries and exposes the inner protective coat or parchment. Then the coffee beans are soaked in tanks and fermented to loosen their covering. This is washed away in fresh water until the beans are quite clean. They are then dried in the sun or by machine and are finally put onto a huller, which removes the parchment and silver skin.

Once the silver skin has been removed, the 'polished' coffee is ready to be sorted and graded by size. Finally, the green beans are packed into 60kg bags for shipping round the world.

The stages of the 'dry' method are that, first, the fresh cherries are spread in thin layers on mats or drying ground. They are raked and turned frequently so that they will dry evenly in the sun. This may take two weeks or even longer. Once they are dry, the cherries are put through special hullers. These remove the dried pulp, the parchment shell and the silver skins covering the beans.

IMPORTANCE OF COFFEE

The exceptional economic importance of coffee can be judged from the following facts:

● Coffee is one of the most valuable commodities in world trade. In several years, its value in international commerce, measured in US Dollars, has been second only to petroleum.
● More than 20 million people earn their livelihood from coffee. Most of them are farmers and agricultural workers whose welfare and security depends on the income received from the coffee they grow, process and export.
● Coffee provides millions of jobs in the importing countries, not only in the transportation, processing, packaging and marketing of the product, but also in the production of the agricultural equipment, factory goods and services sold to the coffee-exporting countries.
● The countries that grow and export coffee are still in the process of becoming industrialised. More than forty developing nations depend in some measure on coffee export earnings for sustaining their economies and for supporting their socio-economic advancement. For this reason, it is a commodity of considerable social and political, as well as economic, importance.
● The production of coffee dominates the economies of many of the world's developing countries; in some cases exports of coffee account for well over seventy per cent of the country's total export earnings.

BIBLIOGRAPHY

All Manners of Food – Mennell – Blackwell
Chambers Biographical Dictionary
The Classic Italian Cookbook – Marcella Hazan – Macmillan
Classic Game Cookery – Julia Drysdale – Macmillan
The Cook's Encyclopaedia – Tom Stobart – Macmillan
Compleat Strawberry – Stafford Whittaker – Century
Greek Food – Rena Salaman – Fontana
Herbs, Spices and Flavourings – Tom Stobart – Penguin
Herbs and Spices – Rosemary Hemphill – Penguin
Italian Food – Elizabeth David – Penguin
Jane Grigson's Fruit Book – Penguin
Jane Grigson's Vegetable Book – Penguin
Le Répertoire de la Cuisine – Jaeggi & Sons Ltd
North Atlantic Seafood – Alan Davidson – Penguin
Food – Waverly Root – Simon and Schuster
Food and Drink in Britain – C. Anne Wilson – Penguin
On Food and Cooking – Harold McGee – Allen & Unwin
Queer Gear – Carolyn Heal & Michael Allsop – Century
Real Food Guide – David Mabey – Quiller Press
The Reader's Encyclopaedia – William Rose Benet – A & C Black Ltd.
The Taste of Italy – Fay Sharman & Brian Chadwick – Macmillan

ACKNOWLEDGEMENTS

The author and publishers are grateful to Suzie Ward, Prunella Harrison, Chris Gilmore, Caroline MacAndrew and Rita Hutt for their considerable research for, and commitment to this book.

NOTES